WILLIAM EVERSON
(Brother Antoninus)

THE CROOKED LINES
OF GOD:
A Life Trilogy

VOLUME I
The Residual Years (1934-1948)

VOLUME II
The Veritable Years (1949-1966)

VOLUME III
The Integral Years (1966-1994)

WILLIAM EVERSON

(Brother Antoninus)

THE RESIDUAL YEARS

Poems 1934-1948

Including A Selection Of Uncollected And Previously Unpublished Poems

Foreword by Allan Campo

Introduction by Kenneth Rexroth

Afterword by Bill Hotchkiss

BLACK SPARROW PRESS ❂ SANTA ROSA ❂ 1997

ACKNOWLEDGMENTS

Certain of these poems were originally published in the following periodicals: *The Ark; Berkeley: A Journal of Modern Culture; The Caravan; The Carmel Pine Cone; The Catholic Worker; Circle; The Compass; The Experimental Review; The Illiterati; Literary America; The Owl; The Pacific Spectator; Phoenix; Poetry, A Magazine of Verse; The Saturday Review Of Literature; The Tide; The Tiger's Eye; The Untide; Voices; Warp & Woof (The Ontario Outlook);* and *Westward.* The Everson Estate also expresses gratitude to the various publishers listed in the Bibliographical Note who first issued these poems in separate editions.

Appendix A credits: Bancroft Library, University of California, Berkeley; William Andrews Clark Memorial Library, U.C.L.A.; Occidental College Library, Los Angeles, Special Collections Department; Scarecrow Press, Inc., Lanham, MD; Selma High School, Selma, CA.

Photo credits: Cover photo of William Everson, Selma Calif., ca. 1938 courtesy of Mrs. Erle O. Shorey (Vera Everson); photo of William and Edwa Everson and photos of manuscript pages of "The Sphinx" and "Chronicle of Division" courtesy of the William Andrews Clark Memorial Library, U.C.L.A.; Photo of Mary Fabilli courtesy of Mary Fabilli.

Black Sparrow Press books are printed on acid-free paper.

LIBRARY OF CONGRESS CATALOGING-IN-PUBLICATION DATA

Everson, William, 1912–1994
    The residual years: poems, 1934–1948: including a selection of uncollected and previously unpublished poems /William Everson (Brother Antoninus); foreword by Allan Campo ; introduction by Kenneth Rexroth; afterword by Bill Hotchkiss.
        p.   cm. — (The collected poems: v. 1)
    Includes bibliographical references and index.
    ISBN 1-57423-055-7 (paper: alk. paper) — ISBN 1-57423-056-5 (cloth trade: alk. paper) — ISBN 1-57423-057-3 (deluxe cloth: alk. paper)
    I. Title. II. Series: Everson, William, 1912–   Poems; v. 1.
PS3509.V65A17   1997 vol. 1
811'.52—dc21

97-43682
CIP

CONTENTS

BOOK ONE:
SINGLE SOURCE (1934-1940)

THESE ARE THE RAVENS (1934-1935)

SAN JOAQUIN (1935-1938)

THE MASCULINE DEAD (1938-1940)

BOOK THREE:
A PRIVACY OF SPEECH (1943-1946)

CHRONICLE OF DIVISION (1943-1946)

BOOK TWO:
THE IMPOSSIBLE CHOICES (1940-1942)

THE RESIDUAL YEARS (1940-1941)

POEMS: MCMXLII (1942)

THE YEAR'S DECLENSION (1948)

APPENDIX A: A SELECTION OF UNCOLLECTED AND
   UNPUBLISHED POEMS

Photographs follow page 190.

BIBLIOGRAPHICAL NOTE

This collection is comprised of the following editions, listed in the order of their respective publications. The years of composition are given in brackets.

These Are The Ravens [1934-1935], The Greater West Publishing Co., San Leandro, California, 1935.

San Joaquin [1935-1938], The Ward Ritchie Press, Los Angeles, California, 1939.

The Masculine Dead [1938-1940], The Press of James A. Decker, Prairie City, Illinois, 1942.

X War Elegies [1940-1943] (Note: This was a mimeographed edition. The printed edition of 1944 contains eleven poems.), The Untide Press, Waldport, Oregon, 1943.

The Waldport Poems [1943], The Untide Press, Waldport, Oregon, 1944.

War Elegies [1940-1943], The Untide Press, Waldport, Oregon, 1944.

The Residual Years [1940-1941], The Untide Press, [Waldport, Oregon, 1945].

Poems MCMXLII [1942]. (This collection was printed by Everson in 1945 as an individual project rather than as a publication of The Untide Press.)

The Residual Years [1934-1946], New Directions, New York, 1948.

A Privacy of Speech [1946], The Equinox Press, Berkeley, California, 1949.

The Year's Declension [1948], The Berkeley Albion,: Rare Book Room of the University of California, Berkeley, California, 1961.

The Blowing of the Seed [1946], Henry W. Wenning, New Haven, Connecticut, 1966.

Single Source [1934-1940], Oyez, Berkeley, California, 1966.

In the Fictive Wish [1946], Oyez, Berkeley, California, 1967.

The Springing of the Blade [1947], The Black Rock Press, Reno, Nevada, 1968.

The Residual Years [1934-1948], New Directions, New York, 1968.

PREFATORY NOTE:

The Residual Years was first used to designate a slight, mimeographed sheaf of poems William Everson issued from the WWII conscientious objectors' camp near Waldport, Oregon, in 1945. It subsequently became the title of a selectively cumulative edition of the poet's work to 1946, published by New Directions in 1948, and again in 1968 in expanded and chronologically sequential format. The present volume not only reissues the 1968 collection, including the poet's subsequent textual revisions, but also includes a selection of uncollected and unpublished poems through 1948. The present collection presents the poetic achievement of the author before his entry into the Roman Catholic Church in 1949. Following his reception into the Dominican Order in 1951, he became Brother Antoninus, the name under which his books were issued until he left the Dominicans in December of 1969, at which time he resumed his secular name of William Everson.

NOTE ON TYPOGRAPHY:

The Residual Years was registered on computer by Allan Campo, Judith Shears, and Bill Hotchkiss, with Times New Roman text and Century Schoolbook and Moravian heads—via TrueType and Microsoft Word for Windows.™ Book layout by Bill Hotchkiss, at Castle Peak Editions, Williams, Oregon. Text proofing by Allan Campo, David Carpenter, William Harryman, Lee-Marie Varner, C. Kate McCoy, Steve Sibley, and Bill Hotchkiss.

FOREWORD: *THE YEARS REVEAL*
Allan Campo

It is nearly thirty years now since *The Residual Years* was published in 1968 by New Directions, bearing as subtitle "The Pre-Catholic Poetry of Brother Antoninus." Fourteen months later, Brother Antoninus left the Dominican Order to marry Susanna Rickson and to continue his career as William Everson once again—a third incarnation in the course of his poetic vocation. Kenneth Rexroth—Everson's long time friend and sometime mentor—affirmed the abiding worth of that body of poetry in his Introduction to the 1968 volume; hence Rexroth's Introduction is appropriately included in the present volume.

Indeed, the poetry of the first phase of his career as poet was, of course, never merely "the pre-Catholic poetry" for William Everson. In his Preface to an earlier *Residual Years* collection published by New Directions in 1948, Everson wrote:

> ...the work of a life is a chronology, drawn from event to event. The years reveal, reveal and recede into the dark residuum that is the totality of our experience, that keeps and preserves the forward-flowing line of growth, the progression of our lives.

Although the years recede, what they reveal remains, articulated in the poems to which they gave birth. Everson himself demonstrated the ongoing relevance of the earlier poetry when, in his first public appearance in Southern California after leaving the Dominicans, he gave a reading at California State University, Fullerton. He read neither from the Catholic poetry that had been his mainstay for some twenty years nor from the new work that limned his passage from the monastic back to the secular life. Rather, he read such poems as "The Impossible Choices," "Do You Not Doubt," "The Answer," and "The Siege"—verse from the early 1940s wherein, as he remarked, "I was trying to find a place where I could stand." Nor should we overlook the fact that his final work as a poet—left unfinished at his death in 1994—was the autobiographical *Dust Shall Be the Serpent's Food*, which would have encompassed those same "residual years"—a major work which must now remain incomplete.

This new edition of *The Residual Years* is not simply a refurbished printing of what has already been published. Even as it is the first of the three volumes that, when taken together, will present the complete poems that comprise Everson's "Life Trilogy" (for it will be followed by *The Veritable Years* and *The Integral Years*), it is, as well, a testament to the ongoing presentness of the poetry.

In order to make this volume a proper collection—correct in text and arrangement, complete in its contents—all of the previous collections and separate editions have been consulted in order to correct errors that have cropped up and to incorporate the changes which the poet himself made over the years (even as late as the summer of 1993, when he assisted in the preparation of a generously proportioned selection of his poetry to be published as *The Achievement of William Everson*).

In addition, a directive he composed for the printing of the 1948 *The Residual Years*, entitled "Note to the Designer & Printer," has been utilized and is included in the present edition.

Furthermore, the principal holdings of Everson's papers have been examined in order to clarify and confirm the chronological arrangement of the poems (which are grouped under the titles of the original collections or independent editions in which they appeared or to which they belong by their dates of composition—with the exception of "The Chronicle of Division" and "If I Hide My Hand," which appear under their own titles, not having been collected or independently printed, as were the other poems).

Finally, and distinctively, my examination of Everson's surviving manuscript material has made it possible to append to the main body of his verse a "Selection of Uncollected and Unpublished Poetry"— addressed in the Introduction which accompanies it. This additional verse serves to round out our presentation of the poetry, thus enabling the reader to gain a fuller awareness of Everson's pursuit of his art during the period in which *The Residual Years* was written.

Needless to say, the preparation of this edition owes much to others for its execution, and, on behalf of both Bill Hotchkiss and myself, various acknowledgments are in order and happily given. Due to the foresight and efforts of Lawrence Clark Powell, the William Andrews Clark Memorial Library of the University of California, Los Angeles, maintains the bulk of Everson's surviving manuscript material through 1948. The Clark Library's staff (especially Suzanne Tatian and Renée Chin) was most amiably cooperative and proficient. The Bancroft Library of the University of California at Berkeley, though principally holding the post-1948 materials, retains some valuable papers from the earlier period. There, Anthony Bliss and other staff members were admirably cooperative.

I would further extend grateful acknowledgments to William Eshelman for compiling and editing the 1938-1946 correspondence between William Everson and Lawrence Clark Powell as *Take Hold Upon the Future* (Scarecrow Press, Inc., 1994)—an acknowledgment that does not do justice to the full value to our efforts of Eshelman's very considerable work. Acknowledgments are also due to Carol Sommer of the Clark Library for ferreting out five boxes of "missing" Everson material; to Steve Tabor of the Clark Library for providing photograph reproductions for use in this edition; to Michael C. Sutherland of the "Special Collections" at Occidental College in Los Angeles; to Daniel Luckenbill of the "Special Collections" at UCLA; to Richard Hughey for securing relevant material on my behalf; to Nancy Bonilla, the librarian at Selma High School; to Tammy Lau of the "Special Collections" at California State University, Fresno; to Judith Shears, William Harryman, David Carpenter, and Steve Sibley for editorial assistance; to John Carpenter for obtaining Everson's personal copies of published collections; to Robert Hawley for his support and assistance; and to John Martin of Black Sparrow Press for committing to the publication of this and the succeeding volumes.

Finally, I offer my personal gratitude to Bill Hotchkiss, who, in addition to his role as co-editor and his contribution of the Afterword, prepared the computer-generated photo-ready copy of *The Residual Years* for printing and publication—while coping with the encumbrance of having a computer neophyte as his colleague.

—Allan Campo
Toledo, Ohio

INTRODUCTION, 1968 Edition: Kenneth Rexroth

It's long ago now, another epoch in the life of mankind, before the Second War, that I got a pamphlet of poems from a press in a small California town—*These Are the Ravens*—and then a handsome book from the Ward Ritchie Press in Los Angeles—*San Joaquin*. They weren't much like the poems being written in those days, either in *New Masses, Partisan Review* or *The Southern Review*. They were native poems, autochthonous in a way the fashionable poems of the day could not manage. Being an autochthon of course is something you don't manage, you are. It was not just the subjects, the daily experience of a young man raising grapes in the Great Valley of California, or the rhythms, which were of the same organic pulse you find in Isaiah, or Blake's prophecies, or Whitman, or Lawrence, or Sandburg at his best, or Wallace Gould, or Robinson Jeffers. This, it seemed to me, was a young fellow out to make himself unknown and forgotten in literary circles. The age has turned round, and the momentary reputations of that day are gone, and William Everson, now [1968] Brother Antoninus, is very far from being unknown and forgotten.

I say this, not in a spirit of literary controversy, but to try to bring home to a time that accepts his idiom and his sensibility, how unusual these poems were thirty years ago. Everson has won through, and in a very real sense this whole book—a new edition of his early poems—is a record of that struggle. It is a journal of a singlehanded war for a different definition of poetic integrity. There is nothing abstract or impersonal about these poems. They are not clockwork aesthetic objects, wound up to go off and upset the reader. T.S. Eliot and Paul Valéry told the young of the last generation that that's what poems were, and the young dutifully tried their best to make such infernal machines, never noticing that their masters never wrote that way at all. Everson paid no attention. He cultivated and irrigated and tied up the vines and went home in the sunset and ate dinner and made love and wrote about how he felt doing it and about the turning of the year, the intimate rites of passage, and the rites of the season of a man and a woman. He used the first person singular pronoun often, because that, as far as he could see, was the central figure in the cast of the only existential drama he knew. And what is wrong with that? Nothing at all, the critics of the last generation to the contrary notwithstanding. It wasn't an alarm clock that meditated in the marine cemetery or suffered in the wasteland of London.

Everson has been accused of self-dramatization. Justly. All of his poetry, that under the name of Brother Antoninus, too, is concerned with the drama of his own self, rising and falling along the sine curve of life, from comedy to tragedy and back again, never quite going under, never quite escaping for good into transcendence. This is a man who sees his shadow projected on the sky, like Whymper after the melodramatic achievement and the tragedy on the Matterhorn. Everything is larger than life with a terrible beauty and pain. Life isn't like that to some people and to them these poems will seem too strong a wine. But of course life is like that. Night alone, storm over the cabin, the sleepless watcher whipsawed by past and future—life is like that, of course, just as a walk on the beach is like "Out of the Cradle Endlessly Rocking," or playing on the floor while mother played the piano is like Lawrence's "Piano." Hadn't you ever noticed?

Something terribly important and infinitely mysterious is happening. It is necessary to hold steady like Odysseus steering past the sirens, to that rudder called the integrity of the self or the ship will smash up in the trivial and the commonplace. This is what Everson's poetry is about—but then, sometimes less obviously, so is most other poetry worth its salt.

I don't think there is any question but that William Everson is one of the three or four most important poets of the now-notorious San Francisco school. Most of the people wished on the community by the press are in fact from New York and elsewhere. The thing that distinguishes Robert Duncan, Philip Lamantia, William Everson and their associates is that they are all religious poets. Their subjects are the varied guises of the trials of the soul and the achievement of illumination. Everson's poems are mystical poems, records of the struggle towards peace and illumination on the stairs of natural mysticism. Peace comes only in communion with nature or momentarily with a woman, and far off, the light is at the end of a tunnel. So this is an incomplete autobiography—as whose isn't?

How deeply personal these poems are, and how convincingly you touch the living man through them. I have read them for years. Brother Antoninus is one of my oldest and best friends and the godfather of my daughters. As I turn over the pages, some of them thirty years old, I feel again, as always, a comradeship strong as blood. Evil men may have degraded those words, but they are still true and apposite for the real thing. Blood brotherhood.

—Kenneth Rexroth

NOTE TO THE DESIGNER
& PRINTER

[This undated "Note" by Everson was sent to New Directions along with his typescript of poems for the 1948 edition of *The Residual Years*.]

In the preparation of this manuscript, particular attention should be exercised to see that the sense of the stanza, or verse paragraph, is maintained. In so doing, it will be helpful to observe the following principles:

A sufficiently wide measure should be established to accommodate all but the very longest lines; say, thirty picas for 12 pt. type. The practice, advocated by some authorities, of establishing a measure based on the average-length line instead of the longer ones, necessitates too many "turned over" lines, which, by their indentations, disrupt the effect of the stanza.

When a turned line is unavoidable, a shallow, rather than a deep indentation, is preferable. No more than 3 ems, I should say. A deep indentation is often confused with a double-space.

For the same reason, when it is apparent that a line will not fit the measure, several words should be turned, rather than the last word only.

Do not let a stanza finish at the bottom of a page unless it is also the end of the poem. This is against customary practice which always strives to complete the stanza on the page, but which, in so doing, destroys the double-space, the only way stanzas are indicated. In like manner, do not complete a page on a period, i.e. the end of a sentence, unless of course it is the end of a poem, and for the same reason. This is an unorthodox request, but one that concerns me deeply. Almost every book of modern poetry has in it pages from which it is impossible to tell whether or not the poet intended a stanza. I have prepared the manuscript so that no page finishes upon a period unless it is also the end of the poem.

—William Everson

BOOK ONE:

SINGLE SOURCE

(1934-1940)

THESE ARE THE RAVENS

(1934-1935)

FIRST WINTER STORM *

All day long the clouds formed in the peaks,
Screening the crags,
While the pines stared through the mist.
Late-afternoon the sky hung close and black,
And when the darkness settled down,
The first large drops rapped at the roof.
In the night the wind came up and drove the rain,
Pounded at the walls with doubled fists,
And hollered in the chimney
Till I felt the fear run down my back
And grip me as I lay.

But in the morning when I looked,
The sky was clear,
And all along the creeks
The cottonwoods stood somnolent and still
Beneath the sun.

OCTOBER TRAGEDY

Do not sing those old songs here tonight.
Outside, the buckeye lifts nude limbs against the moon.
Outside, the heavy-winged herons
Are scaling down into the misty reaches of the marsh.
Bitter is the wind,
And a mad dog howls among the withered elderberry on the ridge.
Bitter is the quiet singing of the cricket,
And the silent pools lie black beneath still reeds.
Go away:
Follow the spoor of a wounded buck,
Over the marsh and deep into the desolate hills.
You must never sing those old songs here again.

---

* Previously, "clamored" replaced the original "hollered" (line 9), which Everson restored in the limited edition *A Man Who Writes* (Northridge, CA.: Shadows Press, 1980).

RED SKY AT MORNING

This room has known all night the brittle tick of the clock,
Beating and beating between the walls.
I lie in the dark,
Listening to the desolate wind banging a far barn door.
Half-naked sycamores bend stubbornly,
Their sparse limbs rattling,
And the loose leaves scrape across the roof.
Through the window I can see clouds pile above the hills,
Blotting yellow stars.
The barn door bangs again,
Screaming distantly on rusty hinges,
And the wind whines off into the west.
From my bed I watch the dawn come groping through the ridges,
Cold and slow,
And smothered to a scarlet smear beneath the clouds.

WINTER PLOUGHING

Before my feet the ploughshare rolls the earth,
Up and over,
Splitting the loam with a soft tearing sound.
Between the horses I can see the red blur of a far peach orchard,
Half obscured in drifting sheets of morning fog.
A score of blackbirds circles around me on shining wings.
They alight beside me, and scramble almost under my feet
In search of upturned grubs.
The fragrance of the earth rises like tule-pond mist,
Shrouding me in impalpable folds of sweet, cool smell,
Lulling my senses to the rhythm of the running plough,
The jingle of the harness,
And the thin cries of the gleaming, bent-winged birds.

FOG DAYS

Through the window I can see the fog
Smothered against the steamy panes of glass.
Fog-cold seeps in under doors,
Numbing feet in a heated room.
There's no keeping it out.
It enters through the tiny cracks of window slots
And soaks through walls.
Place your hand on a wall some heavy morning
When the fog hangs low.
You will find the paint grown damp and chill,
Stealing heat from early-kindled stoves.
On such mornings wood won't burn,
Smoke hangs in the flue,
And the salt lumps up in the shakers over the stove.
Only the cedars do not tire of fog;
They drip patiently through days,
Gathering mist and letting it fall.
I have lain in bed and heard the fog-drip
Tap all night upon the ground,
Given by the silver boughs
In renitent release.

MUSCAT PRUNING

All these dormant fields are held beneath the fog.
The scraggy vines, the broken weeds, the cold moist ground
Have known it now for days.
My fingers are half-numbed around the handles of the shears,
But I have other thoughts.
There is a flicker swooping from the grove on scalloped wings,
His harsh cry widening through the fog.
After his call the silence holds the drip-sound of the trees,
Muffling the hushed beat under the mist.
Over the field the noise of other pruners
Moves me to my work.
I have a hundred vines to cut before the dark.

DO NOT BROOD FOR LONG

Do not brood for long within these doors,
For there has been too much of weeping now.
It is for us to walk beneath the windy sky
And mark the way the willows blur the gloom.
It is for us to tread these fallow fields
Before the low red leaves the west,
And sing the last, slow song.
It is for us to mourn, indeed,
But mourn dry-eyed along these lanes,
Heeding the heron's cry,
And knowing the noisy wind too well to weep.

BUT THERE WAS NO LAMENT

When he walked through the waist-high wheat
And vanished in the woods,
There was no wailing at the house;
There was no sound of wild lament,
Or even of a quiet weeping.
The folk stood round the doorway
Staring at the somber trees,
Never moving, never talking,
Only waiting for the dusk.
When the darkness came
An owl hooted from the barn,
And in the farthest fields a bullfrog cried.
But there was no lament,
No hint of grief,
No sound of any mourning at the house.

THESE ARE THE RAVENS

These are the ravens of my soul,
Sloping above the lonely fields
And cawing, cawing.
I have released them now,
And sent them wavering down the sky,
Learning the slow witchery of the wind,
And crying on the farthest fences of the world.

OVER THE ROADS

Over the roads the country children come,
Swinging their books and laughing across the knolls.
In twos and threes they straggle along the lanes,
Pulling the bright-faced poppies up from the green.
North and west the late wind tramples the grass,
Blowing behind the roofs of barns,
Blowing the shrikes up from the tilting posts.
Country children lean into the gust and laugh,
Picking the poppies out of the green, today.

WHO LIVES HERE HARBORS SORROW

Secluded and dark the few farms hug the creeks,
Dividing the frozen drabness of the plains.
Who lives here harbors the mood of sorrow early in fall,
And holds it heavily, listening to long coyote-howling
Mourning down the wind on moonless winter nights.
These folk breed children strong as mountain weeds,
Teaching them young the patience of the years,
And letting them have no hope
When summer heats the earth to life again.

THE HOMESTEAD

Father and son, and father and son
Have given their sweat to the plough
And the torn earth leaving the share.
It is enough to say this field was turned a thousand times
And the land still young.
It is enough to say four men have broken themselves
Unendingly treading these sun-bleached ruts.

There is nothing so timeless as struggle.
After the centuries have spent themselves,
And the sky-hungry civilizations have sprouted beside the seas
And rotted into the earth,
There will be bent men breaking the ground and scattering seeds.
After the world convulses,
Heaving the hills and the gray-green water,
There will be men warring against the wind,
And toiling lean-limbed beneath the slow span of the years.

THE POSSE

Under the granite walls,
Back of the stripped steel you shall not keep him.
He is a man who has stood hawk-faced upon the clear edge of the sky,
Too long familiar with the streaming wind,
Too taken with the broken buttes to cage indoors.
Deep in the dawn you may drive him down
And blast him into the yellow dust,
But he has seen the moon snagged in the ragged hills
Too long to spend his seasons straining against your stone.

Into his flesh was bred the spirit of stooping hawks;
Hot in his veins is lobo blood,
And the cunning of shy coyotes wailing behind the dunes.
Ride him into the earth and break him, this you may,
But neither your walls nor the wind of your revenge
Can keep for your own the sky-yearning fierceness of his heart.

TOR HOUSE

Now that I have seen Tor House,
And crouched among the sea-gnawed granite under the wind's throat,
Gazing against the roll of the western rim,
I know that I can turn back to my inland town
And find the flame of this blunt headland
Burning beneath the dark beat of my blood.

For I have stood where he has stood,
And seen the same gaunt gulls,
And all the tide come pitching in from Lobos Point
To shatter on this coast.
In going I shall bear the feel of his harsh stone,
The sight of sea-wet wings,
And need no souvenir to rub my memory clean.
There is no keener touchstone I can take
Than my one glimpse of Falcon Tower toothing the Carmel sky.

I KNOW IT AS THE SORROW

I have wondered long at the ache in my blood,
The waking as a child weeping in the dark for no reason,
The strange sadness when the storm-tide lures the leaves
    to the wanton dance.
I know it now as the grief of long-gone women
Shivering in the cliff-wind,
While the lean boats dipped in the fjord,
And the home-returning warriors stooped on the bitter shore,
    bearing the slain.
I know it as the intolerable sorrow of little children too strong to weep
    in the light,
Who could not smother the sobs in the gloom of the Norway pines,
Remembering the Danes from the dawn,
And the bright steel slashing the dusk.
It is the unutterable sadness of the sea;
The memory, deep in the bone, of the flesh straining,
The nerves screaming, but the lips loosing it never;
The unrejectable heritage, learned in the womb a thousand years ago,
And given from blood to blood
Till it lies at last in the secret depths of my soul.

In the lightning-whetted night,
When the thick wind sucks at the eaves
And rides the ridgepole into the wisp of the first dim dawn,
I dream in the dark,
And voice again the ancient song,
And find no joy in the singing.

LET IT BE TOLD

Let it be told in the driving dark of some far night,
When the pine trees stagger upon the ridge,
And the crying killdeer rise through the rifts of the broken sky.
Let it be told in a single breath,
Torn from the throat and thrown to the wind
To shake on his shoulder over the streaming hills.
We who watched in the stagnant dusk of this still room
Heard neither breath nor word,
But only the plaintive bats talking faintly under the eaves,
And the crowing of one far cock, dimly down the wind.

SAN JOAQUIN

(1935-1938)

HERE THE ROCK SLEEPS

Here from the valley floor the long rock sleeps in the sky;
Length over length the steep walls gather and lift till the far top dims,
Majestic disdainful splendor, silently mocking with infinite peace
The frailness of life and of motion,
Drinking the dawns, the torrent of time since the hot world cooled
And this long range rose on the crust.
O enormous mass, eagle-hungry height, bewildering beauty of stone:
El Capitan, Cathedral Spires, Half Dome,
Fronting the wild jumble of peaks and the broken thunder of rock
    in the treeless spurs and the starving sky!

I think it best to leave this place and not come back;
To see it once and turn away, the first look scored on the numbed sight,
The memory kept like a searing coal to startle the nerves
    in the last thin years
When the senses lag and the worn mind wavers toward night.

FISH-EATERS

This blood has beat in a thousand veins,
And mingled redly in too many limbs
To remember the source, the single spring,
The fountain lost in the mist of the years.
Nordic and Celtic is all I know:
Pale-haired giants roaring their mirth on the Norway coast;
Somber Celts in the Irish fog,
Under the edge of the weedy dunes,
Huddling the meager blaze, and no singing.

I think of the men behind the centuries,
Groping down to the sea,
Fish-eaters, pickers of flesh from the salty shells,
Snuffling the wind of the water's edge, the black waves beating.
I think of the withered women left in the stinking huts of the hills,
No glimmer nor a hope,
And knowing no strength but the lips held mutely over the teeth.

O you folk of the farther dark,
This bone and this blood are nothing of mine,
But wrung from your flesh and fiercely born in the dimmest days,
When to live was to lust, to reach for the axe and rise to the fury,
Wade to the roaring thick of it,
Shoulders hunched and the long arms hacking.

Yet, trying my heart I find no hunger for the sword,
This blood drowsy and slow, wanting no war,
Glad for the peace of the hawkless hills,
Glad for the sleep in the sun.

FOG

The gray mask of the fog, the pale plate of the sun,
The dark nudeness of the stripped trees
And no motion, no wave of the branch:
The sun stuck in the thick of the sky and no wind to move it.
The sagged fence and the field
Do not remember the lark or her mate or the black lift
    of the rising crows.
The eye sees and absorbs; the mind sees and absorbs;
The heart does not see and knows no quickening.
There has been fog for a month and nothing has moved.
The eyes and the brain drink it, but nothing has moved
    for a number of days,
And the heart will not quicken.

ATTILA

On a low Lorrainian knoll a leaning peasant sinking a pit
Meets rotted rock and a slab.
The slab cracks and is split, the old grave opened:
His spade strikes iron and keenly rings.
Out of the earth he picks an ancient sword,
Hiltless with rust and the blade a long double curve,
Steel of no Roman nor Teuton king,
But metal struck in the sleeping East and lost in the raids.
He turns it awhile in the thick hands,
His thumb searching the eaten edge, and throws it aside.
The brown strip winks in the light and is sunk,
Winks once in a thousand years, in the sun and the singing air,
And is lost again in the ground.

Attila, you rode your hordes from the Asian slopes and swept
        to the west,
Roaring down Rome and the north-born Goths.
In the screaming dawns you struck the rich earth and left it smoking;
Struck and butchered and lived like the crimson arc of a cutting knife.
Through the reeling years you ran like a wolf,
Side-slashing blindly from border to border the length
        of that bleeding land,
Till your own lust killed you and the dark swarm broke.

In the nights the moon crawls to the west and is hidden;
The dawns bloom in the east;
The fogs gather.

Attila, in your frenzy of life you burned, but for nothing.
You roared for an instant, shook the world's width,
        broke the fierce tribes.
You are outdone: the earth that you raped has been ravaged more foully;
The cities you sacked have been burnt and rebuilt a hundred times;
From your day to this the valleys you plundered
Have known killing and looting, the sharp violence,

The running thunder shaking the night,
A gasping moment of peace and then at it again!

Yet you struck deep: in the fields the earth gives up a curious sword;
The bright-haired folk of a German farm
Regard with doubt a baby born with oval eyes;
In a gusty hut an old man hugs the hearth
And tells an ancient story.

WE IN THE FIELDS

Dawn and a high film; the sun burned it;
But noon had a thick sheet, and the clouds coming,
The low rain-bringers, trooping in from the north,
From the far cold fog-breeding seas, the womb of the storms.
Dusk brought a wind and the sky opened:
All down the west the broken strips lay snared in the light,
Bellied and humped and heaped on the hills.
The set sun threw the blaze up;
The sky lived redly, banner on banner of far-burning flame,
From south to the north the furnace door wide and the smoke rolling.
We in the fields, the watchers from the burnt slope,
Facing the west, facing the bright sky, hopelessly longing to know
    the red beauty—
But the unable eyes, the too-small intelligence,
The insufficient organs of reception
Not a thousandth part enough to take and retain.
We stared, and no speaking, and felt the deep loneness
    of incomprehension.
The flesh must turn cloud, the spirit, air,
Transformation to sky and the burning,
Absolute oneness with the west and the down sun.
But we, being earth-stuck, watched from the fields,
Till the rising rim shut out the light;
Till the sky changed, the long wounds healed;
Till the rain fell.

LINES FOR THE LAST OF A GOLD TOWN

MILLERTON, CALIFORNIA

When they rode that hawk-hearted Murietta down
    in the western hills,
They cut the head loose to prove the bounty,
And carried it here to this slope on the river's rim
Where the town sprawled, but no longer.
In a jar on the courthouse desk it lay for days,
While the wide-wheeled wagons swam in the dust,
And the word ran: upstate and down the folk heard it and sang;
And the head in the jar on the Millerton desk
Sneered through the glass at the faces.

Now the thick grass.
The willow fringe on the water's edge drinks the March sun
    and has peace,
Takes the deep sky, and bird-singing, the low mottled music, but heavy
    with peace.
On the low slope over the stream, with the roof of it thin
    and the windows gone,
The old courthouse alone on the meadow squats in the drag of the years;
Musty, floors fallen, the smell of dead time on it,
Of the killed moment, the stifling accumulation of sheer existence,
Thick in the air, and the wind takes it.

There can be heard over the earth,
Running in deep and vibrant gusts, the broken music;
Blowing, the reverberation of uttered sound,
Of bawd's talk and squaw's talk and the male-throated laughter,
Primal and harsh and brutely intense.
The mind's eye fashions the picture: glare on the night
    and the shacks crowded,
The congestion of flesh, of reeking animal flesh, blood burning,
    nerves blazing.

And one turns to the years,
Through the soft disintegration, thinking:

Where are the seekers and where are the whores?
What has come of the roaring, the lewd language, the riotous lusts
     and the acts?—
Here, where are only slow trees and the grass,
And this empty hulk and symbol of an order jeered at,
Spat at, hooted and scorned in the days of its birth?

Crumbles, the leaf; sags, the used stalk;
Softly, the alteration, the touch....
It has been said, often, tongues hating it.
It has been said.

AUGUST

Smoke-color; haze thinly over the hills, low hanging;
But the sky steel, the sky shiny as steel, and the sun shouting.
The vineyard: in August the green-deep and heat-loving vines
Without motion grow heavy with grapes.
And he in the shining, on the turned earth, loose-lying,
The muscles clean and the limbs golden, turns to the sun the lips
  and the eyes;
As the virgin yields, impersonally passionate,
From the bone core and the aching flesh, the offering.

He has found the power and come to the glory.
He has turned clean-hearted to the last God, the symbolic sun.
With earth on his hands, bearing shoulder and arm the light's touch,
  he has come.
And having seen, the mind loosens, the nerve lengthens,
All the haunting abstractions slip free and are gone;
And the peace is enormous.

**

WHO SEES THROUGH THE LENS

Who sees, through the searching lens on the mountain,
Arcturus and Vega and all those far-swimming millions back
    of the moon;
And leaving at morning turns east to the flame,
Feeling earth underfoot, dust of the leaf, and the strain,
The reach and insatiable hunger of life;—
Finds in the morning no peace, nor rest in the noon.

The cold mind needles the rock,
Fumbles the sleeping seed, pokes at the sperm.
Blinded and burned it flutters at all the candles of the sky,
Fixed in the obsession of seeking, the dementia for knowing,
Immutably gripped in the pitiless frenzy of thought.

Watcher, give over;
Come star-bruised and broken back to the need;
Come seeking the merciful thighs of the lover.
Out of the plasmic dark the repressed and smothered thunder
    of the blood
Will roar to the ears and the white mind drown in it;
There will pound in the throat the incredible song.
Retain the balance; match thinking with feeling.
There is ocean and night that needs never a gleaming,
Nor star for its sky.

BARD

Sing it. Utter the phrase, the fine word.
Make the syllables shout on the page,
The letters form till the line glows and is ringing.
Pursue the illusion. It is sweet to the heart
To think of them listening, to think of them
Thumbing the leaves, the eyes avidly drinking.

You have in your nights the dreams of the older years:
Hearth-side bards in the great halls, singing,
Shouting the tale, chanting the lusty word and the rhyme,
While the warriors stared, the women hushed and not breathing.

It is fine for the heart to think of oneself as the Voice,
The Pointer of Ways.
It is warm in the chest to think of them listening.
Sing the phrase and fashion the line;
Hug the sweet dream in the lonely dusks when the far planes whine
        in the sky and the west deadens.
It is good to the heart, it is fine in the chest to think of them listening.

ON THE ANNIVERSARY OF THE
VERSAILLES PEACE, 1936

Low is the light;
No red in the sky but a yellow stain;
And that killed snake, the sierra, all angles and humps on the filled east.
In the low fields where no song is and the wind dead,
The forces are caught, the wrestlers hang in the wide sky, blended
    and still;
There is no warring nor fury nor flame, but the hush and the balance;
And one watching can nearly accept with hope that gospel of love
    which was Christ's.
But the truce fails; the light spreads, hurling west,
And the sun bursts roaring from the rough hills,
Trampling up sky, and is free.

Cry *peace!* if you will.
There is in the plasm the mood that denies it.
There is in the fist the love of the striking,
And out of the heart the savage inviolate flame.
Life comes to it shining: grass choking, the wolves slashing.
Napoleon, nor Caesar, nor Genghis could have led the hordes,
Unwilling, into the jaws. They ran down singing.
And I who hold the poor dream as passionately as any,
Expect it never. We have sprung from the loins of that mother, the past,
And got something but love from her dugs.

WINTER SOLSTICE

Here with the dawn the sun crawls wanly, takes the south sky,
    the short route, filters the fog.
Over the drift the killdeer cries in it, lost in the depth
    but the notes floating.

Now is the solstice, day of the weak light, the soon-setting.
Now is the time of the waning ebb; feeble the sap, slow is the blood.
We who have sung in the sun and run in it, raced in it, laughing
    with light,
The August-lovers; we, thin-blooded, shivering in the early sundowns—
    this is not ours.

Deep in the east the night comes running,
Over the rim, over the high withdrawn and hidden peaks,
Ridge-haunting, darkening the lift, the far slope...
Now are the days of the setting sun;
Now is the running night.

YEAR'S END

The year dies fiercely: out of the north the beating storms,
And wind at the roof's edge, lightning swording the low sky:
This year dying like some traitored Norse stumbling
    under the deep wounds,
The furious steel, smashing and swinging.

From the northern room I watch in the dusk,
And being unsocial regard the coming year coldly,
Suspicious of strangers, distrustful of innovations,
Reluctant to chance one way or another the unknown.
I leave this year as a man leaves wine,
Remembering the summer, bountiful, the good fall, the months
    mellow and full.
I sit in the northern room, in the dusk, the death of a year,
And watch it go down in thunder.

SAN JOAQUIN

This valley after the storms can be beautiful beyond the telling,
Though our cityfolk scorn it, cursing heat in the summer
    and drabness in winter,
And flee it: Yosemite and the sea.
They seek splendor; who would touch them must stun them;
The nerve that is dying needs thunder to rouse it.

I in the vineyard, in green-time and dead-time, come to it dearly,
And take nature neither freaked nor amazing,
But the secret shining, the soft indeterminate wonder.
I watch it morning and noon, the unutterable sundowns,
And love as the leaf does the bough.

THE RAIN ON THAT MORNING

We on that morning, working, faced south and east where the sun was
    in winter at rising;
And looking up from the earth perceived the sky moving,
The sky that slid from behind without wind, and sank to the sun,
And drew on it darkly: an eye that was closing.
The rain on that morning came like a woman with love,
And touched us gently, and the earth gently, and closed down delicately
    in the morning,
So that all around were the subtle and intricate touchings.
The earth took them, the vines and the winter weeds;
But we fled them, and gaining the roof looked back a time
Where the rain without wind came slowly, and love in her touches.

IN THE SHIFT OF THE STARS

High in the west one falling star streaks on the curve of night;
Jupiter glimmers the dark; the Dipper wheels on the Pole
    as the world turns.
Wind over oat fields;
And the sight gone plunging up in the sky,
Thrown violently out for the mammoth flames,
And drowned in the dark.

On a summer's night in the shift of the stars,
When it comes like that, swiftly, the awareness,
The realization thundering deeper than all the dreaming,
Life turns lonely and small, and all that has been done
    and thought of, nothing;
The breed, nothing; the self and the spirit wretched and whining.

Well, weeper, the fault is not yours.
Out of your parents' passion you came wondering,
A healthy beast, your lusts and your limits, and the saving grace
    of your ego.
That you are lost in the scheme is no matter.
Kiss the flesh and finger the bone;
Temper your lust with the mind's touch, but cherish it dearly.
Laugh and be hearty, the body is good;
And take on the flesh and the careless heart
The sun that is over this land.

CIRCUMSTANCE

He is a god who smiles blindly,
And hears nothing, and squats faun-mouthed
    on the wheeling world,
Touching right and left with infinite lightning-like gestures.
He is the one to pray to, but he hears not, nor sees.

Because the man who is my father chanced to a certain town
    in a certain state,
And met the woman, my mother, and met her again in another place,
    and they loved and were wed;
Because the night she conceived, one sperm and not another, of all that
    he gave her, touched home and developed,
I am tall, not short; and dark, not blond; and given to indolence
    and dreaming.
Because it happened like that through the line of my fathers—
(A meeting here, a touching there,
Back through what shrouded and imponderable journeys of time)
This shape of my life the inexorable brood of those ages of chance,
And I at the peak: every move that I make to pattern the form
    of what's off and beyond.

He is the god to pray to; he sits with his faun's mouth and touches
    the world with hovering hands.
He is the god—but he sees not, nor hears.

✳✳

THE KNIVES

She goes more delicate and gentle than any I know;
Compassionate, sweet as the lark's song,
Sweet as the wind's song: she is one to be loved.
But scorning the flesh she will go lonely through life,
Straining to that ethereal detachment, the spirit's realm,
    the mind's garden;
Bruised on the right and cut on the left;
The body's coarseness dragged stinking behind to blight her forever.

Poor virgin, you forge your own knives,
And whet them too keen to be carried.
The lusts that you loathe, as the soul you adore, were made by the God;
And nothing exists needs praise nor condemnation, but shines
    its own splendor.
The way of your choosing lies sterile and cold, the mind's steel harsh
    in the wincing flesh.
You will go hurt, the wound and the bleeding:
But the knives, the knives—they are yours.

SLEEP

The mind drifts warmly, focused on farther dreams.
There comes over the eyes a vast and immeasurable tide,
With no shore breaking, the lift of a darkening sea,
And the mind goes down to it gently, lapped in the lull.

Now from the sunken brain the freed flesh throbs the deep song;
The bone and the fiber hark the same music;
The blood pounds cleanly, pulsing wantonly through the slack
        and indolent limbs,
Loosed from the mind's hand, the nerve's dominance,
Sprung to the secret joy of release.

It comes to the eyes as a moving tide,
With no shore breaking, the lift of a darkening sea,
And the mind goes down to the depth and the silence;
The loose blood pounds the deep song.

WE WALK THE YOUNG EARTH

Conejo, California

Over the hills the loud sun rolls in the falling sky,
Flames and goes down;
In the wide and cloudless evenings the night comes slipping
    out of the east,
The sun goes down with a drop and a rushing and no paint left
    on the west.
On moonless nights small boys in their beds hearken for train-sound
And hearing the far intolerable whistling stir wanly,
Having over their breasts the feeling of weeping
That lies like the touch of a hand.
They listen at night and the sound finds them.

It is here in these new-broken places
One looking west in the late dusk
Thinks of the wind and remembers;
Looks east to the ridges, naked and lifted,
Looks over the gaunt fields, thinks of the wind,
Remembers the earth ancient and hoary: new-broken, new-seeded.
It is here with no human past to tone it
The desolate wilderness of the earth bleeds from the furrow
To color the air till the thick-planted orchards smother it under
And houses soak it and it loses the smell as a buck's hide
    loses the stench with the years.
Then in that time a man may wander the dark
Not stopped by the wind, not saddened by nostalgia for times past,
Things gone, something no longer near, the thick sound of people.
Then will be girls laughing and the lights close.

       *

What signs can you hold to in choosing a country but earth and the sky?
What ways can you tell it but work there and sweat there and learn it
    by living?
You can tell by the shine of the rising sun whether or not
    it is your country—

By the taste of the air, by the feel of the loam—

You can tell by the color of the shining wind
Whether or not it is your country.

We have the new earth;
We walk on a ground that remembers the grass, and dung of the deer,
        the camps of the moving tribes.
There are in this place no songs remotely sprung from the grief
        of an ancient brooding.
Only the talk of the old men recalling the way a man walked, or a horse
        sprang, or the young squaws naked at dusk.
We walk on the wide fields burdened with light
And the past there thin at our heels.

We walk the young earth,
And out of it rises the whisper, the inscrutable mood;
It comes to the throat in a lift and an eddy.

We walk the young earth—and the thin stars moving,
The deep root feeding,
The far trains haunting the night.

☀☀

ELEGY FOR A RUINED SCHOOLHOUSE

The walls down, the beams shattered,
All the false columns opened like shells;
That hulk of a schoolhouse, pretentious and ugly, spilled to the earth.

To have spent years in the rooms, under the roof,
    between the stained walls;
To have sprouted the earliest seeds of the mind's soil;
To have shaped passions, repressions, the cant and the lean of a life—

For the world it is nothing.
These things grow and come down marking the hub of every crossroads
    village the land over.
There are temples ancient with suffering;
There are cities steeped in human passion generation on generation—
Poems are for those, odes for the oldest!

But for me—my life's in the brick,
In the dust of the saw and the chalk of the plaster.
A brick on a brick, but my life's in the heap,
In the surge of the sun and the night.

NOON

The wind down, hushed;
In the sudden suspension of time and all motion
The sun lies heavily on the hand,
Spreads on the tilting cheek;
The ocean of light that is widest at noontime
Swells on the mind.

And no leaf turning, no flag for the restless eye,
The heart takes softly unto itself
Some deep and voluptuous meaning;
And filling, it flows to the blood like sleep in the veins;
And the thick light floats on the shoulders.

Deep sun, deep sky;
No wind now for the dance of the leaves;
But the light clean on the shape of the neck,
And the deep sound of the heart.

NEW MEXICAN LANDSCAPE

We left Pietown north through a country screened by the dark,
Only the ruts of the lifting track fleeing the wave of our lights.
Dawn gave us vision: mile beyond mile the confusion and maze
    of the ridges,
Nakedly dwindling away to the eye's failing,
Blue-gray and somber, the color of desolation,
Wavering out of sight.

One born of a country loaded with growth,
Where the green blazes of foliage kindle the sun eight months
    of the year,
And the ocean of vineyards a lovely flood for the eyes to swim in—
The farmhouses float in it, the islands of orchards lift their dark hills
    out of the level sea—
One born of the green-lying flood
Chills in the wind of New Mexican beauty.

Though worshiping nature for God,
He seeks furtively out the warmth of his kind—the rich fields shaped
    to the human need,
A life not too naked and lonely to lean in the gale of the earth.
Being more sheep than falcon he turns, however unwilling,
Into the huddle at twilight.

THUNDER

You on the road walk north, your knees bending,
Your body swung on the focal hips,
And your head turned west where the hidden thunder
Pounds in the dragging sky.
You walk north, your head west, the wind on your teeth
    stuffing the mouth,
And the sagittary lightning splitting the low sky down.

You feel through the soaked and heavy leather of your lifting shoes
The earth solid and deep beneath you,
Spread hugely away to the thrown hills and the country beyond.
You feel in your hair the caught rain;
On your chest the surge of the air,
Leaking in through your clothes,
Running in sharp and chilling currents over the flesh.
You walk on that roadway live as a nerve,
Poised and quick as a shaking flame;
And the earth comes in on the waves of sight,
And the hawks of the blood are high.

WE KNEW IT FOR AUTUMN

The wind of that dying year made yellow the leaves,
Sycamore, cottonwood.
Downwind in the faltering air they slipped feebly,
They hung in the spikeweed.
Clouds westward told rain, and three crows weaving the hanging sky
Made in their throats the song.

We lay in the edging air, under the late sun, touching.
There was the waiting thigh, the loose and indolent flesh
     hung on the bone,
Easy with autumn, not burning.
We lay in the sun with the leaves going,
And the smell of that month on the wind.

And being closer to sleep than to love,
We knew it for autumn, that made husks of the fruit,
     that seared off the flowers.
We knew it for that seasonal dying,
And sank to the sand, to the broken leaf,
And focused our eyes on April.

LOVE SONG

There have been women before you for untold ages
Who sobbed in the twilight, huddled weeping in corners,
Beat with their fists futilely the shut doors.
There has been anguish before you time into darkness,
The moaning under the evening star, and no help for it.

You have laid off the armor,
Gone nakedly into the world's war,
Unweaponed, perfectly trusting,
The heart open, the consummate gift.

There have been women before you broken and moaning.

You walk in the sun with your hair down,
And the light laid clean on the rounded flesh;
With your eyes laughing, lips laughing;
You walk in the Sunday sun with your laughter caught on your lips,
And your hair dancing.

Woman, be gentle, touch with the lips and the delicate hands.
Touch softly, give gently—
(There has been anguish before you time into darkness)
Give gently, trust perfectly now.

SPADE

And seeing down the dark and new-cut ditch
Earth rise, the shovel-lifted earth
Leap up and go down, the spades leaping,
Remark in your mind how assuring a thing,
The machine failing now in the fragile growth,
It is again the hand, the fingers wrapped on the toughness of oak,
The biceps' movement, the muscled back;
Remark how, now by the stance and the swinging,
Postures of labor, the end is attained.
We bend, and behind us, in the pictures of our blood,
In the remote and time-hidden motion of the breed,
Are men bending, the arms lifting,
The spade, the spade, the simple tool.
We have leaned to the hulk of the nerveless earth,
And been shaken by weather; have turned in the withering thrust
    of the sun;
And have seen.

WIND WEST

There were signs:
Wind preached it two days,
Mare's-tails wrote it white on the sky before cirrus and the sheet.
What came in from the west, out of the belly of the hidden sea,
Lay to our sky, colored horizon.
We under the stretched and taut ripple of the western gust
Turned to it, surmising inundation,
The falling rain and the roofs of the hills,
And those bent and solitary workers
Yielding to weather, and the stripped fields.

The cities went under;
Words in the wind, and over the face some girl's song,
    and the breathing of toilers.
There was in the shape of it all that lay westward.
And taken by silence, made suddenly aware, beyond our prejudice
    and constraint:—
Humanity, the bond of the blood, the narrow brotherhood
    of the seeking nerve—
We leaned to the push of it, hunting what lay under west.

WINTER SUNDOWN

The fog, that nightlong and morning had lain to the fields,
Earth-loving, lifted at noon, broke to no wind,
Sheeted the sky blue-gray and deadened.
The sun somewhere over the dark height ran steeply down west;
And that hour, silence hanging the wide and naked vineyards,
The fog fell slowly with twilight, masking the land.

And alone at that falling, with earth and sky one mingle of color,
See how this moment yields sameness: December evening
    grayed and oppressive.
You have seen night come like this through all of your growing—
The trees screened, the air heavy and dead,
And life hushed down, this moment repeated,
The dusk and the fog all one.

OH FORTUNATE EARTH

Now afternoon's running.
There are men moving singly and slow, pruning dead growth.
In the cold south-falling light there are teams moving.
High up killdeer, crying, flash white from the breast
    as the sun takes them.

You can see from this hillock towns and their smoke on them,
    roads shining,
And miles under the thrusting sight the slumbrous earth.
That beauty shadows the heart,
Till evil and violence and the tragic splendor of the crashing world
Die on the mind, as thunder fades over a sleeper.
In islanded calmness, in the deep quiet, spirit nor blood will awake
    to the drum,
Perfectly tuned to the heavy mood that breeds in the valley.

"Oh fortunate earth, you must find someone to make you
    bitter music...."
No chanting of mine lures the talons down.
These places rare, and too dear.
The world is the plunder of hawks.

VERNAL EQUINOX

Andromeda westering.
These evenings the sun sinks, beautiful and alone,
In the cleared sky, the wide silence,
For spring's up the year;
The restless sap in the naked vine thrusts at the bud.
To give to it wholly—but the mind sees it ancient and tired,
The old recurrence, the earth like some old jezebel
Annually touched by a stale desire, daubing her lips.
The burst of revival is over the ploughland.
It should be beautiful and immense, as the birds see it,
When the blood in them burns and their mates beckon.
Traitorous mind, having duped nature, willing to dream some months
    longer under the heavy beauty,
You color the vision, that once knew with welcome the growth
    of the bud,
And the coupling birds.

ABRASIVE

You know now the reason,
Since April has shown it, and the young wind thrown you
      its weight.
You know by the answer that speaks in the blood.
In fall resent winter, in winter, spring,
Disliking no season, but torn by the wars of perpetual change;
One part of your nature longing to slip yielding and drowned
      in an ocean of silence,
Go down into some abstract and timeless norm of reality,
Shadow the eyes, the uneasy heart, and be done.

The sun makes a fool of you: the flaunting year shocking with seasons,
Into the desperate sight loading transition.
Having honed the lean nerve, what sheath can obscure it?
The long winds hunt it, sun storms it,
And life grinds at the scabbard its furious weight,
The abrasive of change.

COAST THOUGHT

There is wind from far out, and the moving sea,
And no words for it: what edge of the shining earth
Can be caught singly and sure in the flashing eye?
It takes slow love, the mood of a country seeping the vision,
The mind absorbing the season's turn and the heavy years.

I see the long level, the deep movement,
And remember the flood of that other ocean,
That sleeps in the eye and its shining upon it,
Not troubled by motion, the spread of those vineyards
Knows only the tide of the falling year.

This place has a mood, but that in me strongest is bred of the other,
And cannot be shaken, though gull's cries and salt smell
        hood it a moment.
It sleeps in me surely, tolerant of strangers, smiling to see me
        wooing this rival,
Knowing itself deeper and firmer, and holding the bone.

SUN

Season on season the sun raiding the valley
Drowns it in light; few storms, the hills hold them,
The long hills westward take in their arms the children of the sea.
I speak of the storms for the sound and the music.
Out of the weight of those ages behind us roll furious words,
The syllables of thunder; they break on the lips, beautiful and round.
There has been tumult forever, speech from it,
The names for tranquility lost in the wars.
Sun breaks; it rides the high noons magnificent and forgotten,
Taken for granted, and sinks late;
And wakens a music too mute for the mouth
That hungers the north.

OUTSIDE THIS MUSIC

These verses are lies.
Who bends the hard hand over the lines,
Shaping the words, feeling the gust of an ancient mood
Blow through the room, the weight of the night and the broken hills,
Hammers no truth.

He feels up through the floor the strength that is cramped in the stone
      of the earth
Push at his flesh; the lips stammer on darkness.
Into the delicate substance of the blood
Flows the long wind, deep drives the night.
The eyes will be blind, the throat shattered and mute
In the wave of thunder of the fallen sky.

What lies outside the closed and hollow music of this verse
Runs in the earth, in the plunge of the sun on the summer sky.
There is wind on the walls,
And the feeling of tough wild weeds straining all outdoors,
And the bruised mouth, forming the shape of a word,
Turning toward night.

TRIFLES

The man laughing on the steep hill tripped on a stone,
Fell broken among boulders, suffered his life out under the noon sun.
The young wife, when the tire blew on the Trimmer road,
Took that long crash screaming into the rocks.
By sand slipping, by the shoe splitting on the narrow street,
By the parting of atoms,
By the shaping of all those enormous trifles we plunge to that border,
Writhing under the long dark in the agony of destruction,
The great sky and the flaming west riding our eyes,
Gathering in from the heavy hills, and the tides of the sea.

O poets! sleepers forever under the soil!
You have spoken it out of the bitter mouths hundreds of times;
Your anguish beats from the pages, beats on our bored
        and indolent sight!
But earth yields and a man is smothered,
Wood splits and a man is broken—
Simply, the mute and terrible ease of the function—
And you and your shouting burst up before us;
We taste that wry and sterile bitterness,
And pound with our hands on the dark.

HOUSE ON SECOND STREET

We moved south where the streets turn,
Northeast, southwest: the house half faces sunrise.
In the hush of the night we lying abed feel those great
    mysterious currents
That run up the world, out of Mexico and the jungles south,
Out of the southern slopes and all that bulk and strength
    of the lower seas,
Pouring north through the night,
Hit the house counter, the beams strain,
The house like a ship taking seas on her bow
Moves in the dark, the nailed and hammered wood whines on its posts.
Rising at night see Sagittarius lifting you think due east,
    the wrong quarter.
Baffled by street plan turn back to the bed.
In the charged and quivering air of that room,
When the thick night coils on the walls and your blood deadens,
Listen: the house trembles,
The old wood shifts on its posts.

WALLS

East, the shut sky: those walls of the mountains
Hold old sunrise and wind under their backs.
If you tread all day vineyard or orchard,
Or move in the weather on the brimming ditch,
Or throw grain, or scythe it down in the early heat,
Taken by flatness, your eye loving the long stretch and the good level,
You cannot shake it, the feeling of mountains, deep in the haze
    and over the cities,
The mass, the piled strength and tumultuous thunder of the peaks.
They are beyond us forever, in fog or storm or the flood of the sun,
    quiet and sure,
Back of this valley like an ancient dream in a man's mind,
That he cannot forget, nor hardly remember,
But it sleeps at the roots of his sight.

CLOUDS

Over the coastal ranges slight and indefinite clouds
Moved in to sunrise, rode up the west;
Toward noon the change of the wind strung them to furrows.
Sundown flared late, the close and the heavy twilight of August
  hooded the fields.
They were broken to fragments, and were burnt on the growth
  of the gathering night,
When Venus blazed west and went down.

So common a beauty: the workers over the wide fields hardly looked up.
Under the great arching sky of the valley the clouds are across us,
The trade of the routes of the upper air,
Their temporal splendor hawked on the wind for some listless eye.

Cirrus and stratus: the fringe of the distant storms of the sea;
December wanes and the nimbus are driving.
They are scattered by dawns, or are killed on the heavy fists
  of the peaks;
But the wind breeds them west forever.

THE MASCULINE DEAD

(1938-1940)

ORION

Remote and beyond, lonely farms on the shoulders of hills
Sleep in the night. Seaward-running rivers,
Draining the continental flanks,
Pour in the dark, pour down the mountains,
Suck silt from the plains.
On inland ridges timber stirs in the cloud,
And far down the channels of the southern sky
Those arctic-loving tern are crossing the islands.
Mist gathers; the long shores whiten;
The midnight stars on the central sea
Lure the morning stars over Asia.

Light seeps at the window;
A faded chart of the used season hangs on the wall.
There are mats, worn, the thin bed,
The bare stand holding its chipped jug.
Glow from the alley colors the room: a dull stain.
The tension strung in the nerves of the city
Trembles the night.

Under the crust the massive and dormant stone of the earth
Swings at the core; bulk turns;
The weight turning on the tipped axis hangs to that line;
Atom-smashing pressures war at the center
Straining the charged and furious dark.

We, come at the dead of night
To the stale air of a drab room
High on the edge of the empty street,
Feel under the wind of our own compulsion
Those seekers before in the drained ages,
Daring the dark, daring discovery in the shut rooms,
Secretly meeting at river's edge under scant stars.
They sought and were lucky and achieved fulfillment;
They hung at last on the old fury,
And ground with their loins,

And lay sprawling and nude with their hearts bursting,
Their emptied flesh,
The spent mouths gasping against the dark.

They pound in our limbs at the clenched future.
They drive us above them, beating us up from that dead time,
Thrusting us up to this hanging room,
This toppling night, this act of their need
Forming again from the sunken ages.

Orion! Orion! the swords of the sky!
Forever above the eastern peaks they rise and go over,
Burning and breaking in the random years.
Under their light and the lean of a roof
The eyes drown inward, the blind eyes sinking,
The blind mouths, the great blind currents of the blood
        pulsing and rising.
Here in the room the streams of compulsion
Have formed in the rhythm of these gathering loins;
And feeling behind them the tides of all being—
Betelgeuse his bulk, and the yeared light, and the high silence—
They suck into union,
A part in the torrent of those shattering stars,
And time and space a waveless sea, and the dying suns.
Beyond all the sources of that breeding light
They strike and go out,
To the presence inscrutable and remote awake at the last,
Music that sings at a star's death,
Or the nature of night, that has border nor bulk,
And needs nothing.

Sleep, flesh. Dream deeply, you nerves.
The storms of the north are over Alaska.
This seed of the earth,
This seed of the hungering flesh,
Drives in the growth of the dark.

THE RUIN

The year through September and the veils of light
Broke equinox under; south darkened;
The wind of no rain, northwest and steady,
All day running the valley,
Swung with the dusk, strengthened,
And the cloud gathered, raiding the open sky.

Under the whisper we watched it come over,
The raisins heavy yet in the field,
Half-dried, and rain a ruin; and we watched it,
Perceiving outside the borders of pain
Disaster draw over,
The mark of the pinch of the coming months.
There was above us the sheet of darkness,
Deadly, and being deadly, beautiful;
Destruction wide for the dreading eyes.
What was hardly of notice another month
Now burned on our sight;
And it rode us, blown in on the wind,
Above and beyond and the east closed under;
It let down the ruin of rain.

THE ROOTS

England, gaunt raiders up from the narrow sea;
In the dark of the ridges,
Broken under the waves of conquest,
The shattered tribes;
Those gazers out of the stricken eyes,
Under the spell of that moody country,
Shaping the sounds: from the ruinous mouths
The core of existence caught on the tongue,
And the words fashioned.

They are lost in the years of that unknown time,
But the single rhythm of the ancient blood
Remembers the anguish, the hate and desire;
The lips shape a word, and it breaks into being
Struck by the wind of ten thousand years.

And I, not English, in a level valley of the last great west,
Watch from a room in the solstice weather,
And feel back of me trial and error,
The blunt sounds forming,
The importunate utterance of millions of men
Surge up for my ears,
The shape and color of all their awareness
Sung for my mind in the gust of their words.

A poem is alive, we take it with wonder,
Hardly aware of the roots of compulsion
Quickening the timbre of native sounds;
The ancient passion called up to being,
Slow and intense, haunting the rhythms of those spoken words.

FEAST DAY

Peace was the promise: this house in the vineyard,
Under the height of the great tree
Loosing its leaves on the autumn air.
East lie the mountains;
Level and smooth lie the fields of vines.

Now on this day in the slope of the year,
Over the wine and the sheaf of grain,
We shape our hands to the sign, the symbol,
Aware of the room, the sun in the sky,
The earnest immaculate rhythm of our blood,
As two will face in the running light,
Ritual born of the heavy season,
And see suddenly on all sides reality,
Vivid again through the crust of indifference,
Waken under the eye.

East lie the mountains,
Around us the level length of the earth;
And this house in the vines,
Our best year,
Golden grain and golden wine,
In autumn, the good year falling south.

THE DANCER

for Gordon Newell: the stone he cut to a Jeffers poem

I have in my mind the dark expanse of the northern sea,
And the storms across it,
Moving down from the arctic coasts,
Gray whirlers, the knees of the wind.

I have in my mind the stone block and the splendid thighs,
Turning in on themselves in a beautiful dance,
Moving to some incantation sung from the run of the changing sea,
Dancing the wind up out of the waves,
Poised and turning,
Dancing the music awake in the depth.

The mood of the stone is alive in my vision,
The mood of the sea,
The mood of my own inclement blood.
The wind of the rain is awake in the granite;
The clouds are alive; the tides are alive.

Low drumming of thunder in the murky north,
Gray dancer, gray thighs of the storm,
Gather us up in the folds of darkness;
Come over us, solemn and beautiful music,
Mindless, the pivoting thighs,
The song of the thighs, and the dance.

THESE HAVE THE FUTURE

So sleep the vines, as the vineyards of Europe,
Feeling back of them, hundreds of years,
The intervals of silence dividing the wars,
Now gather their strength in the cold weight of winter
Against a new spring.

They have the past but these have the future.
The towns will be altered, roads break,
The rivers shift in the grooves of their beds,
All through the valley the subtle and violent forms of transition
Work to their ends, but the vineyards thrive,
Come time and war and the links of quiet,
As now to the eyes in the low winter light
They yield the good presence of peace.

South lies the sun;
The year's coming over;
In these wakening fields the hordes of the weeds
Will go under the throats of the April ploughs.

In the long time hence,
When those tides of the future have formed and gone down,
Some poet born to the voice and the music
Will live in this land, it will sound in his verse,
And waken the sight of the men of his time
Who before had no eyes, but for splendor.

THE ILLUSION

The low wind talks on the boards of the house,
Gains and recedes, night deepens.
And feeling it round you,
The touch of this peace on your full spirit,
You know the illusion: men in the world stronger than you
Bleeding under the roofs, falling under the wheels,
Pitching down from the sky to lie in the fields under blunt stars.
Hear in the night the long wail
Calling the cars to some roadside shambles.
Remember him who lay on the mountain,
Holding his shattered foot, and the axe.
Think of the torn mouths begging release down the groove of the years.
Sit in your peace, drinking your ease in a quiet room,
Soft in your dreams—and the men falling.

The cities are shining.
The great ships west in the welter of seas hunt out the islands.
You feel the high, impregnable ranges of earth leaning in darkness.
You feel the texture of your living flesh
Wince on the bone.

You rest in your peace.
They pitch and go down with the blood on their lips,
With the blood on the broken curve of their throats,
With their eyes begging.

You rest in the ease and fortune of your dreams, and they break.
In the solitary towns, on the long roads high in the folded hills
The night blows over them rushing and loud and they fall.

THE SIDES OF A MIND

Can a man hide fire in his bosom, and his garments not burn?
                                                    PROVERBS VI:27

I

He lay on a ridge of that frozen country,
By the broken guns, by the smashed wagons.
He lay gasping raw mountain air.
He saw in the valley the thin line of the rising troops
Waver, the sticks that were men topple and fall.
He lay coughing, rasping, in the pain and fever of his one dream:
The new cities, those clean wide streets and those shining mills.
"And now I lie at my death's edge while they lunge to the slaughter."
He coughed. Blood roared through his brain.
High and bright in the upper air
A squadron tipped on its wings in the sun's eye, and plunged.

While a poet, leaning above his futile poem:
"I close my eyes and feel the steep wave of affirmation
Crash and thunder on the reefs of my mind.
I feel the power rising out of the dark sources,
Those unknown springs in the sea-floor of the self.
I open my eyes and the arrows of beauty strike and plunge in;
The light roars over; the gales blow down from the strongholds
        of the north.
I have only to let them pour through these poems,
Deep and controlled, and men can touch their strength again,
And taste the old wonder.

"But the theme! the theme! Every motive I try
The thin mind stooping above it searches and tests: the theme fades.
Every hope I have come to is smiled down,
Belief made foolish, the pitiless hunger unfulfilled,
The mind crying for anchor.
Our lives are haunted by the wealth of a past we no longer own.
Wherever we turn, our hands encounter the husks of forms
That lost their meanings before we were born.
We, obsessed and fevered, a dry fury eating our lives—

But these empty poems that would gather the millions:
Lies, and I am their liar."

But another, up from the alleys, furious:
"You sit in your rooms stammering over the terms of abstraction
And outside your doors is the source of the power
    that is shaping the world.
Whatever the beauty you may have desired, no poet has sought it
But the veering wind blew through the room
The smell of misery and rot and the filth of the poor.
You have seen them, risen out of their holes,
Wearing the common look of need.
You have hunched in your rooms all the years of your kind,
And begged crusts, and shivered with cold,
And died, and your bodies lost in nameless graves—
And you sit here, the choices of action plain at your hands!

"We have time no longer for the seeds of your doubt.
We have time only for man and man
Facing together the brute confusion of the stubborn world.
Man and man, and chaos beneath us resolving to order
Under our common hands."

But another, where the poised lens stared at those whirlpools of the sky:
"When you have it; when you live at last in your shining towns,
Your children tall in the sun and the fat land teeming;
No war among you; no poverty ever to shadow your people;
Your lives clean and strong in the flower of your dream—
Then face the mirror; look in your eyes;
Turn then your questing eyes to the light;
Know only the eddies of your searching minds
For that cold comfort.
Low in the west swim the constellations that fostered an age,
That had gathered on Thebes and would blaze on Rome;
That are spending yet down the steep sky,
Burning their own way out into nothing—
Breed, build cities, alter the oceans;
But there is no God, nor was ever a God,
And that is the root of our trouble."

Yet one, who heard the sound of great spaces,
Smiled in his room,

And placing pen on his paper, wrote;
And out of that page, music,
The strains like light in the quiet air,
And the walls shook;
And the wind that had lain on a hundred hills
Swung on the house;
And he, smiling:
"I will not be hedged by their carping minds,
For I have the means to elude them."

Low, beautiful beyond belief,
The soft sound of music grew in the room.
I had leaned to the earth,
Listened under the rifts of the hills,
Lain in the pools of the valley streams,
Listening, leaning for music.

Low, beautiful beyond belief—
And all the substance that makes up my limbs,
The veins, the quiet bone in the sheath of flesh,
Every thread and fiber of my seeking self
Lifted to meet it.
There was soft to the marrow what I could not know,
And blind on my eyes, the vision.

II

Father, whatever you hoped for that first deep night,
With the seed of the future
Sown in the living loam of the moment,
Dreaming a son to carry the world,
Some stormer and breaker to grasp it full in his two hands,
And shape it after his whim and his fancy—
Whatever you dreamed,
The years that came after cheated you dearly.

I am not what you wanted.
I sit hunched in a room,
Wrapped in the narrow folds of my self,
Knowing the facets the world distrusts:
The love of seclusion,

The cold staring of the inner eye,
The twist of mind that smiles at your hopes,
That sets me bitter against your likings.

Where can I find the means of achievement
Locked in the orbit of what I am?
Now in the night,
Hearing the secret hammer of my blood,
I see the veins,
The arteries strung in the texture of flesh;
I see the nerves, the floating lymph,
The cold white bone.
(Watch how the blood behind the eyes pulses and changes!)
And I rise, under the goad of my own anger,
And facing see only the pale wall, the pale ceiling.

And I think of you, father:
I, your son, the stuff of your loins
Sprung into life.
I think of the land you left, and the men behind you,
Shouting, the fierce past of your race—
And I have them within, they are cramped in my blood,
But I know not the locks of release.

III

Darkness coming, darkness out of the eastern hills,
That I, a child, engrossed in my gaming with the autumn leaves,
Suffused with their odor, was never aware of—
Until night upon me, the worshiping trees,
The reaches of silence gathering up
To that solitary and unwatching star.

I stopped. I had laughed under it all my life
And had never seen.
I lifted my face in wonder and silence.
I lifted my unseen and wondering face,
And the wind, blind as an underground beast,
Touched at it; and I fled, wide-eyed,

To the room and the light and the warm stove,
And the voices of parents.

I crouched in the heat
Listening to hear if the wind still hunted the trees.
I looked up in my mind to the thin star, lone in the sky,
That could not see, hanging in darkness forever.

I, bully and braggart and coward,
Thieving, lying, whispering, whimpering:
I looked up out of the engrossment of my self,
And saw high in darkness the blind eye,
The beast of the wind,
The dark devotion of the straining trees.
That night in my bed I felt the thin roof
Fragile under the sky.

IV

Watching her move I said: "This is my mother.
She bore me month after month in the cradle of flesh,
And brought me forth in her desperation
That morning early as the east split—
And now I am grown, and she, older."

And I suddenly thought of that withered womb,
The wet walls, the rubbery sides of aging flesh.
I cried out in my heart: "Why should I love?
She is that noisome place from which I have come,
The symbolized blackness of the earlier grave,
Horrible inhuman darkness that thrust me bloody and panting,
Drinking the air, breaking the hold of the inner night!"

Oh, mother, mother!
I am your hope and your pride.
You would go down to the night and never doubt.
You would twist to the last tearing ribbon of pain
That I might live.

Mother, forgive me.
I have agony and frustration and knives of my own;

And the rivers that run from the springs of my self are deep,
And too wide for my swimming.

V

All day, working, I felt underfoot
The teeming cities of the summer ants
Stamped on and shattered,
The fragile torsos of weeds broken,
Their seeds bursted,
Their structures wasted back to the earth.
Eating at noon, the plasm of life went under my teeth;
Every sucking breath that I drew
The long border of warfare ran down my lungs,
Furious soldiers of my blood warring and killing,
The people of the air plundered,
Their castoff bodies buried in dung!

(All day you are careless and happy;
The light pleases;
The warm wind nuzzles the caves of your ears.)

Oh, speak of salvation!
Offer your worship to the staring sky!
Deep in your very blood they are dying,
Killer! Killer!
Under your heels the agony, the death rattle!
And your laughter loud in the sun!

VI

I sat in the dusk of that cold room
And knew something beyond me.
She leaned in the gloom,
Calling them down from the shining air.
She held up her hands and called them.
They came like birds.
They slid from the night and the quaking stars.
I felt them shifting and floating,

But they made no sound.

I watched her swaying in her abstract rite,
She who had crossed the border of death
To play with these beings.
I knew myself isolate and alone in the cold dusk,
Foreign, hot-fleshed and scarlet-blooded,
In the closed limits of my earth-fashioned bones,
And I could not speak.

For they have the knowledge.
Free in their thin and transient beings
They see down the past,
Up the rifts of the future.
They watch the far scenes kindle and flare.
They see our blindness, the limits of our minds,
And know the foolish and earnest error
That sends us fumbling through our lives.

Feeling their presence we sense suddenly the levels of time,
The riptides forming in the sheets of the wind.
We crouch in the night with the odor of danger rising across us,
And turn, and all our passion and the temper of our rage
Break, and the sky looms.

We go twisting and begging into the earth.
We hang in terror at the opened earth,
Hugging our own, the forms, the rites,
Sucking in anguish that need for the known;
Until all we have seen, and all we have done,
Is gathered at last from our eyes.

VII

They lie in the trapped darkness of my loins
And hunger for life: formless inchoate voices,
Aching whispers of the tidal dark.
They lie blindly through my years

In the unborn darkness of pre-existence,
And dream the future.

Poor dupes and children that I never shall get,
What could I give you?
A soul scalded by the self-conscious and acid inward-peering eye;
Inordinate desires, inordinate appetites for non-existent foods.
I would give you hunger and fury and fear,
And set you staggering blind down life,
Breaking your fists on the frozen rocks.

I feel around me the urge and tension of the rolling air.
I see the storms that hung off Hawaii
Bloom in the west, open their folds,
Take on their throats the upward-stabbing sword of the wind.
I, loving life, drinking the dazzle—
But each shiver of pain they ever felt
Would ripple in to the moment of my act,
And I will not yield.

They stir in the dark,
Their blind hunger aching for life.
I have closed the door, severed the cord.
Let them dream in their darkness forever.

VIII

Here on my hand the thin hair leans,
Crowds on my arm,
Runs heavy and long up my leg to the hip;
Hair of the pubis tangled and rank;
On the small of my back a little patch
The size of my hand.

Hair of my body grows from my flesh
Each with its life,
Seeking its need through its own function.
Locked in my skin the little roots
Suck at survival,

The small lives flourish.
I shave my face and they thrust again,
Blind as the grass.

In the Arizona dark
The manseed burst in the black channel
And I came into being.
In the California dawn they broke the bond.
I bolted down food and my limbs lengthened,
The lean ribs grew in the slender chest:
All the frightening acts and needs of my body
Rushing me up to the growth of a man.

This morning, rising from stool,
I looked down at the dung of yesterday's feast
And knew what I am.
All over my body the pores are oozing;
On the soles of my feet the dead skin sloughs;
My nails grow;
My heart hammers its own rhythm year after year;
I go down in the nights into blind sleep
And nothing is altered.

I sit in this room
With one small portion of a pulsing brain
Directing my hands to make marks on a sheet.
For this the pores yield?
Do I eat beeves and make dung to hunch in a chair
And loose myself in the sprawl of these words?
I feel the shout and pressure of the blood of my race
Stop in my veins;
The hunger of those who fought and endured,
Bled out their lives,
Beat their way gasping, choking,
Through the closed nights of force and resistance—
For what?
That I may squat in a wooden room

And scrawl on a paper?

You, McKelvy, can you tell me better?
Watkins, you've read all the books!
Carothers, you've flinched already to the world's fists!
I see your faces cold in the gloom
And you do not know.
You cannot tell me.
You do not know.

I feel the blood in my throat
Start down the channels beyond my control,
And I know the last terror:
That we have no say,
We are not asked;
That life feeds on life:
Between my hand and my mouth
Its hope and its hunger and its mindless need
Pass into nothing.
This is the whole substance of our thought,
Its term and its triumph.
The nights draw over,
The long streams start in the fissures of the rocks,
And water runs only downhill.

IX [December 31, 1939]

Flow, night; roll, river;
Sea on the steep of the western ridges,
Eat at your reefs.
Now in the span of a single hour
The decade that tempered the shaft of our lives
Wanes to the past.

That saw us in love and doubt and anger;
That watched the fever of our adolescence
Gain richness, resolve into order.
I see in the focus of my mind

The innumerable acts rising before me,
Rising to press themselves into my eyes.
I smell the odor of a new wind, broader,
My knees in the seep of draining time,
The locked nights yielding the east.

Roll, river.
Night of the past and the one future,
Suck and go down.
The wind's with the runner,
Throwing its weight through the last hour.
The decade wears itself out.

THE MASCULINE DEAD

PROLOGUE

Day after day the naked sun on the upper ocean
Rides the blank sky.
The dead sea washes, lazily piling into the reefs.
Gulls feel the still air thick on their wings
And, high in the light, see level beneath them
The stretch of the distance studded with islands,
The coast of Alaska a curving arm.
No wind fills the sky; mist burns in the noons.
The dead calm hangs on the whole of that region
Closing the face of the waiting sea.

Then cold wind forcing, units of air
Fat with heat and heavy with moisture
Drift upward, cool as they rise, thicken to vapor.
The wind picks at the water, warming and rising.
Clouds form, hang full and thick and smother the sun.

That is the time the wind breeding out of its northern cradle
Starts the storm down.
It meets the firs on the iron coast and bears inward,
The trough of the continent sloping it south.
High in the massed and limitless woods
The warning stations send out the sign.
The black bringer of rain crowds the northwest and drives over;
It flies on the valleys; it tears its belly on the granite peaks.
Women on lone Montana farms
Stand at the doors with wind on their knees
And watch it come in.
On the span of three states the great hub turns.
The rain loosens.

THE MASCULINE DEAD

Now it is fall we feel once more
The far-streaming wind ride down the world.
We see the seeds, hardly alive in the shells of fiber,

Watch through the loam.
The stubble that stood so long from the cutting
Feels the new weather:
Stalk rotting to earth, root changing to mould.
All over the fields the live and the dead
Have heard that old summons:
The trumpeting loud on the northern horns
That the rains are here.

AN OLD WOMAN

Aye, the wind's rising—watch the low sky.
There's scud in its weight and the Lord's light
Snapping out of its paunch.
The dead'll be walking the woods tonight.
The dead'll be clamoring under their stones
And the earth won't hold them.
All the rock in the world can't hold down the dead
With the sky breaking.

THE MASCULINE DEAD

Beautifully over the tops of the trees
The first clouds come.
We see them low toward the north gathering through haze,
Swollen and black, rolling down from the smoking sea.
We hear the wind in the weeds,
Sweeping and plunging in the useless stalks.
We lean together, feeling all the old autumns
Rise up again and cover our eyes.

A GIRL

It was out on the road in the April noon
When the hills were green.
The road runs by the river, and climbs,
And the old flume that came out of the mountains
Was still by the stream.
He sat at the wheel, laughing,

His blond hair flattened by wind;
And we came through the hills,
They were beautiful and green,
And the sun was on them, and the birds,
The birds rose from the river.
There was a rut in the road we did not see till the car struck,
And the whole world went out from under,
The tipped sky dragging its trees,
And then that crash, and the car rolling,
My flung body crushing the weeds.
I crawled in the stalks, and called him;
He did not answer;
And looking, I saw his smashed face and his eyes.
I got to the road; I stopped them;
And they went down, and lifted him;
And bearing him up that heavy hill his head rolled back,
The throat strained upward, white and weak,
The cords standing under the clear skin,
And the bruised mouth open.

THE MASCULINE DEAD

We could lie like this on the open fields
Year after year if there were no fall.
When the thick light sleeps through the summer days
We rest in the reeds and have hardly a dream.
We do not remember our long limbs,
Nor the bone in them,
Nor the blood that crept down out of the heart,
Filling the flesh,
Feeding the brain all the old wonders.
But wind coming out of that northern country
Breaks up our sleep.
We think of the fingers supple with life,
And the teeth we had,
Crushing the pulp of the golden fruit.

A WIDOW

When eleven struck and he had not come home
I went to bed.
I lay in the cold sheets,
Trying to hush my mind into sleep.
I could hear the clock,
Lonely and alive in the silent room,
In the dark of the room and the quiet of the house
Marking the hours.
I thought of the still and empty halls beneath me,
The rooms lying silent and cold,
The beams keeping the strain through all those years and not settling;
I thought of the wind,
Rising and falling against the eaves,
And I dropped into sleep.
I woke with the phone ringing on and on in the empty hall.
I felt the floor cold on my feet,
And the cold stairs, and went down;
And there in the dark I learned what had happened.
Back in the room all I recall is the face of the clock,
And the hands pointing ten until three.

THE MASCULINE DEAD

And rousing, we dream the eyes of women out of the dusk.
We see them leaning, curve of the head, round of the throat.
We see them, and know once more
The importunate rush of those shut nights,
The strain of the nerve that could not abide,
And all that it meant, more than the eyes,
More than the answering tilt of the lips.
We see time closing in to the moment under the elms,
The moment under the eaves,
In the silent rooms, in the soft of the beds.

A YOUNG WOMAN

I stood on the corner a full three hours
But he never came back.
The night wore by, and the day after,
Then all the days passing and not a sign.
Some nights of the week I'd go to a dance.
There were fellows I knew, and we danced till day;
But it never mattered who I was with,
I was always watching.
That was May, I remember.
May went into June and June to July.
Out in the yard those summer nights
I'd lie on the lawn
And hear far down the street
Some man on the walk.
I'd lie holding my breath, and listening,
And the steps would grow,
Get louder and louder,
And come to the house,
And always go by.
I'd look up into those yellow stars,
And know how lonely they were,
How far and still, strung in the sky.
Then the nights got cooler,
The stars moved over behind the house
And strange stars came.
I knew by that it was autumn.

THE MASCULINE DEAD

We see the eyes, the knees, hands loosing the silk,
Lips turning to meet us parted in haste and desire.
We see the bared breast and the naked thighs,
The bodies beneath us sloping and soft;
And we watch from out of this pale abstraction
Our plunging loins, our glued mouths,
Our flesh sweating in the lock of love.
We see the blood gather out of its old source,
And rise, and break, and our limbs hush,
Go slack and soft, our lungs gasping,

And our eyes opening out of the ranges of night
On those faces beside us tender and soft,
Beautiful in their white peace,
And the splendor of completion.

A WIFE

That was the night we crept out through the fields
When the wheat was high;
There was deep in the east a full moon,
Round as a disk, and few stars, and no one was near:
Mile after mile all we could see was the waving grain.
He slipped his arms beneath my own,
And the wheat went over our heads like a wave
As he drew me down.
I lay on that black and breeding earth,
And what I was doing cried out in my mind,
But this man was there.
I felt him leaning against the dark,
The need in him trembling his urgent limbs;
I knew he was going far away,
And would not come back;
That this would be all;
That never again would the two of us meet.
I knew what he feared,
Bending beneath that naked sky;
And I knew I could not refuse.

THE MASCULINE DEAD

Or drunken with wine we mounted the stairs to the dim rooms.
They met us, painted mouths and the false smile.
We put our hands in their clothes.
We took them naked and laughing in our aching arms,
And crushed them against us,
Pouring our strength in their blind wombs,
And left them, swaggering,
Our money hid in the secret drawer.

THE OLD WOMAN

Hi! how they're shouting!
They're singing behind the hammering panes!
The wind slipping and scrawling across the eaves
And the young dead in it.
There's never a woman safe in her bed when the wind's up.
There's never a woman safe in the night
With the reckless dead caressing the eyes,
And twining their limbs in the lovely knees,
And kissing the lips.

THE MASCULINE DEAD

And there rises before us the childhood moment
When, staring out of our wondering eyes
We saw the pattern open its folds,
Show us the wide land lonely and broad between the oceans,
The little towns on the high plateaus,
Making so tiny a light in the dark.
We saw the forests of earth and the long streets;
We saw the wind in the frozen womb of the north,
And those tidal forces under the sea that alter the future;
And knew in the flare of that opening glimpse
The sudden awareness of what we were.

And it comes, it rises.
We see ourselves in the good strength,
Arrogant, loving our quick limbs and our wit,
Ignorant, singing our bawdy songs,
Shouting with pride and assurance in the plenty of our health.

Till over us crowded the load of darkness,
Slipping like shadow across the sun.
There was one long look of the turning sky,
And our knees caved, the spring-tight nerves
And the strained thews snapping and fraying;
And we fell: urine burned on our legs,
The broken lights and fragments of our dreams
Raced on our eyes.
Then only the night, shoreless,

The sea without sound,
Voiceless and soft.

We lay for a time on the edges of death
And watched the flesh slip into the earth.
We watched the eyes loosen their holds,
The brain that had hungered,
Known fury and pride,
Burned with lust and trembled with terror.
We saw our sex vanish, the passionate sperm,
All the future children of our loins
Be nothing, make mud,
A fertile place for the roots to plunder.
After a time the bones were chalk,
And the banded rings we wore on our fingers,
Corroded and green.

A WOMAN

They were all like that,
Good riders and runners,
Quick on their feet,
Free with a girl on either arm, and merry.
I went with them every one at Troy.
I went with them all,
And danced with them all,
And more than that,
And I don't regret it.
They're dead.
They died early and young.
They died with most of their lives before them,
And got only a taste of what should have been theirs.
I think of them laid out under the ground,
And whatever they did comes to little enough.
I think of them laid out under the earth,
With their poor blind skulls;
And remember them under the lights at Sleed's,
And under the bridge at Freighter Creek.
I'm near enough to the grave myself
To know what the difference is.

THE MASCULINE DEAD

Under the earth are the windless lakes
That lie forever beneath the trees.
The roots drink down to them year after year,
Burrowing in through the loam and the gravel,
Groping between the hidden stones.
The moles cruise there in the under darkness,
Eyeless and slow.
Innumerable hordes of the breeding worms
Rush through the obscure function of their lives,
And live, and pass, and remain forever.

We slumber among them and watch the endless flux of the living.
We see the hare spring from the bush,
The plunge of the hawk,
The talons strike in the small of the back,
The great killing beak.
We see the weeds put up in the spring,
Full of their tough hope and their hunger,
Go under the hooves and be trampled to pulp.
We see the women in childbirth,
The infant closed in the black womb,
Turning in torment, groping out toward discovery,
Pitiful and small and fragile with life.
In the shallow streams, the fish that have fought for a hundred miles
The rocks and the falls and the hidden traps
Replenish their kind on the clear bars,
And, rolled on their sides,
Drift broken back to the waiting sea.
The rush of survival blows through the earth like a deep wind,
Forever, the goad, like a heavy wave, the flux.

High rides the darkness,
The storm on the states hangs like a mask,
The white serpent of lightning flickers and plays,
The great trees break.
We see high over the heavy sheet the thinning air,
The darkness widening up to the stars.
We see the northern fields turning toward winter
And the fields of Australia turning toward spring.
In the South American jungles

The Amazon pours through its centuries,
Dragging a continent into the sea.
All over Asia the tribes are forming.
The races of man rise from the dreaming hills of their homes,
And wander the earth,
And hammer their will through war after war
On the nations about them,
And go down at last into dissolution;
Their people scatter,
Die one by one in the secret cells
At the world's end.

The men who supplanted us measure their strength
        on the stubborn earth,
And bend to the brunt:
Negroes staggering under their loads,
They can break in their arms the back of a ram;
Tall golden Swedes whose nostrils suck the smell of the sea.
They try their muscle against the earth,
But strong as they are the earth beats them.
They try against stone; they try against steel;
They take it into their hugging arms,
And fall, and come back bleeding,
And whine with the bursting strength of their youth.

We see them, and rise, remembering the past.
We look at them out of the eyes of death,
Tasting the salt of that old anguish,
And want only this:
The importunate nerve, the blood surging in splendor,
The famished breath sucking into the lungs
The sweet stuff of our lives.

THE OLD WOMAN

Poor shattered throats,
Poor knees so fond of nuzzling the blankets....

THE MASCULINE DEAD

For we are the men who, young and hot-blooded,
Fell under the blow,
Were knocked speechless and stunned,
Our dead eyes and our open mouths
Facing the sky in the changing weather.
We are those who stooped, who sprang,
Who were lost and hunted and never found,
Who slid through the luminous curtains of sea
To the middle depths where the weight held us.

We see the old, who lived their full lives,
And died in peace on quiet beds,
Go down into darkness with hardly a sigh.
We are the tortured and the damned,
Forever doomed to rise through the autumns,
Hungering the wealth of the broken lives
We never fulfilled.

Oh, far and far the violence of earth
Opens before us,
The torrent starting and the high stream,
The rain-swollen rivers smashing themselves
In the groins of the mountains.
In the upper lanes the storm-baffled geese
Scatter in broken ribbons of flight,
Crying their lost mates down through the dark.
We on the earth rise out of the rubbish of fallen sticks,
And shout once more,
Seeking with disembodied passion
Some shred of the joy that shivered our flesh.

High as the eagles, fleet as the gulls,
We float the long channels,
Singing the remnants of the old songs,
The lonely melody of lost life.
And the song falls,
Pulsing and soft,
And the reckless men in the dim rooms
Sense it, momentarily,
Under the belly of the wind,

But they do not hear;
They reach with their hands to the toppling moment
And drag it into their arms.

Oh, give us salvation!
Grant us the tools of resurrection!
We throw ourselves upward,
Beating our boneless hands on the air,
Clapping dead mouths on the speech of our need.
We huddle together,
And gather upon us the stored hunger of all we have dreamed
In the heavy earth,
In the heavy night,
Under the grinding rivers of the world.

And the hills go down;
The mountains go down to the heels of the rain.
In the storm-darkened canyons
We jostle again, the old promise of fulfillment;
But the rivers
Cough up their clog,
And stagger down to the sea.

Selma. California

BOOK TWO:

THE IMPOSSIBLE CHOICES

(1940-1942)

Let breath keep to the lung.
She'd never believe,
Had soul for her sung,
Mind gonged, or the bell heart rung.

Not one tongue-tolling word
Would she believe.
Though high court heard,
Sealed the assent, and the State averred.

What deficit at birth
Blinded her eye?
What scant, what dearth
Blanks out her own, her immeasurable worth?

**

THE RESIDUAL YEARS

(1940-1941)

THE IMPOSSIBLE CHOICES

No, not ever, in no time,
In none of the brooding age of the breed,
Have the wings of salvation
Enfolded in triumph the living self.
There are those who cough up the rot of their lungs;
There are those strengthless divers of the sea,
Their bleeding ears in the pressure;
Those leaned to the lash;
Women split by the butting heads of their sons—
And all those webbed in their own desire,
Dragged through the bleaches of every sensation,
Who never attain, and who die forsaken.

Against the outer extreme or the inner compulsion
The flesh crumbles and breaks.
The bone is not strong.
The riotous nerves drink their own death in the roiling air;
Or the endless North grins against them its ready muzzle,
And reaps what it can.

One seeing his shadow
Thrown on the shape of that double doom
Looks to his method,
Sorting the chaos of all endeavor
For the narrow moment between the acts.
Fronting lust and revulsion
He painfully fashions the mode of survival;
Between the intolerable climaxes
The blossom flowers before his eyes.

He turns in the end to a mean, a measure,
The impossible choices hung at his hands,
And he leans between them,
Breathing an equinoctial air,
And lives in that weather at last.

THE PRESENCE

Neither love, the subtlety of refinement;
Nor the outrider, thought;
Nor the flawed mirror of introspection,
Over all the age labored up from the ape,
Let light down that dark.
In the wilderness between skin and bone
There bulges the presence we do not know.
In the spun space between minute and minute
The will collapses;
The shape stoops in the mind, hairy and thick;
And the norms vanish,
The modes of arrest and the taut adjustments
Whirl down the years.

Women giving themselves in the summer nights to unknown men
Seek only the male hunger,
The masculine flesh;
Locking their knees round those dark loins
They couple in lust,
Are left in the weeds depleted and gasping,
Their bellies burdened with strange seed.

And those, cold and imperious, forging their lives,
Nursing their bitter precepts of will,
Enduring years of denial, years of restraint—
They too, they too will know in a bursting night
Their blood and nerve and their smothered need
Erupting like lava,
Their beasts' bodies doubled and lewd,
The gross voice of incontinence
Bawling along the vein.

They will lift up their knees
And that slogging plough will find the low furrow.
They will bear against it their gaped wombs,
Driving their flanks and their bending backs,
Driving their loins,

Throwing their bellowing flesh on the tool
That eases the rutting sow.

In the anguished awareness of all that it means
They will labor against it,
Seeking to kill in one ruinous act
The failed years, the spent endeavor.
Sobbing and lost they will plunge with their groins,
And fall broken down the dark.

They will be used;
And bleeding, will find it cold comfort to know
That what they went down to is greater than they had ever feared;
Than they dreamed;
Greater than their stubborn pride,
Or their pitiful will,
Or their racked bodies;
As great almost as that which watches beyond the bone,
And puts out the eyes,
And blackens in time the faces.

THE VOW

The sky darkens;
Lights of the valley show one by one;
The moon, swollen and raw in its last quarter,
Looks over the edge;
And I kneel in the grass,
In the sere, the autumn-blasted,
And seek in myself the measure of peace
I know is not there.

For now in the east,
The flyers high on the rising rivers of air
Peer down the dark,
See under the flares the red map of the ruined town,
Loose cargo, turn,
And like north-hungry geese in the lifting spring
Seek out the long way home.

The low freighters at sea
Take in their sides the nuzzling dolphins that are their death,
Burst and go under;
Their crews lie on the rafts in the deep fogs,
And will not be found,
And will starve at last on the blue waste.

And I dream the delusion of men twisting in death
Without honor or love;
I feel the unresolvable tension forming within me,
Knowing myself of the same breed,
And I shatter the hollow weeds.

For yet in my blood are Leif the Lucky,
And Njal, and the daughter of Hoc,
Who saw son and brother pierced by the spear,
And that firece old king who fought in the walls,
Going down at last with his skull split,
His great beard bloody and stiff.
There are the stunned eyes and the gibbering mouths,
Those who endured crazy with hate,

And who bore in their loins the warped seed
That never forgot.

I, the living heir of the bloodiest men of all Europe.
And the knowledge of past
Tears through my flesh;
I flinch in the guilt of what I am.
Seeing the poised heap of this time
Break like a wave.

And I vow not to wantonly ever take life;
Not in pleasure or sport,
Nor in hate,
Nor in the careless acts of my strength
Level beetle or beast;
And seek to atone in my own soul
What was poured from my past;
And bear its pain;
And out of the knowledge of dissolution
Bring my pity and bring my ruth.

Delicate and soft,
The grass flows on the curling palms of my hands.
The gophers under the ground
Fashion their nests in the cool soil.
I lift up my eyes,
And they find the bearing that swings the sky,
And I turn toward home,
Who have gathered such strength as is mine.

Autumn, 1940

NOW IN THESE DAYS

In our easy time,
Those days of delight unfolding behind us,
In solitude and quiet,
Nursing the seed-like mind into light,
We sought to resolve in the wrestling soul
The old intractable contradiction;
And however we faced that hard decision,
All that we learned of it stands to the test.

For we are the ones
Who, outside the narrows of nationalism and its iron pride,
Reject the compulsion;
Who stamp our allegiance only at last
On a concept wider than it can hold,
Denying the right of its militant creed,
Its arrogant will,
Its ignorant laws and its dangerous myth;
Who, facing the edges of that decision,
Will pay the wry price,
Will reap the loving reward of faith,
And pray as we reap it that time and its pain,
And the deadly erosion of will,
Traitors us not to our need.

And each in his room
Smiles the rue smile against that future,
Unwilling to preach,
Disliking the odor of any crusade,
Knowing only as each man unto himself
Perceives its truth will the Peace come;
Only as each man sees for himself
The evil that sleeps in his own soul,
And girds against it,
Will the Peace come.

We would wait in these rooms and watch them go down,
The raiders hawking the low sky,

And see all about us the forms we have loved
Blasted and burned, nor rise against it.

We would wait in these rooms
And accept the degradation of slavery and want.
We have seen to the central error of fighting.
We know only by love,
By the act of contrition,
By the humble dreamers of all lands
Enduring misery and hurt and holding no hate,
Can the agonized race
Climb up the steeps to the last levels.

Now in these days,
The tag end of peace,
In the amplitude of soul that sees pity
Heavy behind the hate,
We watch the gathering days,
The gathering doom,
And read in our books and hear in our music
The high morality of those dauntless men who could never be bought,
The indestructible will rising through sloth,
And we know we have not been alone.

Winter, 1941

ONE BORN OF THIS TIME

One born of this time,
Growing up through his childhood credulous and soft,
Absorbing the easy creeds of his sires,
Their bland assumptions,
Their ambiguous faiths;
But gaining his strength,
Seeing the deadly myth and the lie,
Seeing indeed the buried ages
Hurled up bursting before his sight,
The implacable sky whistling with death,
His traitorous dreams and his false assurances
Paper-like peeled from the frame of his mind—

Let him not, therefore,
Crying that none can escape his time,
Seek power and seize,
Imposing his terrible order about him;
Nor bitter and callous turn in on the nerve;
Nor, lacking even the fiber of that decision,
Whimper before it,
His gaunt hands screens for his eyes,
His pale mouth moaning delusion,
And his terrorized tongue.

But let him, rather, turning to past,
Seek out that iron rib of conviction
Bearing beneath the steep thought of all times,
The unbending belief of men holding to truth
Through wave upon wave of unreason and doubt.
Let him be like those dreaming infrangible Jews
Fronting their centuries.
Let him build program for action based on repose,
The tough and resilient mind
Gazing from out of its central strength,

Rock-like, the beam of morality holding it up against terror, oppression,
The howling fronts of revolution and hate.
Let him dare that;
And let him know in his daring
He has all any man ever had.

Spring, 1941

THE UNKILLABLE KNOWLEDGE

Churchill: the sound of your voice from the eastern air,
Borne on the singing lanes of the sky,
And caught in this room.

What we hear: the old imperious English speech,
That out of its wealth and its rich evocation,
And out of the singular English past,
Broaches the heritage
Boned in the structure of our common lives.
Your terrible warning and your crying appeal
Blow through the mind.
We suddenly see in its vast implication
The leveling of London,
And the implacable voice
Speaks on in its rigor,
Speaks on in its need,
And breeds of that need the slow indignation,
The rock-rooted anger that fosters resolve.

But draw as you do on all the right,
It yet is not yours;
Though with blood you bind it,
Not yet is it yours.
For even beyond your tenor of soul,
Beyond your courage, your strength, your incomparable speech,
Resides a morality deeper than any your cause may claim,
An insight sheer through the animal manifestations of terror and rage,
Beyond nation, the divisions of race,
The smouldering heritage of hate,
To coil at last at the final unkillable knowledge
That lives among men.

Shout down the sky.
Who listen beyond the hammering tongue
For the eloquent fallacy wound at its root

Are not to be wooed.
Drawing all the detail to one iron focus
They watch with eyes wide;
And they wait.

Spring, 1941

THE HARE: AN EARLIER EPISODE

The hare running for life in the sparse growth
Broke cover,
His ears low and his legs driving,
But sure blew the shot,
And shattered and mauled he thrashed in the rubble,
His entrails sprawling the red ruck,
And those angered ants at their work.

Then surely that time
Evil hooded my heart;
Surely that time
The source of all hurt and harm and heavy woe
Pinioned me high in the frozen air,
Gazing far down the blue height of my indifference,
My ears stoppered against those piteous cries
That swam up about me,
My stone eyes cold in my iron face,
The central terror and the separate hurt
Far at my feet.

Between that time and this
The subtle and transigent forces of growth
Have altered my mind;
Nor can I now say the way that it was,
But ice thawed,
Height dwindled,
The dwindling height threw me racked on the ground
     by that bleeding hare,
My torn flesh and my splintered bone
Tangled with his.

Against the frozen impossible fact of redemption
(No act undone,
The hare mewling and jerking
Down time from now on)

I draw all my strength,
And wear as I can the measure of pity,
The meed of forbearance,
And the temperance fathered of guilt.

LAY I IN THE NIGHT

Lay I in the night,
Hearing the rain at the raw roof,
The wind breaking its knees on this hurdle, the house,
And plunging beyond.
Thought I of those wide and winter-soaked fields
Verging on spring,
Their mushrooms rising into the rain,
Bearing leaves, sticks,
Loose crumbs of earth on their table-tops,
Their stumps soft and brutal with life.

Thought then: I also lean on the verge,
My young time pouring across me,
Flesh violent with love,
Brain coiling and breeding these germinal poems,
All my power and all my need
Bursting me into the full of my life.

Thought then: so let me now,
Confronting that future,
Bring to it all the edge I am able,
Feeding my brain and my drinking nerves,
Bearing my mind against rust and ruin and sagging sloth.
Let me not waste myself on impossible flights,
Nor scatter my strength in self-pity and fear;
But let me turn to the tide of this forming time,
Dredging beneath the blind surf of events
For the stone levels I know are there.
Built on such base,
Let consciousness load through the gates of my mind
All that my being can bear.

A WINTER ASCENT

Climbed, up stone slope and its runneled rifts,
The shade-heavy side of a winter hill.
Under our feet the rain-ruined flints,
Over our heads the birds scarce in the air
And the air widening,
The air spreading about us—
Time-eaten England, her hanging doom
Washed from our brows.

So blood beat;
So backs rising stone over stone
Bore the full sky;
So sight sprang, when, gaining the crown,
Knew far in the valley its first farm,
Shrouded, as in some airman's straining eye
The Orkneys, small on the sea, draw him down.

THE APPROACH

Breaking back from the sea we ran through low hills,
The long deserted pavement falling and winding,
Lonesome farms in their locked valleys,
The coastal range, ancient even as mountains,
Moulded by wind.

Till inland we curved to the far converging city,
Seeing it laid at the hill's heel,
Whirlpooled, the long lines of its power,
Beacons for planes revolving the dusk,
The black trails of concrete slipping down grade
To the first clusters, to the city,
Thick in the gloom with its few lights showing,
With its veils, its myriad roofs,
And its heavy pounding heart.

DO YOU NOT DOUBT

Do you not doubt, being lonely of heart,
And bleakly alive on a wrinkling world,
The fate that so forces?
Men doubling on death
Deny with their eyes the joy that drew them;
And the cursing girl,
Twisting about her central hurt,
Breathes oath on black oath
Before she fails.
These turn at the crux;
But one whole of mind and firm of flesh,
Flinch as he does his aching eyes,
May yet bear brunt,
Unholy and harsh though it beat against him,
May yet bear brunt.

For the scope, the sweep,
The balancings and continuations of our lives
Extend beyond us.
However we spaniel to wedging fate,
The inherent choices of human attempt
Are opening yet.
What has to be taken take with mind wide,
Dragging wholesale armies into its maw,
Sorting the masses of heaped confusion,
Dealing with doubt and that lonely fear.
And though the spectacular agitation of pain
Quench you at last,
Be yet prepared to use as you can
The augmentation and heritage of the race,
The continuity of mind beyond mind
Grappling with truth,
As if all who have hammered against the dark
Beat from your brow—
Then hard-handed force,
The exactitude of that final fate,
Such even as that may be faced.

THOUGH LYING WITH WOMAN

Though lying with woman,
Taking deep joy from her rich knees,
Or threshing that dream in the lonely circle of masturbation,
Or seeking it locked in a boy's limbs;
Though lurching with wine,
Though craftily teasing the beggared tongue,
Though dazzling with speed the wide and staring flowers of sight—
Be sure that over those eyes,
Back of that brain,
(The terminals where meet the quick nerves)
Be sure there exist the subtle levels of comprehension
These never can know.

Be sure your joy breeds from a beauty
Existent beyond it and out of its reach,
Showing for him who has broken the smothering triumph of touch,
Of the swinging sight,
Of the pale and delible uses of taste;
Who, gazing from out of an ampler vision,
Beholds in the fastnesses of his mind
Some manifestation wrung through the web of the roaring senses,
A hulking dream pervading its power across his thought,
The edge of some transigent revelation
Unfolding behind the nodes of response
Its glimmering shape.
Beyond such a time,
Though caught in what craving,
An untouchable portion of his awareness remains aloof.
The mind looks out of its own involvement,
Across the yammering tongues of all desire,
And finds finality there.

LAVA BED

Fisted, bitten by blizzards,
Flattened by wind and chewed by all weather,
The lava bed lay.
Deer fashioned trails there but no man, ever;
And the fugitive cougars whelped in that lair.
Deep in its waste the buzzards went down to some innominate kill.
The sun fell in it,
And took the whole west down as it died.
Dense as the sea,
Entrenched in its years of unyielding rebuff,
It held to its own.
We looked in against anger,
Beholding that which our cunning had never subdued,
Our power indented,
And only our eyes had traversed.

THE RESIDUAL YEARS

As long as we looked lay the low country.
As long as we looked
Were the ranchos miled in their open acres,
The populous oaks and the weedy weirs.
There were birds in the rushes.

And deep in the grass stood the silent cattle.
And all about us the leveled light.
Roads bent to the bogs;
Fenced from the fields they wound in the marshes.
We saw slim-legged horses.

We saw time in the air.
We saw indeed to the held heart of an older order,
That neither our past nor that of our fathers
Knew part in the forming:
An expansive mode remarked through the waste of residual years,
Large in its outline,
Turning up from its depth these traces and wisps
That hung yet on through a cultural close
We had thought too faint to recapture.

POEMS: MCMXLII

(1942)

THE ANSWER

The bruise is not there,
Nor the bullying boy,
Nor the girl who gave him the bitter gift,
Under the haws in the hollow dark and the windless air;
But the rue remains,
The rue remains in the delicate echo of what was done;
And he who labors above the lines
Leans to an ache as old almost
As the howl that shook him in his own birth,
As the heavy blow that beat him to breath
When the womb had widened.

For boyhood bent him:
Awkward at games he limped in the offing.
Youth yoked him:
The tyrannous sex trenchant between his flowering limbs,
Nor strength to subdue it.
Now manhood makes known the weaknesses flawed
      in the emergent soul:
Guilt marring the vision,
The whimpering lusts and the idiot rages.

And the years gnaw at him.
Deep to the dawns does he marshal all skill at the intractable page,
But nothing converges;
Grown pudgy with time he takes blow and rebuff,
Is baffled,
Hugs to the rind of his crumpled pride,
Endures only out of an obscure persistence
Grained in his soul.

But at last comes a time when, triggered by some inconsequent word,
The breath of an odor,
Some casual touch awakening deep in the somnolent flesh
Its ancient response,
The inner locks open;
And clear down its depth
The delicate structure of that rue harvest

Trembles to life.
The thought stirs in its seed;
The images flower;
Sucked from their secret recesses of mind,
The shadowy traces of all intuition float into being;
And the poem emerges,
Freighted with judgment,
Swung out of the possible into the actual,
As one man's insight matches mankind's at the midpoint of language;
And the meeting minds reduplicate in the running vowel
Their common concern.

Then here rides his triumph:
Caught in his doom he had only his anguish,
But the human pattern imposes across his stammering mind
Its correctional hand.
What was vague becomes strict;
What was personal blooms in the amplification of art;
And the race pronounces;
Out of his mouth there issues the judgment of all mankind,
And he touches attainment in that.

HOTEL

The aged are there,
And the infant in arms,
(Each woolened, each dreading draughts)
The soldier schooled in such ruinous skills,
The barber, the broker,
The pervert wound in the tenor's trance—
All dance indeed on the yokel's eyes,
Who, out of far counties,
Gapes and ogles,
Fumbles his hat on the gaudy plush,
His feet thick in light leather.

But women go by and his eyes assail them.
Suddenly swept, his dream drives up,
Where, high in the honeycombed hotel,
In the reared rooms,
Mouth against mouth in their sightless swoon
The lovers embrace,
Their twinging thighs and their stinging sex
Joined in great joy.
Speechless, lost in the latitudes of the bed,
They grope out through the arched enveloping flesh
Into each other;
While he, who below them giddied his mind, looks out at last,
Aware of the dimming down of the lights,
The hollow street,
And the emptiness within.

EASTWARD THE ARMIES

Eastward the armies;
The rumorous dawns seep with the messages of invasion;
The hordes that were held so long in their hate
Are loosed in release.
The South shakes,
The armies awaken;
High in the domed and frozen North the armies engage;
They grope through the hills to the hooded passes;
They meet in the blue and bitter dawns,
And break up in the snow.
To the West: war, war,
The lines down,
The borders broken,
The cities each in its isolation,
Awaiting its end.

Now in my ear shakes the surly sound of the wedge-winged planes,
Their anger brooding and breaking across the fields,
Ignorant, snug in their bumbling idiot dream,
Unconscious of tact,
Unconscious of love and its merciful uses,
Unconscious even of time,
Warped in its error,
And sprawled in exhaustion behind them.

Spring, 1942

THE OUTLAW

I call to mind that violent man who waded the north.
He imagined a slight,
Killed for it;
Made outlaw, lay in the echoing waste;
Fled to far cities;
Knew dangerous about him the subtle strands of communication
Ticking his doom.
Cornered at last he knelt in the night
And drew like magnet the metal loosed in the acrid air.

And so went down.
Nor ever knew that what brought him such bounty
Was only the wearing out of a way—
He and the wolves and the dazed tribes
Numb in their dissolution.
Blind in their past,
The past betrayed them;
The trees of tradition screened from their sight
The enormous forest of the waiting world—
As we, we also, bound in our patterns,
Sense but see not the vestigial usages grooving our lives.
Like some latter-day outlaw we crouch in our rooms,
Facing the door and the massed future,
And draw doom down on our heads.

THE RAID *

They came out of the sun undetected,
Who had lain in the thin ships
All night long on the cold ocean,
Watched Vega down, the Wain hover,
Drank in the glimmering dawn their brew,
And sent the lumbering death-laden birds
Level along the decks.

They came out of the sun with their guns geared,
Saw the soft and easy shape of that island
Laid on the sea,
An unwakening woman,
Its deep hollows and its flowing folds
Veiled in the garlands of its morning mists.

Each of them held in his aching eyes the erotic image,
And then tipped down,
In the target's trance,
In the ageless instant of the long descent,
And saw sweet chaos blossom below,
And felt in that flower the years release.

The perfect achievement.
They went back toward the sun crazy with joy,
Like wild birds weaving,
Drunkenly stunting;
Passed out over edge of that injured island,
Sought the rendezvous on the open sea
Where the ships would be waiting.

None were there.
Neither smoke nor smudge;
Neither spar nor splice nor rolling raft.
Only the wide waiting waste,
That each of them saw with intenser sight
Than he ever had spared it;

---

* First stanza, fifth line: in Everson's personal copy of the '68 edition, the poet writes in "glimmering" to replace the original "weakening."

Who circled that spot,
The spent gauge caught in its final flutter,
And straggled down on their wavering wings
From the vast sky,
From the endless spaces,
Down at last for the low hover,
And the short quick quench of the sea.

WEEDS

All night long in the high meadow
They shielded the city-light from their eyes
Under towering grass.
Weeds warded them:
Dock hung in his hair;
Mallow marred with its subtle stain
Her rumpled skirt.
Near midnight air chilled;
They drew about them his heavy coat,
(Soldier's gear brought to such usage!)
And hoarded their heat.
Toward three they dozed,
All cramped and cold;
And went down in the dawn,
Limping under the early eyes,
Went their way,
Went out to the world,
To the War,
Bearing mallow, dock,
The odor of weed and the weed stain,
And the harsh print of the earth.

MARCH

The lovers, fast in their longing,
Lay high on their hill and looked out into March:
Fields all flooded and the rutty lanes,
Three farms, two teams,
Kites set to the wind, and the kiter's cry.

Lay high on their hill and looked out into spring,
The sensitive season,
Their throats so throbbing,
And their thieving thighs,
Lax on the hill in the thoughtless weather,
Their listless love.

Looked out into spring and the open air,
The lying lovers,
Beholding through their unseeing eyes
New form for old fancy,
Dawdling their languor,
Nursing the slow and crowning mood
For the push past gingham to the sprawling hug
Where each tries each,
And the shy recessive sex,
Grown bold and brutal,
Meets its own coarse kind.

INVOCATION

Year going down to my thirtieth autumn,
Year through the spring and the soaring summer
To the equinoctial season of my birth,
Yield me the breadth and the crowning measure;
I now have need of your last bestowment:
The deferent strength,
Nurtured through many a somnolent season,
Bold in the formed and final bloom.
Yield me that blossom.

I aimlessly wander,
And everywhere that my chance eye falls
Behold in the multiforms of life
Your summer fulfillment:
The sap-swollen grape and the peach in its prime;
The melons fat in their August fullness;
Even the shy and outcast weeds,
The fugitives of the summer ditches,
Strew their teem for the wind's hazard;
And the quail are grown;
And the blackbird,
All his lucky brood
Replete in their prime.
These in such fortune
Shine with the flush of your rich excess—
The inexhaustible plenty
Poured stintless out of spring's fructification.
Such am I seeking.

For only now, in my twenty-ninth year,
After all my ragged attempts and dispersals,
Am I sometimes given the means to perceive
The mode of progression and the subsequent cost.
Behind lies the past,
In its disproportion,
In its crippling mistakes;
But before gleams the mesh of the knotted future,
At every point its distinct resistance,
Its veiled withdrawals eluding discovery,

All its encounters to be undergone:
The manifold forms,
Remote and timeless,
Disposed in the pattern of the yet-to-be.

And I? What am I?
My singular forces,
My ruinous flaws?
The soul that sleeps in the definite frame
Has hardly been limned.
Only the skimming surface storms have blundered about it,
While the howling heart swept on in its dance.
I go forth to a war
In which neither the foe nor myself is known.
Only as I have encountered the past
Can I measure the margins of what I am.
The secrets of time,
The ambuscades and the pitfall pains
Will alter and shape,
And cautery cleanse,
And the sly hurts and the babbling distractions
Will wreak their harm.

But only by such is the test enacted.
As the mind gropes out toward new disclosures
The world is waiting to try its worth.
With pain for its power,
Mordant and sharp the world abides—
Pain in its fictive graduations,
With its hosted allies,
The little weaknesses flawed in the flesh,
Carping demands of all habit and use,
And the loud senses, pampered in past,
Baying the fief of an old indulgence.

For the war endures,
The war seethes and endures.
Though ease enshroud it,
Though pleasure obscure it,
Yet will it remain.
Not alone with the lusts,
The self-engrossment bawling within the fat tendrils;

But rather with that obscurant harm
Stemmed of the nature of duplicity:
The shortsighted good,
That carries within it its murderous seed;
The innocent joy,
That never regards in its rapt progression
The chaos sown of its reeling run.
Not ignorance only,
But its commoner kin,
That closures the mind,
Till knowledge, grooved in its simple channel,
Wheels the known rut.

There runs the war,
In the half-perceived but unattended,
There at the marginal edge of perception,
There must it be met.
There at that line let me level the screens from my blindered eyes:
The habitual framework of human use
That man in his labor has builded about him—
The needs of the past
Not forming the choice of the altered present;
The hand stayed in its strike,
The foot in its fall;
And pressed through the crust of old inurement
The goad of conscience,
The goad of guilt.

And let me not truckle indifference.
Never, in the flush and height of contrived sensation,
Too long forget its prerequisite cost:
Those who, in the avalancial years,
Knew nothing of ease and yet fashioned my own,
Painfully shaping the mode of survival,
Their minds wrapped in the terrible mantle of fear,
Seeding enlightenment.
Let me never forget the sick child,
Runted by famine and the killing cold;
And the mothers,
The shrunken of pap,
The withered of loin,

Going down again to the bloodstained bed and another birth.
The ages are there,
The uncontrollable past that resides in its welter,
Vast and shapeless and not to be known.

And let me never,
Beholding providential food on the loot-loaded table,
Put out of my mind the great steer steaming in his own blood,
The hooks that haul him head-down and dripping,
Clinched in his hocks;
Nor hide the hurt of the soft calf,
New in the knowledge of his sudden doom;
Nor the hung hog;
Nor the lamb that looks at the suckering knife,
And cannot foresee;
Nor fowl;
Nor frog;
Nor down-diving fish on the line's treason—

Was I not fish?
In the windless womb,
In the Wilderness,
Was I not frog?
Turned I not in the turtle's torsion?
Crept I not in the snail's span?
I hold at the heart,
At the timeless center,
All features,
All forms.
And wrung on the rack of what mutations,
This stringent flesh?

And let me never forget the tuber torn from its own fulfillment,
The globular wealth of genetic wheat
Crumbled to meal;
Nor forget the great horse hooked to the plough,
His generational strength nurtured thousands of years,
Sire to son,
For no profit of his.
Nor ever see fur on the shoulder of woman,
But mark how she paces,
Bright in the blood of a hundred miseries,

The pelt-plundered carcasses
Heaped on the balance her beauty breeds.

Thus seeds the pity.
Thus of the pity its further perception:
The spirit cleansed,
The ego chastened,
The bawling senses hushed in the fury of their animal roar.
The multitudes in their terrible might
Grope up the levels of evolution,
And locked in the self the extensional conflict,
As the emergent soul
Clotted and clogged in the hampering frame,
Stares out in its need,
And perceives that there,
In the partial attainment,
Can the great toll and wastage of the past
Be somewhat redeemed.

Year going down to my thirtieth autumn,
Year through the spring and the soaring summer
To the equinoctial season of my birth,
Yield me fulfillment.
I see life in transition unfold its ever-extending veils;
But not for nothing;
No, never for nothing.
It exacts its proportionate due.

THE SIEGE

Failure came first,
By the slight and unknowledgeable means it enforces,
As the vote failed him,
As the vote, in its meager margin,
Wavered against him.
He rose that morning fumbling the husks of half his life,
And saw thereafter power fade,
Fortune dwindle and poverty gain,
Bearing within it its harsh fruit:
Wife plotted the base adulterous bed;
Daughter, touched by the suck of disintegration,
Showed the deep flaw,
The mother's defect;
Son, dazed in that wreckage,
Cursed father, cursed self,
Sent the brute bullet roaring the road to the inner engine.
There followed the long parade of disease:
The subtle rot,
The insidious itch,
Establishing each its baleful rule,
Imposing upon that vulnerable frame their permanent mar.
These he endured;
And old age found him maimed but intact,
Regarding from out the inner fortress
The long list of ragged attacks,
The patient siege.

For time, that had spared him his forty years,
Sealed also his strength.
What would surely have shriveled his soft youth
He painfully carried,
Seeing always outside the local assault
The wider war that is waged beyond.
He took wave upon wave,
Each of them schooling in some subtle way
His means of response,

And stood at last in his surface scars,
In the benign and limitless central peace of the old fighters
Who know what war is,
How constant its means,
How vast its scope,
And how obscure are its ends.

THE MASTER

The furious cripple,
Who raged in the circle of his wounded pride
And so governed an age;
The painter, powerful in his premonition,
Knowing year upon year the patient encroachment
Inch up his flesh;
The leper, outcast on his island;
The cancerous king;
And my mother, who bore in her breast the pus-pouring lung—
These, these in their bondage,
These in the durance of imperfection,
These hover my mind.
Each stoops in his shackle,
The indigenous monitor perched forever in the faulty flesh;
Each watches, beyond his earnest endeavor,
His extravagant hope and his pitiful yearning,
The great chastening presence
Obtrude its dominion across his life.
And each, even in this, has his restitution:
The primal volitions live side by side in the burning body,
Forbidding excess.

We others, reckless with health,
Engrossed in the rapture of the ringing nerve,
Thrust through existence,
Ignore the dour master,
Shunt him off to the dusty closets of mind
To mumble and sulk,
Pronounce his blunt warnings,
Brood all the eighty years of a life—
And rage through the rooms in the end.

NIGHT SCENE

"After the war," he thought, "after the war—"
And crossing, traveled the street at a long angle,
So late it being and no traffic now.
High fog had come over,
Botched stars,
Laid its mark on the moon:
A halo's hoop.
Pursed he his lips for a thick whistle,
But felt the naked unutterable desolation of the sleeping city
Breathing behind the shuttered shops;
And saw the weak sign,
The horse-turd ripe in the raw street;
And mounting the curb
Saw with that sudden cold constriction
Soldier and girl,
In their surd tussle,
Sprawled in a jeweler's door.

THE CITADEL

The janitor knew;
High priest of the wastebasket,
Bridging the outer and inner worlds,
The janitor knew—
As did also the staff,
The auditors and the higher clerks;
Even the salesmen,
Those casuals of the corridors—
All knew, all knew but Norstrem,
Who, blithe in his function,
Worked on unaware.

Resourceful, diligent,
Abler no doubt than the men who survived him,
Neither his special brilliance nor his general worth
Would at last avail.
For in the upper office,
The citadel,
The shrouded vault in the maze of rooms,
The fabulous center he had not seen
Nor could ever aspire to—
There in that sanctum his fate was decreed.

He worked for weeks,
Absorbed and unknowing,
Serene in his ignorance,
Constructing his proper place in that world;
Until the sharp morning,
Cryptic with frost,
His manager blandly summoned him in,
And told him what all knew but he.

THE REVOLUTIONIST

His enemies learned.
In the small of the nights,
In the pre-dawn chill of the swart streets,
What once they despised
He taught them to dread.
The smouldering eye in the iron face
Marked many a man.
He wore the zealot's heart,
And such was his gift
Power poured to his use.

But his enemies learned.
At cost, with error,
They bled, but they learned.
Learned late, but learned well;
Learned, indeed, only at last,
But learned in time;
And they too mustered;
They too mastered the means of the small hours,
His stratagems, his known deceits.

He made over the roofs,
Half-naked and injured;
Skulked by day in the hedges,
The intrepid face glaring out from the stones with a beast's bale;
Traveled by night the desolate lanes;
Crossed with the moon the hostile border;
Wandered for weeks;
Found far haven.

For a time he aspired.
Men remembered his terrible face,
And plotted his triumph.
They were hunted down.
Under that fierce remorseless bane his cause withered.
He grew old in time,
Subsisting on scraps in a bleak room,

Hating about him the foreign tongues, the foreign faces.
Fixed in his thwartion,
Like some banished lord,
Like Bonaparte, sick for his sovereignty,
The wind of whose want
Poured out of the waste of the South Atlantic
Toward France and fulfillment,
He fastened the past within his grinding heart,
And eked out his life on its gall.

THE BROTHERS

Well-husbanded, staunch,
No man but her own could compass her eye.
She moved among them,
Wound in the trammel of his male appeal,
Loving the heavy cast of his head,
The resilient limbs,
The soul that looked from the somber eyes.
Sown with his seed she grew big of that burden,
Brought forth from her body the man's stamp,
His miniatured mould,
And loved it the more in its replication.

The eighth year of their life,
His brother, home from far cities,
Abode in the house a six-months' span.

Then it was that, touched by the lave of association,
She came to perceive in the frame of the brother
Her husband's shape, but in modulation;
The duplicate face, moulded by life to a variant pattern;
The selfsame eyes,
But burning behind them another fancy.
She saw old love
Opening out into other extensions,
The boundaries of her exploration
Thrown suddenly wide,
Through the half-beheld and hence alluring:
New modes of perception,
Remote progressions of touch and response.
She whom disparity never had troubled
Lay snared in duplicity's intricate web;
And she wavered between,
Caught in a tuggage she could not control,
She could not contain;

Till the past-ploughing night,
Stricken with guilt,
The rupturing strain of allegiance and betrayal
Cleaving the numbed and speechless mind,
She crept to the brother's bed.

THE FRIENDS

They had spoken for years,
Meeting at times in the late cafés,
Chancing together on the hosted street,
A passing word.
Over the casual cups of coffee,
In the years' flux,
In the seasons' motion,
Their friendship deepened;
And one fog-folded night,
Seeing her home through the emptying ways,
The slow concatenation of time
Turned at the outpost of her porch,
And he did not go.

The room breathed of her presence.
Undressing beside her,
In the high mounting of his perception,
He had the sense of total conjunction
With all that she was.
He watched the well-tempered body divesting its sheaths,
Saw the sculptural back,
Knew the flare of the hips from the waist's weal,
And the hair-darkened hollow,
Where all the body's inleading lines
Sucked toward center.
She made no evasion.
The cup they had carried so long atremble
They let pour over,
Drench down;
And such the reciprocal nature of trust,
They could beg no lack.

For time sustained them.
The subtle progression of minute means
Rose now in its recapitulation,
Enriching the present,
Yielding it amplitude and scope,

Providing out of its vast reserve
Its bountiful wealth.
Having fashioned the present out of the past,
The past and its promise achieved fulfillment.
They endured no regression,
Who knew that even in this—
The tidal dark, the volcanic night,
The rash eruptive rush of the blood—
The discriminate mind makes its choices.

THE DIVERS

Wifeless at thirty,
How else can he dream,
In the cold bed,
In the empty covers,
But grope in his mind her known loins,
Her familiar knees?
How else can he dream,
But her plundering mouth,
Her body's beat?

Nor brand him base,
No, nor deem him insensate,
That these of all moments should center his mind.
For could she waken within the grave,
Could the small jointed bones resume their links,
The fallen flesh refind its old form,
And she strain upward,
Sunder the root,
Break the cold clod,
And spy once more the liquid light of the frosty stars,
Would she hasten home,
Burst door, climb stairs,
To roll in the rapture of that embrace.

In love they lived;
But like deep-dredging divers,
Who trudgen down to obliterate depths,
And yet rise unto air,
By air sustained;
So these in their concourse
Followed the undertowing torrent
To the deep dark of such descent,
And yet rose up,
Rose up renewed,
To sight sea-dapple,

Its living light,
And gulp the good air.

Let him dream as he does,
Her night-garment winding his chill knees.
In the deep sorrow that hollows his heart
The years return:
Her features,
Her flank,
Her torrential tongue
Looting along his own,
And the unaccountable days—
He hugs them all to his harsh breast,
In the numb knowledge of loss.

THE STRANGER *

Pity this girl.
At feckless fourteen,
Glib in the press of rapt companions,
She bruits her smatter,
Her bed-lore brag.
She prattles the lip-learned, light-love list.
In the new itch and squirm of sex,
How can she foresee?

How can she foresee the thick stranger,
Over the hills from Omaha,
Who will break her across a hired bed,
Open the loins,
Rive the breach,
And set the foetus wailing within the womb,
To hunch toward the knowledge of its disease,
And shamble down time to doomsday?

---

* At line two, "feckless fourteen" replaces "callow sixteen"—a change Everson made during his editorial work with the projected *The Achievement of William Everson* during the summer of 1993.

THE DIVIDE

He came in the room at day's end;
His eye took in its measure the closet, its clutter,
The empty open chest,
All sign of her rude peremptory exit;
And he knew in the certitude of his loss,
That though she return,
Blithe to his bed in the false dawn,
And they try once more their worn renewal,
A week, a month, a year's quarter;
Though she creep to his cover in guilt and remorse,
Easing his ire,
For him she was gone.

Too long had he wavered.
In even the best,
Burdening bed as the west blackened,
Inching their love to the hung noons,
Trying its mettle their multiple ways and finding it firm—
In even such utter consummation,
He was never willing to fasten his trust.
He was never willing to speak the word,
Pronounce the vow,
And bind in his own and the world's eyes
The worth of his pledge.
Wanting one foot in freedom,
He found in his dolour that freedom comes dear,
And would carry the mark of that mistake to the grave's lip,
Never immune,
Vulnerable to a dream's shift,
Memory's mischief gusting the past through his crippled soul.

This much can be said:
His was the error of introspection,

And its hurt would not heal.
But what can be said of those pitiable men who slobber affection,
Live at the edge,
Wed a baby's face, a doll's body,
And slowly discover their wives?

Selma, California

BOOK THREE:

A PRIVACY
OF SPEECH

(1943-1946)

Somewhere the daylight drowses in your breast
Whereon, as of a dream, I strove and slumbered.
Your body deeply breathing, breathing deep,
All passion slaked, and the spirit unencumbered.

How could I know what yearning charged your soul?
I could have known, but the griffin of man's pride
Takes all for granted; I heard your throttled cry
Only as someone's singing at my side.

We learn too late. A truth was touched and known,
A music we should have kept, might simply have been.
But the slow murmur of the years, denied,
Whispers away, and is not heard again.
                                        *

---

* This poem was written on January 16, 1968, and included by Everson as the prologue poem
for Book Two of the 1968 New Directions edition of *The Residual Years*. The poem's drafts
are included among the Everson papers at the Bancroft Library.

CHRONICLE OF DIVISION

(1943-1946)

CHRONICLE OF DIVISION

PART ONE

I

That morning we rose,
Who, man and woman,
Rose one from another our spacious years.
But now no more—
    The face puffed with sleep,
    The tousled crown,
    From the dream-found clasp withdrawn,
    The smeared mouth—
But now no more.
There was haste to be made;
Yet neither would scant the last ritual of breakfast
From what it had been,
But bit bread,
But smoked cigarettes in the slow-chewn silence,
But saw all about the casual leavings of our lives,
Where the fly fed,
Delicately,
With small touches,
Cleaning his wings.

The one: there was cut through his mind the ribbon of road,
Its sharp declivity a part of his life
He had yet to acquire.

The other: how could she hold off hollow tomorrow,
Her shoes doomed of their echo
Tolled back from the wall?

For this, we had nothing,
As the patient,
Prone on the table,
Cannot encompass the massing years
Divorced of his limb.
We clung in our trance,

In the mastery of the huge event,
Till the clock,
That had dragged itself toward its ultimate hour,
Struck once in its orbit,
And toppled the avalanching wave
That taught us the knowledge of loss.

II

The bus begins,
And brings the traveler his known cities,
His familiar fields;
But these are outrun.
The sun draws down to inexistence,
And night closets all.
The eye being blind,
The ear resumes the brain's injunction,
Brings him the matron's murmur,
The salesman's oath;
While the bus,
Mad for miles,
Devours distance under its iron,
Till a restless fantastic semblance of sleep
Glazes the mind.

But dawn brings him sight and a new country.
The bus breaks on toward some vast abstraction,
Some dominant myth,
Lurking and harsh behind great woods.
What fastens ahead?
What powerful gravitation,
Unseen but controlled,
Tugs at the roaring winding car,
And pulls North, ever North?
The traveler abides,
Without volition,
While faces about him blur and converge,
Lifeless masks of the one suspension
That wear the same look;
Till the final stop,

When glimpsing out through the smudgy glass
Its secretive roofs,
He alights to another life.

III

This, then, is our world.
Having entered the gate,
Who is there to measure the length we will stay?
The factors that manage that endurance have yet to be formed.
This much we know:
Blood will be poured.
The world in constriction must loosen, unlock,
The tides withdraw,
And all the wide chaos,
That dwarfs our meager participation,
Must have its great way.
Yet the impassive calendar governs our minds.
And the gate remains,
Broad for departure,
To pass if we choose.
Some of us do,
Openly asking the consequent hurt,
Or by stealth and deceit in the moon's blindness.
Only rumor returns.
We others remain,
Holding within us the vast temptation and the obscure threat,
And nurse the wide cleavage of will.

IV

The newcomer marvels,
Beholding about him wherever he enters,
The direct head,
The declarative face,
That wears its look like an open hand.
For him in his newness,
Fresh from the world,
No bitterness breeds,
None slander,

None thieve,
None rail in anger nor smoulder in hate;
But the abundant leaven engendered of trust
Earns of itself its reciprocal usage,
And endures no abuse.

This he had dreamed
In his glimmering visions,
Projecting the shape of some nebulous life—
And here he would hold it,
Till time taught him less,
Revealing the brittle bias,
The unseen error that makes human the saint,
Thwarts the idealist,
Marks the martyr,
For none is immune.
What the soul strives for is not to be had.
That too would he learn.
But here for a time it is true.

V

The pacifist speaks,
Face to face with his own kind,
And seeks to fashion a common course
That all may mark.
But whatever he offers,
Finds already framed in another's thought
A divergent approach.
The binding belief that each allows
Is cruxed on rejection:
Thou shalt not kill.
But for all the rest,
What Voice shall speak from the burning bush,
In the work-site noons,
When the loaf is broken,
And brief and rebuttal countercross,
And no one wins?

Apart on his rock,
The forester sucks his sufficient quid,

And never hears,
At one with the landscape
That crouches behind its masked firs,
Its skeletal snags,
Brooding upon the lost myth
Created once in its unfathomable past
And never regained—
But it wants to,
It waits, it waits,
Its immense obsession—

And when speech runs out,
When the rebel lays down his irksome axe at last,
And takes his stand,
The crude pencil,
Moistened with spit and tobacco juice,
Has only to scrawl the offending name,
And the man and his reasons
Converge toward those walls at the world's end
Where all questions die.

VI

For most, there is prayer.
No food passes lip without the mute blessing,
And the black book carried against the heart
Assures, assures.
By daylight their faces,
Placid with trust,
Reflect the hushed mind.
They sound the song of the heart's plenty.

But by night they implore.
The bodies, doubled beside the beds,
Invoke redemption.
The faces, knotted in need,
Thrust up toward attainment.
The eyes that have wept on a fabulous vision
Pierce rafter and board of our circumscribed lives;

And the straight lips,
That were always so certain,
Halt on the brink of articulation.

We others,
Who suffer our god to move unmolested,
Turn silent away,
Ashamed to perceive,
As one shuns the violent coupling of lovers,
Finding the naked soul too harsh to behold.
They are unaware.
Engrossed in that vision they are saved and lost,
Are indeed transfixed,
Who abjure the sanction of doubt.

VII

For all, there is Woman.
Some, virginal, keep only the face,
Unreal and resplendent.
Others clutch in the mind the swollen thighs and the belly's bend.
For most, she is sin,
Shut from their light,
But curled in their dreams,
A white worm in the meaty core.
Whatever we do she makes herself known,
Her secular presence enforcing the mind.
As angel she smiles,
Beatitude flooding the fond face.
As devil she ripples her soft flesh,
The white fork of desire.
All pin up her picture.
Her motionless features watch over sleep,
The photograph only the image of what exists,
Off there, in the distant cities,
Beyond our brain.
She also reclines,
In the vacant bed bound too in her loss,

Or joined to another by the fierce root that circumscribes faith.
We do not know.
That trouble endures,
Cloudy athwart the drenched mind,
Till daylight decrees our day.

VIII

No man is alone.
Side by side in the long room we mingle and touch,
Nudge at the table,
Shout on the walks,
Lie head to heel in the close beds.
Even at stool we squat in our row:
The private act revealed and made known to the corporate eye.

Yet after a time the mind erects its own defenses.
The tongue chatters,
The mobile mouth smiles and flouts,
In the steaming baths the nudists dance and wrestle with joy;
But behind the bone wall
The spirit whistles and sings to itself,
Keeping its inward motion and its solitary grace
While the bodies touch.

But the body itself,
Though it turns and cavorts,
And schools forever to the avid throng,
Does it not tire?

Will it not also,
Some subsequent day,
Aware of stillness and a strange peace,
Be glad to be wholly alone?

IX

The man struck from the woman—
That is the crime.
As the armies grow

So gathers the guilt,
So bloom the perversions,
So flower the fears,
So breed the deep cruelties and the secretive hurts.
And each, the man and the woman,
Too much alone,
Age and grow cold.

Let the man touch the woman.

Now the husband dreams of the wife,
Recalling her clear singing and her solitary grace.

We are not whole.

And she?
Sadly apart she stirs in sleep and makes moan,
Turns and makes moan,
Needing the all-encompassing arm
That now is not there.

X

Can the photograph teach?
This simple snapshot,
Made to send home—
Three friends grouped in the lambent morning—
Can it know and instruct?
See the smug youngster,
The posturing fraud, and the bearded crank.
Is this what we were?
No, no! We were humble and good!
We were filled with the pleasure of being together,
In our earnest joy and our natural pride,
And not this, not this!

Yet the moment is gone.
Only this endures,
In its consequent proof;
And the future,
Chancing across the faded square,

Will snigger and point,
As we ourselves taunt the ludicrous past,
That has now no defense.

But the camera—what does it see?
Something was there,
Tangent to our lives;
And the shrewd lens,
Probing and delving,
Has perhaps laid bare.
It mocks without mercy.
We suffer ourselves to its casual whim,
Its malice, its scorn, and its fun.

XI

To sunder the rock—that is our day.
In the weak light,
Under high fractured cliffs,
We turn with our hands the raw granite;
We break it with iron.
Under that edge it suffers reduction.
Harsh, dense and resistant,
The obdurate portions
Flaw and divide.

From the road in the dawns we behold the sea,
In its prone slumber,
Holding the west with heavy ease.
The rock closes it out,
Narrows our sky,
In the morning thaw lets fall its sparse rubble.
We wait, suspended in time.
Locked out of our lives we abide, we endure,
Our temporal grievance diminished and slight
In the total awareness of what obtains,
Outside, in the bone-broken world.
Confronting encroachment the mind toughens and grows.
From this exigence both purpose and faith achieve coherence:
Such is our gain.
We perceive our place in the terrible pattern,

And temper with pity the fierce gall,
Hearing the sadness,
The loss and the utter desolation,
Howl at the heart of the world.

XII

But at length we learn,
Finding the chastening pattern to school desire:
Not tamper with time,
Neither rowel the future nor finger the past.
The world wars on,
Our subsequent fate involved in its toil,
But the abstract voice that spills from the box
Cannot bring it clear.
Even the purpose by which we have come loses distinction,
With the lover's face and the wife's affection,
Here, in the wilderness,
The waste of the world,
Bounded between the continent's back and the absolute West.

We rise in the dawns,
Enter the day.
We eye the weather and watch the sea,
In its manifest purpose,
Marshal itself for another assault.
Whether or not we are heroes or fools
Is hardly the point,
Who have learned in this that all achievement
Is only attained by the thick sequence of forced beginnings
Composing an act—
As the soldier,
Crouching and killing,
Must also know,
Bent by his gun.

Having fastened on this we can only endure,
Immersed in the chorework of the will
And wade up time,
Where the glacial future,

Frozen and fixed in the stone ranges beyond our sight,
Yields but the iridescent trickle
That bleeds from its throat.

Waldport, Oregon

PART TWO

I

Each evening, the mail,
Flown from the regions of our desire—
The forbidden South, the unattainable East—
To alight in the box,
Like the blue pigeons the boys keep in the bird-lofts of home.
There it awaits,
As yet incomplete,
Each one with its name,
Needing the final cognitive act
To resolve what it is.

What do we want?
What is it we ask of the penciled page,
Trooping in from the dusk,
From the nude ridge and the wind's suckle,
To crowd like feeding fowl at the box?
Some revelation?
Some great benediction to bless us with being,
Make whole our desire,
Balm the hid hurt and the guarded fester?

What we seek of the letter is not its to give,
Or only in bits.
The man, scarcely served,
Clumps emptily off with his mere portion,
Already tipped toward tomorrow,
Seeing far away in the intricate world
The one packet approach,
Unique in the multitudinous bags,
To hover in to his hungering hand
And proffer its magical cure.

II

And the man,
In from the dusk,
Will pluck from the box his sealed hope and be glad,
Remarking the free familiar hand that spells out his name,
And the soft fragrance,
Kept on her flesh,
Confirming it hers.
It lies in his hand like the sheath body,
That may be possessed in the act of entry,
But is never enough.

But this one will hurt.
This one, loaded,
Cryptic and sharp,
In the terrible wounding way of the honest;
This one will sear across his sight,
And leave him,
Detached from his past,
Alone in the wilderness of the self,
Where the lost child wails in the thorned circle
And the night crouches.

The man does not know.
Flushed with delight he tucks it into a snug pocket
And shambles off,
In search of some wholly private place
To draw forth the light burden,
Pierce the soft sheath,
And gently unfold his fate.

III

Does the adulteress grieve,
Framed in her guilt,
When the act is over,
And the lover's head
Nuzzles in sleep the abundant breast
The husband once haunted?
Is something done when a rite is broken

That shatters and tears,
Some stark violation
That cries from the act and is heard?

For the husband, yes.
And alone in his musing,
Suddenly stilled in some common task,
He will stare down the wind and not see,
And say over his rote:
"What then is love,
That it once ruled its world,
And is now nothing;
Or, if yet, overcome by a fiercer?
A need and a wanting.
But no more, nothing more?
Say only the need,
The dumb wanting,
That comes and governs and maybe departs."

But for her, having all,
There is only the now,
And faith is a word.
Her lover is real.
When she gathers again his dominant solace,
He is the fact.
What is the past against his hand?
His mouth breaks across time,
And out of his flesh grows the future.

IV

The man nurtures his hurt.
But searching the past for the harsh word,
The injurious act that turned her away,
Will not find what he seeks.
Nothing was done.
His loss does not gather from what he is,

But from what he is not.

For no one is whole.
Who in his being embodies all the aspects of mankind?
The man, gazing into her eyes,
Is unable to see the continents sunken behind her sight,
The whole regions of being
His limited presence can never disclose.

She who declares: I will be true,
Cannot govern her oath.
Somewhere in the world moves one laden with power,
Who one day may come and merely stand near,
And the darkness will break,
The subterranean ranges rise from their depths and be known,
Guttering time down their sides,
Spilling the waste and wreckage of the past,
Its motives, its needs, its great pledges of faith.
Against such a day the man has no wedge,
Being then not enough.
She will not wait,
But will pack her small bag—
All that she wants of his once world—
Will pen her terse note,
And will go.

V

The man, in his time,
Though he hugs deprivation,
And feeds at the root of so central an anguish,
Knows of his need he can touch no recourse.
Is one ever another's,
Though he wholly consign,
And set the seal of the master motive
With all that he is?

We are rather the world's,
And incident to its grave demand.
Seen in the long perspective of loss,
Recalling the kept motion,

The pure prevailing grace,
He is dumbly aware that this is his luck:
For a time they touched;
Large in his life she merged the antipodes of his mind.
But that which meant most was not his to have;
He could only behold,
And learn of its presence
What soft revelation life can make clear.
There his claim ends,
As the Parian torse,
Regardless who owns,
Resides forever in that great holding the past has bestowed,
And is not to be bound.

The richness remains.
Such she engendered and may not remove.
He has made it his own.
And he holds it,
Shown in the deep retentive face,
To bear down his time till its close.

VI

Is this then his find,
Who had set himself for the time's fee:
Patriot's spite, the mob's jabber,
Or penal pain, its walled world, and the raw dread?
Of that there was nothing.
But now the new ache,
That swift without warning
Can sidle between two turns of a word
And make bare.

So the soldier,
Fixed in his error,
Under the skimming stones of extinction,
Waits on his death.
And through all the unspeakable role of destruction
Hardly is touched,
But comes limping home from those howling hills,

To hold in his crooked and shaking hands
The seen waste of his life.

The measure of trouble has no prediction,
But makes as it merges,
And demonstrates by what smooth indirection
The heart may be hurt:
How easy a victim.

VII

Yet must the man marvel.
For see, what a magical thing is the mind,
That seizes a hurt,
And clings to it,
And draws at that bruise to practice a use:
Not the healer's art,
But to finger, probe,
And learn of its twinge a teaching in loss.

Thus does it prosper,
Bearing its ancient wounds within it,
To touch and remind,
As an old hurt of the hand
Will wince and warn long years of a life
When its owner errs.

Who but is snug in his limitations?
The foetus, shielded and warm,
Loves its little world.
It lags and resists when time nudges,
Shaping its mute mouth for the moan
It yet cannot make.
But it crawls through the terrible gates toward its dawn:
A requisite birth.

The man looks down his life,
And regards from his vantage that obsolete hope.
It is canceled out.
But yet remains the possible future,

Like some huge new world needing discoverers.
He touches again his crude corrections,
And masters his hand to proceed.

Waldport, Oregon

PART THREE

I

All the long evening the man,
Upright on the seat,
Regards from his place the blind landscape.
It flows on the glass,
Lucid and green,
The time being spring,
The season disclosing its tentative blossoms,
Its suave air and its light.

Guarding within him his vulnerable core
The man stares from his place,
Not to be touched.
Let the bus bear him back,
As he knows it must to its destination;
But what he will gain and what he will lose
Are not now in his mind,
Regarding the landscape,
Its squat barns and its frog-loud swales,
Slip past at his eye.
The soldiery of a dozen fronts
Sprawl in the postures of fatigue.
The slack faces,
That already have seen
More than the human sight should behold,
Are flaccid in sleep.
The man muses among them,
And reflects how he too carries his wound,
A private possession,
Under his shirt,
And now being healed
Like them must bear it back toward its source

And another risk.
Would the soldiers sneer?
But who may measure the hurt within
To the hurt without?
He tries to call up his few cuts
And cannot bring them back.
But think now the soldier,
Going out again to his fatal sector,
Where terror is whole,
And pain the one constant;
Where the jungle,
Carnivorous,
Wafts its fronds on the lax air
And eats its dead—
Let him pull comparison out of the belly of a screaming man
If he thinks he must.
But the great ingrowing cyst of his woe
Works within him,
As if all his knowledge of human hurt
Burned in its bile.
He stifles it down:
That much has closed.
He has shut it out and cannot see her face,
But only the fixed abstraction bred out of motion,
And the fluid earth,
In the clean evening,
In the smooth air,
The bus bearing south,
At the year's blossom,
The troublous spring,
That sets the blazing bud on the limb,
And the cold root in the clod.

II

In the station's swarm,
His scanning eye
Roves and goes hungry,
Devoid of her face.
The replicate failure:

Her own appointment
Scotched no doubt for the keeping kiss,
And a lover's nudge.

Then the bright visage
Burns in the concourse of the crowd.
She looks in his face her long moment,
And has nothing to say.

How can they speak?
How can the words come out through the lips,
Or aught of sound,
Between these two,
The wife and the husband,
Mated for years and then broken,
Thrust by the blunt hands of event
That never consult?
What can they have to say to each other
In that shrunken time,
In the crowd's gabble,
The throng's press,
Face before face
And their past upon them?

The man does not try.
But out on the street,
The lights alive on their tall posts,
And the soldier's jostle,
His heavy gaze
Searches the small familiar face for some new sign
And finds it there,
A tracery that is nothing of his,
A soft demarcation his eye may not measure,
Nor his wish preclude,
Nor all his endeavor erase.

III

That evening they fed,
Who, man and woman,
Fared one with another their gracious years,

But now no more—
    The fish uneaten,
    The sherbet spooned on the plate,
    Only the coffee kept and savored,
    The tilted cup
    Worn like a mask across the mouth,
    While the eyes above it
    Watched and waited,
    And got no answer.
The glib tongue,
Schooled in dissemblance,
Took up its task,
And after the making of those months
Each had enough to glut a meal.
But what of the diffidence kept between,
Between their faces,
Between their eyes,
Between the skin of their hands
When at last they touched on the late table,
The provident brew having thawed at the ice
That landlocked the heart?
What of the deep accruent doubt,
That each kept covered,
And neither would claim?

It was not for that night.
Time would be eaten,
The dawn broken with bread,
The noon tempered with wine.
Not for that night nor yet for the next;
But in the wrought context,
The one with the other,
Was it to be known;
And then only its edge,
Disclosing itself in the unguarded glance,
The abrupt gesture stayed in its start,
While the other stared,
Seeing at last its revelation
Shine in the pure unconscious act.

They went out of that place
Still shy and half-speechless,

Like new lovers,
Or friends who have met but a moment,
And must wear the mantle of their reserve
To shield the small self in its fear.

IV

That night in a dim low-raftered room
The thought stood in his mind:
I shall not touch.
But watching her put off the rich wool,
Lay aside the silk,
The body supple and good in its round wonder,
Where was his resolve?

They lay each to each.
They heard through the wall the late traveler toss,
Like a huge swaddled infant bound in his bed.
They lay in their fitful isolation;
And what was to stop his hand in its glide,
Or the speechless mouths from coming together
In the old kiss,
The known embrace,
They long had practiced?

It was so ancient an act between them!
And the bodily needs,
Do *they* ever question
Whether or not they are to decide?
He planted his knees,
And, bent above that unleechable hurt,
Its huge desolation swollen within him,
He made the blind entrance.
And in its raw moment,
When the heart and the brain and the tongue could not utter,
The body reaved its hoarse throat and gave cry.

V

But after the body has had its word,
What then of the heart
That had not spoken?
What of the mind?
What of the tongue,
Speechless between those locked lips
And nothing to say?
What of the eye,
That looks in her own,
And sees in its orb another's face?
His frame lies between.
His presence is there,
Tensile with strength,
Like a dominant block he cannot pass.
He looks in her eyes,
And nothing he finds that he can fathom.
He looks in her face,
And what can he see that is meant for him?
She smiles and stirs;
And something strikes from the skull
Down the tall column to the vulnerable heart
A terrible blow.
He crumbles and falls.
And thrusting his shrunken face to the wall,
Drawn from this woman his lawful wife,
Knows that he, now he, is adulterer too.

VI

Let the year turn under.
Who has known in the ordering of his life
Certitude's secret?
That is a phantom that fleets through the mind
When the body's fed.
But he who is stripped of his cloistering past,
That man perceives.
Alive in his newness the edges merge,
The lines flow and lap over,

And the heart rasps on in its old anguish,
Loss! Loss!
While the mind clasps and reaches,
And wherever it turns
Finds nothing it needs.

The man must not wait.
He will go out to the border that breeds the night,
And face the high-hanging distances kept in its span.
He will drink through the mortal means of his sight
The lain sea,
Like a beast in its smoulder,
Wide on the latitudes of the west,
That breathes and is vast.

Let the heart be dumb.
Let the tongue go speechless.
Stopper the lips that long to say.
Man, man, are you youngster?
You saw it all plain!
Does the verification
So murder and tear?

Thus does it, indeed.
For the precepts hang like high abstractions
Till pain proves them.
He turns back from his brink,
And sees off in the world her apparitional face,
Filled with the knowledge of discovery,
And her own hurt in her eyes.

Waldport, Oregon

PART FOUR

I

They met once more in the ended autumn,
When frost framed the ground,
When winter's bite in the blue air,
That hurt the bare hand,
Hit too at the heart where it clumped and fumbled,
Hemmed about in its raw region,
A polar realm.

They stood face to face in that cold kingdom,
And the man, who looked in her eyes,
Saw only the ghost of a gone time,
Its feature and form,
But dead, all departed.
The spectral hand,
That hovered a bit within his own and then withdrew,
Told too that the past was not to be had,
Could only be glimpsed through the ghost smile,
The ghost glance,
That wore what it was from another time,
And could not restore.

They left one another,
As those who after too great a grief
Leave the house of the dead,
Glad to be gone,
Glad for completion,
Glad for the season and its spite,
Glad that they now have nothing left
But to set the mark on the statutory page
That tells to the world they are through.

II

And the man, gazing into the glass,
Will study and ask:
"What woman will want?"
Regarding the loss-beleaguered eyes

That time has entrenched,
The deep indented face,
Bearing its black tooth in its mouth,
A visible mar.
What is there here of that suave definition
The eye looks for in its first appraisal,
When the fate of all future correlation
Hangs on the governing glance?

So does he say:
"Is then what I have
Not of woman's wanting?"
Oh, do not declare his dream invalid,
Recalling the sudden hands,
The low look of love,
Her spumed pleasure,
Her bated moan!
Do not declare for him
Nevernomore such soft rapture!
For who but will grow all old and abject,
Lacking that slow music,
Forever denied so thick a passion
To soften, subdue the rude male mouth,
By keeping of curve, by caress?

III

But what of his hope that time would temper?
He had thought that such a piling of days
Could make its amends,
That the drainage of time
Could so assist the backward-bending gaze
That what had been done
Could settle within the memory's frame
In the rich integration the mind makes
Of its mutable past.

Had the cut been clean it could have happened.
But she, who rang indeed to the lover's strike,
Had tuned too long to her husband's hand
To ever forget,

And in his blank absence
Was not to be sure that what she had found
Was of permanent worth.
He was there in a past
Reaching half the length of her life behind her,
And she turned,
She begged involvement,
A thick fancy,
A troublous thing she must follow out,
And so explore,
So fix and establish,
She could know her own need.
But not yet to be likened
To what had been theirs in the gone days,
Before war's intervention
Carried the man to his cut-off camp;
Before the blow that broke Europe
Broke also them,
And sent the spheres
That had clung and spun double those multiple seasons
Lurching alone,
Like two solitary planets,
Sunless down space,
Susceptible to the dominant draught of any orb.
Caught in such tuggage she yet was not sure,
Came crying out of her huge confusion,
To beg the simple ounce of forbearance
Till time could make known its intent.

The man had concurred.
Was he one to wear convention's cloak,
Pull the cuckold's pride,
Nurse a fat grudge and cut forever?
The past had provided too tempered a thing
To be so sudden.
The central strength that had always been theirs,
Was it not her most need?
Who then played betrayal,
If honorable in her every act,
She sought out forbearance and found it denied?
He could not plant that pain.
And all his old hope,

He had carefully packed away and buried,
Burst its deep hole;
Set root,
Broke blossom;
And sent the fostering crown in its thrust toward light:
A shimmering head.

He made his choice by the mind's measure;
But he reckoned without the reasonless heart
That balks at all burden,
Keeps a grudging sulk.
For the heart has its kingdom,
And though the tolerant mind smile and agree,
And advance its plain reasons,
Something else remains.
Something remains that may not be scanted.
It will wait out its time.
And let for a little its weather go bad,
The truculent monarch heaves in his kingdom
And sets his decree.

The man kept his peace.
But neither the excellence of the past,
Nor the clemency of that charitable act,
Could narrow the fracture of separation.
The impatient senses cannot resurrect,
They can only respond.
And the lover was there.
Bold in her bed he could fill her fancy;
He could make it good.
The multiforms of association build a past of their own.
What she assumed as tentative license
Endured as demand.

Her letters lessened.
And only then,
After all his astuteness,
Did bitterness thicken;
Did the rancorous heart
Make its emergence;
Did the deep-starting springs

Go dry in her drouth.
Not that she injured,
But victim indeed to her own indecision
Held the hurt too long,
Fed hope and then starved it.
She left him too little:
A spare word in a fortnight,
Scrawled on a slip between appointments;
And gave him the gulfs between the lines
For the mind to widen,
For the heart to hit,
For the truth to toll,
Its great echo pound out of the page,
And no denial,
But only the piecings the plundering sight
Could construct and deduce.
On that he broke,
Made his swift cleavage;
And they met,
And the damp stifle of such a death
Eddied them in.

And what is the nature of alteration
That all its returns should cancel out?
That a rare regard
Should follow love down a funneling loss?
That one who had thought to make of misfortune a final gain
Should gloat,
Should be glad,
That all he held dear was dead?

IV

And she?
South under stars,
The roofs in their huddle
Fending the dark descendant air:

In a room where the water drips all night in the shallow pan;
In a room where the moth braves the hot wick and will die;

In a room where the crust dries on the sill,
Its satellite crumbs—

> *Oh, bitch and bastard!*
> *Clasp in your coupled rub and make mad!*
> *Suck!*
> *Lay cheek by jowl in the scuttler's tilt!*
> *Fucking's your fun!*

Brook no denial.
Stanch no wounds now in such struggle,
Master and mistress,
Shrewd wrestlers,
Closed on extinction.

Now no dawn discovers.
Her mouth,
Bitten to blood,
Mewls in the throes of transformation;

And is assuaged.

V

But bitterness too may have its uses.
Now in his rancor the man may discern
How a gathering hurt too big to be borne
Breaks sideways out to the innocent hand:
The frame of an act.
And he who ruled violence
Out of the text of his life's prospectus,
Now, on his hill,
Alone with the wind,
Over gray sea and its gulls,
A gaunt nature,
Can feel his mind,
When it touches that trouble,
Flare and go white,
Soon past and put by,
But there,

In the blind center,
The strike.

And where lies the line that draws division,
The wish from the act?
Christ canceled it out.
But only he who had naked slogged through the heart's great hell
Could have so discerned.
And the man,
In his need to know,
Inches the white flare back to his mind,
Looks in its core to learn what he is
And finds murder there,
The pure substance,
That puts down pity,
But takes in the flexed incriminate hands
The lyric throat,
And wound in the imminence of the hug,
The wrapped joinure,
Where desire and death forever obtain their fierce definition,
He clenches, cramps,
Till the plunging features
Bulge and go black,
And all his old hurt
Lies healed on the bed.

Could this be—himself?
His the humped shoulders?
His own, the blunt hands?
Indeed they are,
Though he never so use.
And all over the world
The embittered and the damned
Come in to their own in the man's mind,
Calls this one brother,
That one friend,
Who were once wretch and rogue.
The face he confronts on the glutted street,
Cartography of an ancient anger,

Reveals in the flaws of its old erosions
The weathers of pain.
He knows such a land.

He knows such a region.
He has limped into it,
And dumbly perceives he may never go back,
But must learn to live on the plain food that country avails,
And remarks with surprise
How some even grow fat on its fare.

VI

He will be given again to the indifferent world,
Go south to a city,
Muse over coffee in small cafés,
Take the usual room,
Hear from his bed the buoy grieve in the harbor,
Like a lorn bull,
That moans and bellows,
And though sea birds circle
Will not be consoled.

He will stare up the dark through the tall invisible storeys above him,
Where men and women place mouth to mouth in their old exploration,
And will watch through the roof the small hard and unquenchable stars
Make their overhead arc;
And think what a curious thing a life is,
That brings and discloses,
But never quite what had been expected,
And never quite what one wanted to know.
It keeps for itself its anterior knowledge
As of no concern.

So the man will stare,
In the space before sleep;
Or over the mug on the stained table,
Where the butt in the ashtray
Leaves its carmine smear on his mind;
And will turn when the tapping plucks his ear,
And see the blind veteran enter,

Bearing his unrejectable cup;
And will then understand
How the gnarled event must be weighed in its world,
Under the havoc-holding sky,
Under the iron,
Under the catapulting dead,
Who grin in the metallurgic grip
And eat their answer.

It will ring like the guilty coin in the cup.
It will be taken aside,
And secretly appraised,
And found insufficient.
It will be tucked away with the piece of string,
With the match and the nickel,
In the little pocket above the groin,
Where the maimed genitals,
In their soiled truss,
Bear the seed of an oncoming age.

Waldport, Oregon

PART FIVE

Sea:
And in its flaw the sprung silence,
Weighted with dusk,
Margent,
Tufted with shadow,
The skypuffs born of sundown.

Resides:
A vast withholding,
A reticence,
Consuming;
And beckons,
Fleering its white drift,
Its lavish formulation.
Beyond those long stooping ledges,
Those breakers born of the wind's mouth,
The half-light cast like a slick skin

Wrinkles in motion.
And then,
Slowly,
The plumed piling,
The drop,
And the deep west wide-broken,
Split up and spilt,
And the shy casual serene disclosure:
A film at the feet.

What had it done in all its ages?
The same.
Only the same,
Through its grave figuration,
Only the same.
And he nuzzles against its fresh draught,
Turning back and back,
His squinted eyes picking toward west,
Probing its weftage for what it could mean,
For what was in it,
What it held for him,
A possible surcease
From the shadowed doubt
And the shrewd question,
Inhabitant of his heart.

But the letter is there,
Under his hand in the shabby coat,
Like an overlooked clue
In a case disposed long since and forgotten,
Turned up in court.
He fingers its fold,
As if the tips could read for themselves
The dumb script,
Bent in the sheath that bears his name,
That sought him out,
And now mutely waits,
As a restless messenger lolls at the door
Invoking reply.
He makes only the head's gesture,
Shaking off doubt;
The face tilts to the wind,

The searching sight
Preys on contingence,
Its transitory role.

The film.
The long stooping ledges.
The drop.
His eye roves against sundown,
Sets the frail moon in its sky,
That makes its mark,
Emblematic,
In the hesitance of the dusk,
In the approachment of the night,
That swart footfall.
What is he?
Which man of his modes,
Of all he may be,
Shall have knowledge enough,
With the thin sheath in his fingers,
To make any reply?
Not to her, but himself?
Now that the old volcanic hurt,
In its black upheaval,
Buried the civilization of the past?
Now that the Peace,
Breached in the air over Nagasaki,
Lays its ash on the world?
The myriad fragments that make up a war
Come asking home,
Like the unanswerable letter,
In from the islands,
Back from the reefs,
With the foreign sun on their faces,
With the foreign blood on their hands;
Back from the blind insouciant sea,
That sulks and champs and is unconcerned,
Self-caresser,
Forever involved in its own immolation:
Seminal jell on the dappled shore

Sufficing: its adequate own.

The film.
The long stooping ledges.
The drop.
And the vague sand run through the fingers.
But the solitary self under the wind's eye.
The self and the self,
The divisible selves,
Ill-eased with each other.
There mumbles the sea.
(Dip down, dip down)
There mumbles the sea,
But a mnemic speech that never comes clear.
And the solitary self
Broods on its track,
The footprint on the glistening berm,
Easily erased.
A sandpiper,
In his hunched run,
Looks over his shoulder.
(Dip down, dip down)
The lurch rhythm and the dull beat
Tramp out the pace of the blood's scansion.
The dead warriors of all the past,
In a ragged surge at the raw future,
Plunge and fall back.

His slow hand picks up a stone,
Thumbs the scuffed edge;
Wave-work,
That has taken away,
Left its crease and its wrinkle,
And restored nothing.
But brings out a beauty.
See, yes, the fine seam.
A flaw, yes, but of beauty. *

---

* Though this line concludes with a period, it does not mark the end of the stanza—which continues on the next page.

His.
If he wants.
If he wills.

He raises his head.
The wondering face
Turns and deflects.
And the sudden hand
Hangs like a hawk
To broach an exacerbate need.

The film.
The long stooping ledges.
The drop.
And the hand falls,
Rips open and enters,
Invading the storehouse of the breast,
Where the old acquisitions
Lie heaped in its hold.

Dip down! Dip down!

Raids and ransacks,
Rakes up its rich hoard,
The greenful seasons,
Vineyard and valley,
The good and the glad.

Dip down! Dip down!

The face in its speechless joy,
Caught up and made whole,
Seen,
Flung in the wind's fluff,
Brought back.

Dip down! Dip down!

And the clear song,
And the plenitude of touch,

And the face.

Dip down!

And the rapturous body,
Its naked divestment,
Its total request.

Who claims this guilty?
Who brands this bad?

Dip down!

The plundering hand,
Like a mad king,
Reels through the rooms,
Seizes and shakes and finds no clue,
Loots to the last,
Descends to the sunken tomb in the self,
The trapdoor clamped in the murky cellar,
Heaves open its hole,
Drops keening down;
And there discerns,
On the tumorous wall,
Like a human skin
Peeled from the flesh and stretched up to dry,
The raw map of the world.
The shorelines, etched like flaring nerves,
Chart their red coasts.
In the meridians of death
The veined rivers bleed to the sea.
Blotched through the hemispheric zones
The purplish bruise of a total war
Festers and seethes.

How comes it here?
Who made it, the map,
Skinned from the torn flesh of the world,
Hung up in the heart
To blanch the face and blind the eye?
Is this his own handwork,
Who grubbed out the years in the squalid camps

With the men who denied—
Cried: No! Cried: Not to make murder!
Sucked in asleep with a fat wage and a mother's kiss!—
Who lived to verify the slave
And lip the pauper's oath?

Oh, ask up an answer!
And if this be guilt
Strike innocence out of the human page!
Ask the illiterate dead,
Parched and rotten in the clogged earth,
Mummied stiff in the black tombs,
Ploughed in the sand,
Chewed and tattered in the gnawing wave,
Dissolved in the high exploding air
To sift on the cities themselves had burned!
Ask each and any!
Jehovah, who lulls them all in his hallowed palm!
Dealer in mercy and dealer in wrath!
Sweet Jesus, boned and gutted on the phallic tree!
Open your blood-filled mouth and speak!

The sandpiper's cry,
Flung over his back,
Stringes the sea-voice.
The round eye
Gams and glitters,
And stares him down.
In the necropolic heart,
Where crime and repentance
Merge in the attitudes of fear;
Where pity and hate
Grope together and are one;
Where wisdom,
Sprawled like a bayoneted priest,
Raises its face
To speak once more and once more be struck—
The great hide of the map
Oozes and drains,
And all the forsaken immitigable dead

Groan in their fitful sleep.

Why? How and by whom?
What blind intercession
Culls precedence out,
Stalks through the cleftage of event,
Tracks finally to earth?
What merciless equation
Couples A with X
To prove B guilty?
What savage disseverance
Rives agent from act,
Leaves the pregnable seed
Its huge germination,
Its terrible fruit?

Oh, deep down and dredged!
The sanguinary laughter,
The immoderate mirth!
The thick guggle of all taken attempt,
Deflected endeavor,
Swept out and dispersed,
Ground in the black bowels of decision
And heaped on the strand!

He chokes.
Cramped in convulsion he coughs, he gags,
Hacking the phlegm up from the heart,
From the heavy lung,
That breeds its deep bile,
And is spat;
And steps over that stain,
And leaves it there on the glistening shale
Where the sea bird shat,
Where the sand crab's sucked pathetic shell,
Ironic chrysalis,
Heels in the blistering wind.
                              *

---

* "Wind" marks the end of this stanza. New stanza begins top of next page.

The great trampling rote.
The outward-running suck.
The huge silence hung over sound.
The excoriate eye.

The self's knowledge in the self's lack,
And the riddle of error.

The hand checks and falters,
And is withdrawn,
Shriveled.
Deep in the west the open range and pasture of the wind
Ripples and flows;
Those palisaded cliffs that flank the south
Will be ankled in dusk but their crowns gilded;
Far out now and under
The pouring light drops ever away,
The black racer sweeping along the sea,
A sliding wedge,
And the wedge widens,
The blade,
Made steep,
Thickened,
The coast covered,
All taken,
Blacked out and bound,
Wholly annulled
In the swift totalitarian seizure of the night.

Not yet, not yet.
Nor all the impulsion of the mind,
That beggars completion,
Fans it the faster.
And daylight or dark,
It's all one to the sea,
That has beach to dapple.
And yet, when the wind's right,
And the voice muffled,
Maybe deep toward dawn
When the sad moon lays on the sea its glimmering track
And the great bulk shuffles,

Then, then does the self,
That so needs knowledge,
That so wants to know,
Draw as on some shimmering dream
That long ago had steeped the mind in its potent drench
And been forgotten;
And glimmers again in the moon's track;
And is maybe the meaning of the self,
It, too, oceanic,
A central rest and a surface trouble,
And always at flux,
From pleasure to pain,
And out of the pain to painful pleasure,
And so back to pain.

But never for sure.
Not on the shoreline,
Where the shells,
Loose change in the wave's purse,
A counterfeit coin,
Rustle and toss;
Nor far at sea where the cormorant steers his undeviate course
To the specific rock;
Nor among those banded gulls,
Keeping their careful withdrawal,
Their fleeting shadows ghosts of the wave,
Holding that shifting dangerous edge
Severe in the tilted bill and the tucked feet—
This too,
These too,
Would write,
Like the wind,
Upon his heart
Their uneasy answer,
And watch him over his mute years,
With the round regarding eye,
And keep their distance.

Such would he know,
And hold the disconsolate disclosure under his hand,
To wear the incertitude,
Thin glove against guilt

That sleeps,
Like the winter bear,
In the cavern cut in the heart
By the impassive year.

But now the thunder is all converged for sundown,
And the wind smokes on those ledges,
In that wild beckon,
The whitecap's unquestionable wish,
Where all consequence lurks,
Inchoate,
Like a possible synthesis of the self,
And is so revealed,
The metaphor in the sea's mouth,
And is his reprieve.

The film.
The long stooping ledges.
The drop.
He lifts up his hand,
Its shadow flitting between the indefinite face and the down sun;
And he turns,
And goes then,
With the salt smell in his coat,
With the crumpled letter,
With the restless pebble at odd's end in the bare pocket;
And will watch once more from the flinted path in the cliff-cut,
Where it lies out there now far away as in sleep and untroubled;
And weeks later,
Risen at dawn,
Will trace in the rife electric air
That imperative presence,
And suddenly all the tensile might
Will shift and settle;
He will kneel to its print,
Its fluent gesture: the fine sand
Strewn on the rug from the fluted cuff,
From the frayed cloth.

Cascade Locks, Oregon

✳✳

William Everson and his wife Edwa (Poulson) Everson,
Waldport, Oregon, 1943.

Mary Fabilli, ca. 1944.

Nov. 2, 1943

At length
~~At last~~
~~the time~~ we learn.
~~Though at last we learned,~~
Finding the chastening pattern to school desire;
Not tamper with time,
Neither revel the future nor singer the past.
The world wars on,
Our subsequent fate involved in its toil,
But the ~~urgent~~ abstract voice that ~~speaks~~ from the box
Cannot bring it clear.   speaks
                          of
                          spills
Even the purpose by which we have come
Loses distinction,
With the lover's face and the wife's affection,
Here in the wilderness,
The waste of the world,
Bounded between the continents back
And the absolute West.
We rise in the dawns,
Enter the day;
~~We~~ Eye the weather and watch the sea,
In its manifest purpose,
Marshal itself for another assult.
Whether or not we are heros or fools
Is ~~not~~ not now or conceived
   ~~the~~ hardly the point,
Who have learned in this   minute
That all achievement is measured at last by infinite means,   June 5, 44

As the soldier,   That all acheivment is only attained
Crouching and trilling,   By the thick sequence of fixed
Must also know,   beginnings
Bent by his gun.   composing an act,
Having fastened on this we can only endure, As the soldier, killing
Immersed in the churnwalk of the will,   crouching and ahead,
And wade up time,   must also know,
Where the glacial future,   Bent by his gun.
~~Formed and forked in~~
Frozen and formed in the stone ranges beyond our sight,
Yields only the iridescent trickle
That ~~seeps~~ bleeds from its throat.

June 5, 44

That all attainment   That all ~~attainment~~ acheirement
is only acheived   is only ~~attained~~ ~~acheived~~ small thick dull
By the 'uu sequence   by the ~~deliberate~~ ~~tiny~~ ~~dull~~ sequence
~~That~~   of ~~tiny~~ ~~fixed~~ attempts beginnings
                           ~~that make up the act~~
                           composing an act

New line-up, Dec 2, 1943.

I. That morning we wept
II. The bus begins
III. This then is our world
IV. The newcomer marvels.
V. To sunder the rock
VI. In time we learn.
VII. For most time is prayer.
VIII. For all time is Woman
IX. No man is alone
~~X. Break the man from the woman~~
XI. Can The photograh teach?
XII. Each day brings a letter
XIII. And the man, in sin the dusk,
XIV. Does the adulteress grieve?
XV. The man nurtures his hurt.
XVI. The man in his time
XVII. This is his finding
XIX. Yet does the man marvel—

Draft of "Chronicle of Division" Part 1, Poem 12 (1943-1944).

1 All day my mind has fixed upon your face
4 Of *song* bleached of casuistry
2 ~~And~~ of its graven image masklike made
3 ~~And~~ round its graven image wreathed its wraith

5 All day my mind has fixed upon your face
Of ~~sorrow~~ severed, and of casuistry unknown
Of ' ∪ ' ∪ ∪ ∪ / ∪ /
And round its graven image wreathed its wraith
The whisper *sawin* on the carven stone

~~When in that stately dance we softly trod~~
~~And nursed the body~~

Our years between us like twin rivers lay,
~~And~~ The dance we danced was on each nother shore   gestured.
Our bodies followed, but could do no more,

And were conjoined in music only
Conjoined in music only
The years drew down between their desultory roar.

Now in the dance's afterthought I lie
Who asked for your embrace, and was refused
Your face, like Europe, saddens in my eye

Now in the dance's afterbeat I tread,
Lame with constraint, and shuffle at its pace
The ragged measure beats about your face

Shuffle the ragged measure
Beat on the body

Now in the dance's afterbeat I tread,
Stiff with constraint, and shuffle at its pace
The leaden rivers shu *image about* on your face,
As round the syphinx the sands
As round the sandy sphinx the latent dead
Flow to their ∪ / ∪   place
Drain to their

A PRIVACY OF SPEECH

(June 1946)

A PRIVACY OF SPEECH

I

Cried out all night,
What the wind cried,
What the wave cried to the rock,
What the nightbird said in the crumbled gully,
Spoken purely of self,
Catalyst toward a cold morning,
What the leaf said.

Eye cries to the eye,
In the insufficiency of speech,
And lip lacks,
Not favored of sight.
Could part know part in the gangling structure,
Could hand howl,
Could sex sough,
Could it sigh,
Name its clear need—

Nightcrier! Nightcrier!
Prism-maker!
Yoker of tangents!
Be shorn of commitment,
Be shrived of that folly!
One placed against one
Act trembles toward motive,
And all things are.

II

A privacy of speech:
It will tell all—
A recipe of no reason.
Why hand,
How heart,
Whence of the brain its massive dream.
Verb cries to the verb and noun trembles:

It is exposed.
Hand gropes toward hand,
Drenched in its deed,
Cajoled with reasons,
Never enough,
But reasons.

Night holds.
Is prime.
Whence all began that sought beginnings.
And the blind noun shook to the breathing verb,
And was exposed,
Was drenched by doing;
Shakes yet to the verbal heart,
Shakes ever.
One sucks toward one.
In time's dense conjugation
Act trembles toward motive.
Or nothing is.

III

Nor was, ever, but by that instant,
That tippage of time,
When all goes over.
The screech owl,
Dead in the wimpled grass,
His underwing wakened with russet,
Edged in beige,
He knew it.
There was only that instant,
Always,
And all went,
Irrevocable,
Was done,
The act soughing out its eternity of flaw and conjunction,

And the sigh:
Nevermore.

He did not hear it, but we do.
We are that sigh.
Going out, going over,
Trailing our hands in the backwash of time,
Where the leaf floats,
The leaf and the fallen stem,
Wheatseed,
Kernel of oat,
Bearded barley.
Where the wave cries to the rock,
We trail our hands there,
We are that sigh.
The screech owl,
Stiff in the wimpled grass,
Broke like a beak into something other.
When did it die?
What instant, split with convergence?
Of that instant and in it
What could death be?
In the pure contingence
What transformation?
The eye lidded over,
The claw crooked at the sky,
The loose feather in the lank grass.
For it: all.

IV

But not for us.
In the sigh of our going lurks all was-not;
The instant not ours,
Not whole—
We too something other,
But premature,
Before our time.
And at that tippage
Cry out, complex;
Look back and about,

Forever elsewhere.
Everything drains,
Seeps out, weeps away.
Everything alters but nothing transforms.
We grow old.

And the old man gnaws his leathern nail,
And the old woman weeps,
Inconsolable.
Who may be consoled of the unmanageable past
That is its answer?
Who may be spared that abject subservience?
Our sole sadness,
Our single sorrow,
Our metaphysic,
Our whole philosophy.
We have none other.
And the old man fingers his wart,
And the old woman weeps,
Each earlier,
Each elsewhere,
What-not and which-ever
Rubbed in the palsied hands,
A crotchet reminder.
The sigh,
The human sound,
Adam's answer,
The bell's doom,
The tocsin's clang:
Rhetoric of the unconvinced—
Nevermore.

V

But at that ray,
That ray of refraction,
Where light bends,
The moon's gleam in the gleamed gully,
Where the instant
Twains on that racing edge
And is annulled—

It happens.
Of it runs all ruin, inexpectation;
Of it all attainment,
By it achieved.
Contingence, consequence;
Convergence, completion;
Webbed in the riddled framework of time
And broken with being.

For the outlaw,
Trapped by the bursting bullet,
He perceives.
In the trajectory of event,
Over the hill by the runneled ditch,
Where the wave
Cries to the rock,
Where the nightbird utters,
There, it occurs.
The bird whispers and twits.
The screech owl stiffens in the wimpled grass.
And the snub-nosed pellet,
Arced through the avenues of event,
Dips and enters,
Its own explication.
In the threshing vest the watch quivers, ticks,
Is undeterred.
It will not put off.
Then only the fob dangles and turns,
Its dull medallion
A glint for the moon's ray.
But the heart has ceased,
Bursted with revelation.
And the bucktooth,
Bared to the nightwind,
Dries its speckle of froth
And waits for morning.
The guilt died in the head, purged.
The eye, fixed on its final disclosure,
Cuts the course of the wearing stars.
Each is appraised,

And passes over.
Each is absolved.
And dawn draws,
And dries the dew on the sallow cheek,
Where the crow's-foot of an ancient care
Lives stubbornly on.
It will not be divorced from its own.

VI

And dawn draws,
And brings one from the thicket,
Where he hunched all night,
Alien himself to the cold air,
But fearful to move,
Till sight could verify his luck
And the bullet's breve.
He comes out from the boulder,
Limps from the bush,
With the metal means held yet in his hand,
To that chill place,
Where the suit lies mussed in the damp morning;
Looks down from the remote withholding self
That stares and stares and only sees;
Reads the bare detail,
Writes his brief report,
And sighing goes.
The bucktooth grins in the wind.
The fob dangles.
In the wet pocket the shrill watch
Runs out the race with the closing instant,
Runs on, runs on.
It will be parceled aside,
Sent as the rueful reminder,
Where the old woman,
Inconsolable,
Will weep upon it,
And tuck it away
With a photograph of its late owner,
Long before its time,
Uneasily united—

As in the museum of all worldly loss
The hapless objects of a plundered past
Cry out at the ludicrousness of their lot—
But now in the vest it ticks and quivers,
Confident,
And its chill reiteration
Greets the siren sound on the hill,
As the Black Maria
Wheels in the shale to the narrow edge
Where luck plays out
And all things end.

VII

Where all things enter.
Where dawn draws,
Where the footprint fills in the wind,
Where the bloody stain in the wimpled grass
Dries with the feather,
Where the nightbird
Abdicates to the dark covert
And the daybird drinks.

Where all things enter.
In the bare bush of the nightbird's whisper
The daybird flouts,
Ruffing his feathers,
His throat swollen on song,
The rapturous torrent
Breaking forever out,
Upward and out,
Steeped in the extension of feeling,
The bright blaze
Where the verb refracts on its own impulsion
And splinters aside.
A blacksnake lurks in its dank burrow
And watches the bird.
The song splits and shatters,
In the areas of all exposure,
Beyond control,
Beyond reason, doubt or the five failings,

Bleached of joy,
Extracted of sorrow,
Closed in the wide portion
Beyond choice or withdrawal,
And all of its own.

The song stops.
The bird snaps in the air where the mayfly hovers.
The blacksnake listens.
In the wimpled grass the loose feather
Lifts and settles,
Lifts and settles.
The bird begins.

VIII

The bird begins,
But not the unimpeachable heart;
It has sung forever—
The mayfly crushed in the grinding craw
Gleaned of its instant.
But the forever song,
Immortal in the bursting throat,
Binding bird to bird,
Breaks with that wild welling;
Forever outward,
Forever away,
The clear expenditure
Seized up out of the mayfly's juice,
Spilled and spoken.
Over and over and never done
The instant endures.
The nightbird broods and dozes, awaiting its dusk,
Its dull ear scarcely attuned to the rapturing torrent
That blots transience out,
Blots time,
Leaves the bare energy of the expending throat
Wide on the wind.
The blacksnake quits his cold tunnel,
Twines in the bush.
In a bare room

The eyes that watched the migratory stars,
That saw dawn draw,
Saw cirrus, snared of the light,
Turn smoke-color,
Dove's-breast and dun,
Lie under their lids
And see no more.
The watch falters once in the limp vest
And then runs down.
The flesh waits on for its old earth
And another try.

IX

The flesh waits on.
And the blind event,
In its far formulation,
Holds off,
Plays for its proper time,
Feeds incidence in,
Stays for sunfall,
Till the fugitives from their own pursuit,
Of the self condemned,
Of whom the guilt
Grinds in the body of a wholer need,
Can bring to the grass
A briefer blindness,
There, by the gulch,
Where the wave cries on,
In the otherness of its old want,
Its endlessness.

The man faces the woman.
Hand gropes toward hand,
Cajoled with reasons,
Seamed with the transient years of attempt,
The anxious search for the naked future,
Bearing its useless ring of fidelity,

Only token the body brings.

The woman faces the man.
And the word that dies in the strict throat,
The solitary noun—
What would it have said,
Wrung from the hopeless context,
Killed of the insufficiency of sound,
And caught there,
In its twisted need,
Cramped in the knowledge of its own ruin,
And its lost accord?

In the universal flesh
The selves that have lain,
Locked in their salt suppression,
Bondaged under a rude mandate,
Stir, they quicken,
They seek fulfillment,
They sense their time and their time draws,
They await conjunction,
When all will erupt:
The raw reasons made manifest,
The restless springs pouring up and out to their permanent summer,
Broke through into being,
Like the screech owl's beak in the blind future,
Like the song eternal in the splitting throat,
Drunk with the moment's death,
Rapt in the instantaneous endurance
Beyond the ecstasy of flight.

Bare in the bush the blacksnake glistens;
From the deadened west the light leaches and fades.
The screech owl's mate,
Impatient,
Quavers once from the covert,
Cocks its head for the duplicate cry
That does not come.
The woman opens her eyes,
In the last look,
And gazes up to the stone visage,
The hooded male of the blind orbs

Fixed on their own incomprehension,
Bleached of joy,
Extracted of sorrow,
The area where all things enter
And no thing lasts.

Night thickens.
In the black covert the screech owl's mate
Hoots and quavers,
The questioning cry of the lost identity seeking its own,
Its other self.
The skirt, rumpled,
Is figured now with the fallen leaf,
Wheatseed,
Bearded barley.
The man rockets through time.
In the exigence of event
The woman lifts up the stiffened face,
Blind with extinction,
The bullet blunt in the heart,
The flesh blared in the flesh,
Blown to the broken center
Beyond the black cave of the fissioned self
Where all obtains.

Touch.
The hug of conjunction,
The sulk of desire,
Leading beyond the last pulsation,
The terminals of pain.
These. These.
Where will it be broken?
At what point only?
What waits there,
Holding conclusion in its windless depth?
Far back where the voice died,
Far back where the sight failed,
Far back where the touch
Shattered to its red extreme and was dissolved,

The myriad life in the streaming vault
Streaks toward attainment.
There is no returning.
Something comes back but not the other.
Something else returns,
Struggling back into bondage,
Borne on the ever-resuming ebb,
With the lap and the murmur,
Strewn on the shore between life and death,
The dim edge of the night.

And all about there,
Fixed outside that delving dream,
The components of its stretched locale,
Object by object,
Maintain their precinct.
The whispering wind,
The erect and tensile filaments of weeds,
The fallen leaf,
Half-consumed near the igneous rock,
All keep accordance,
Strung on the rays that leave no trace,
But sift out the hours
Purling across the deaf stones,
While the exactitude of each entering star
Chronicles the dark.

These. These.
The wheatseed snared in the stained skirt.
The opening eyes.

X

Cried out all night,
What the wind cried,
What the wave
Cried to the rock,
What the nightbird said in the crumbled gully,
Spoken purely of self,

What the leaf said.

A privacy of speech—
And the noun quickens.
Vibrant between the breathing verbs
It gains its dimension.

And the anxious hand
Gropes again toward its dense future.

Loose in the grass
The feather lifts and settles,
Lifts and settles.

The bird begins.

Cascade Locks, Oregon

IF I HIDE MY HAND

(June 1946)

IF I HIDE MY HAND

I

You who found the yokeage of friendship
Too heavy to have,
Worn as a pain,
As a pain cast—
That other hurt,
Does it not come to you now with its injured hand,
There, in the palm,
Where the throb lives on in its mute why?

Remember the seabird that cannot sing.
You saw its mouth,
Reaved at the cloud,
Flecked with the sufferer's loss
And the sufferer's gain.
It does not ask for understanding;
You do not need it.

And if I hide my hand—
How can I hold it forth,
The human gesture
That plants in your palm
Another nail?

II

Reject.

Because you hate impurity
And I am impure.
Because you hate sickness
And I am sick.
Because you hate weakness
And I am weak.

And having cut my cancer out of your flesh,
And being free to walk

Where the heron walks by the river-mouth,
Of such plumage as kings would wear,
And of the pace of kingship;

Be of good countenance again,
Who have God's leave to dare
Where all others are punished,
And wear His sign
Everywhere about you.

Be set aside, and not of such need.
Of all others,
Out of the common bond,
Be freed.

III

Nor make a reckoning between us,
Favor for favor.
Of the past's pure mutation
Make no mention:
Whether my hand's curve toward error
Wavered your arm;
Whether your singleness of heart
Left me for the better.

We are not equals in this matter.

But given your spirit's clear persuasion
And my reason's ruin,
Declare all over, and no more
Walk where the wave won out;
And on that shore
Not listen now who listened there before.

Cascade Locks, Oregon

IN THE FICTIVE WISH

(Summer 1946)

IN THE FICTIVE WISH

I

So him in dream
Does celibate wander,
Where woman waits,
Of whom he may come to,
Does woman wait,
Who now is
Of his.

Does woman wait.
Not wife now;
Long gone,
Face fading;
Of her once surely,
Whom best he knew,
But not now.
Nor any girl in his life known.
Of them too as of wife maybe,
But not wholly;
And now not.

In him lives alone and is his;
Was always,
Who looked for her outward.
Mistook her,
Wife's face and friend's;
This one's pace and that one's saunter;
Finds now,
In long abstention,
Own form and feature,
Not others,
Laughing behind his thought;
But solemn mostly,
Waiting within.

Once on a paper he drew her face;

First knew then her nature;
His in himself.

Water-woman,
Near water or of it,
The sea-drenched hair;
Of gray gaze and level
Mostly he knows her;
Of such bosom as face would fade in;
Of such thigh as would fold;
Of huge need come to;
Man out of heart's hurt come,
Of self divided.
Her certain shape:
Of such body, yes, and of such croft,
Where ache of sex could so conjoin,
Could so sink,
As soul sinks enfolded,
In dream sunken;
Of such cunted closure,
Butt broad in the love-grip;
As of bed,
Broad,
As of width for woman;
And of belly
Broad for the grapple.

But of grave smiling eyes,
Of gaze gray,
Veiled;
Of such soul;
Oh, surely of such other self,
As he in life sought so to have
And could not;
So looked from such eyes,
Of such gaze made;
And of mouth
Lipped for laughter;
And deep-breasted,

As all women would be:
Of such, she.

But never of need,
Nor begs;
Waits only,
As does water,
And may be entered.

Wader,
Watcher by wave,
Woman of water;
Of speech unknown,
Of nothing spoken.

But waits.

And he has,
And has him,
And are completed.

So she.

II

But masked of the self,
And in it,
What is she?
Who?
Of wife's face divested,
Of friend's feature,
What must she presage?
Fair-countenanced she,
And the bodily grace;
Sleep-comer;
Lurker behind the veils of thought,
And is laughing;
Or grave-smiler there in his deep trances.
Not composite?
For seems she rather
As if was always,

And herself seized on image
When it came near
For use of it,
To make it her own.
Was not all he did
With that other, his wife,
Whom in time he loved wholly,
His huge effort to make them one?
All his watching,
Over their fruit in the sun-filled mornings,
Or in lamp's light of evening
When night laid its indivisible mark on the world,
Was it not surely his need
To find the woman within
In the woman without?
All his rapture in love,
Was it not precisely
When such an accord
Was most complete?
Then most was her breast
Ease of his need,
And the thigh a solace,
And the sudden laugh he loved,
When what looked from her eyes,
As of some clarity of self
Unbeknownst even to her,
But was there,
And he saw it,
And it was—
All transformed!
Then was she not
Most wholly embodied
In what was his?
Till celibacy's long withdrawal
Let down the mask;
And he came in his dream,
Or even in waking,
There in the gloom by the swart tree,
Face to face with one
Stranger than any,

And dearer,
And indeed the pure substance
Of all he sought.

III

But now having seen,
And known at last of his own and none other,
Does she not frighten?
When he leans to embrace,
To merge him into her,
Nurtured of need,
Her deep-biding grace and her bodily essence,
Of grave-smiling aspect and of comforting gaze,
Then does she not terrify?

For whom now may he love?
Whoever incites,
Knows only of her,
And hence of him,
And not another;
Of such multiple visage,
Yet not another.
Blue eye or gray and the body's breathing—
What wonder of woman,
Now that he knows,
In whom touch dwells,
And all emptiness fills,
Can he come to;
Of such utter unlikeness,
In that hope of the heart,
Achieved at last in its own desolation,
Such wild reparation!
Nursed in the mind,
And so disheveled!
None! Oh, none!
She lives in them all,
In his eyes looking out,

Herself emplanting!
Her glance is there!
Her firmness of tread and her sure survival!
She lives!
And the master motive,
Her womanhood's weal,
To so dissemble,
To so disenchant of his huge rapture,
Being of dream only,
And not of his having,
Save there,
Where no substance is,
Nor touch obtains;
But the skinnied heart
Wisps out its want in the fictive wish,
And is revealed;
And in that revelation
Betrays.

IV

Wader,
Watcher by water,
Walker alone by the wave-worn shore,
In water woven.

She moves now where the wave glistens,
Her mouth mocking with laughter,
In the slosh unheard
When the sea slurs after;
In the sleepy suckle
That laps at her heel where the ripple hastens.

And the laughing look laid over her arm,
A tease and a wooing,
Through that flying maze when the wave falls forward,
From its faultless arch, from its tallest yearn
To its total ruin.

Lurker,
She leaves with laughter,

She fades where the combers falter,
Is gone where the dream is gone
Or the sleeper's murmur;
Is gone as the wave withdrawing
Sobs on the shore, and the stones are shaken;
As the ruined wave
Sucks and sobs in the rustling stones,
When the tide is taken.

Cascade Locks, Oregon

BOOK FOUR:

A BALM
FOR ALL BURNING

(1946-1948)

THE SPHINX

All day my mind has fixed upon your face
That drew me in the dance and was alone,
Saddened with a sorrow of its own;
And round that carven image wreathed a wraith,
As rain is wreathed across the graven stone.

Our years between us like twin rivers ran.
The dance you danced was on a nether shore;
Our bodies gestured but could do no more;
Like mutes we looked across that double span.
The years drew out their desultory roar.

Now in the dance's afterbeat I tread
Still with constraint, and shuffle out its pace.
The sandy rivers merge about your face,
As round the monolith the rampant dead
Drain to their dim and unrevealing place.

THE BLOWING OF THE SEED

(Fall 1946)

THE BLOWING OF THE SEED

The wind bloweth where it
listeth, and thou hearest
the sound thereof, but canst
not tell whence it cometh,
and whither it goeth.

JOHN III, 8

PROLOGUE

Whenas the woman,
Come out of her own ascendancy of self,
Some inner intensity unbeknownst to herself,
Cries out, cries out in love toward the man,
Who turns the head,
Turns from the isolate heart
Trapped in the injury of the breast;
Turns the dense compacted face;
Hears; puts forth the hand in its blind touch,
Its confirmation; is reassured.

What speaks there?
What cries from the self in its utterance of love?
What voice, held abeyant for years in some interior region,
Lifts up in its time and declares, cries out, is heard?
Does the long discipleship of doubt,
The self in its seeking,
Its search and rejection,
Returning, returning for such assurance,
And not favored—
Does it not order its own withholdance,
And wait on, ever?

Until such time,
As what has been heard,
Far off, its whisper—
When it stands in its season and speaks,
Cries out to the self, the other self,
Seen across long riftages of life,

Cries out of its inward-holding need, its huge hope;
Declares itself;
Affirms and accepts;
Vests its huge hunger;
Leaps upward,
Leaps out!

Oh, harbored in what haven of heart you heed now,
The man to the woman,
You cry out!
For see, she comes flying out of her dark past,
Her years broken with injury and that soul's search,
Her face beaten,
The mark of her heart's blood smeared on her brow.
She comes with her mad mouth and her flashing eyes,
Out of her fabled and ruinous past,
And is affirmed,
Is seized on and shaken.
She beats with her mouth his shagged head.
In such righteous rejoicing,
Of pain made and pleasure,
Of need known and unknown,
She cries and is heard,
Gives and is given!

And he, that maleness
Measured, of pools
And entrances, deepnesses,
Up out of darkness,
Steep holes, wells, black springs
And cisterns of the self,
Out through the pierced
Peripheral flesh,
Does start, does strike,
Is struck, up
Stroked, brims!
Brims and breaks over!

And hence purged,
Passed through,
As all night is,
As is dark,

As of all blackness,
As of death.

Till in its time the oncoming sun
Drinks and dissolves.

I

I speak
Who am come down from a glacial region north of here,
Where a cold river
Cuts its way to a colder sea,
Leaves the brown stain of its mark
Far out, it is said, for the feeding fish.

I speak, I speak.
I speak from the chattering lips of a cold man,
A man cut to the core;
Speak from the numbed mouth,
Blue in its dearth;
Speak from the hobbling frame,
From the limp of a cold place,
A cold region.

I speak from a cold heart.
I cry out of a cold climate.
I shake the head of a cold-encrusted man.
I blow a blue breath.

I come from a cold place.
I cry out for another future.

II

Darkheaded,
And of the olive flesh,
Your arm, in its encirclement,
Like the pure prevailing wind,
Blowing for miles from its deep equatorial zone,

Blows to the center of myself,
Thaws.

You of the wide south,
Chinook,
Wind of the containing warmth,
Did you know, in your entrance,
What a breath you blew through a heart's dungeon,
Set wide the cells,
The numbed prisoner
Agape in his rust,
In his ruin?

When you loosed that look,
That leaping,
A long way off to lay its mark,
Like sun on snow,
On the bitter places—

Did you know how it hit,
What broke in your coming,
And what you set free?

III

When the rains came over they wetted the forest,
The open slides of the granite peaks
And the little thickets.

They wetted the salmonberry and the leafless vine.
They wetted the rough trunks of the prone trees
Where the treefrog creaked in the branches.
They wetted the place where the hermit hunched,
Fumbling his thumb.

The owl,
In the tamarack,
Whoops on, whits.

The mouse, in the leaden glade,

Gnaws, scuttles.

There is left in that place a little ashes,
The butt-end of sticks and the blackened rocks.
There is left in that place only the small leavings of a frugal life,
Too tiny for the flit pipit
That skits in the thicket.

There is left in that place
Only the smell of a little smoke,
And a little ashes.

IV

If you were to try to say,
Half-closing your eyes in the way you have,
Your mouth pulled in a bit in its pre-speech purpose....

If you were to turn your face to me,
That sudden look of inward revelation,
When out of so much of thought, so much of thinking—
Out of your nights, as you lie abed and pick up the pieces;
Out of your days;
Over whatever task it is you are doing, in whatever place,
Going about your unguessable business
With that air of half-abstraction,
Half-involvement....

If you were to lift up your face,
And from so dense a demand, so deep a denial;
From your hemmed and hampered past,
When your world was weak,
And all your instance
Turned on the tremble of a touch,
And you had no grip, no grasp....

If you were to break,
The tears beat from your eyes;

All your hard hurt broke open and bared
In its sudden gust of bleak exposure....

If you were to try....

Under my hand your heart hits like a bird's,
Hushed in the palms, a muffled flutter,
And all the instinct of its flight
Shut in its wings.

V

And then that humming,
In the tenseness under the skin,
Where the little nerves
Mesh, merge:
In that fabric, that suture,
Where time runs out his rapid dance
And pain poises—

There. There.

Under those roots the running of it
Wakens a wind to skirl in the grasses,
A rain dance of wind;
A long passion forming out of its farther region;
A past of such pain,
Of such deprivation;
Out of such hunted hope when none could be had,
But yet the hope, the hunger;
Out of such starting
That wind widens,
That wind weaves.

Cry out, cry out,
Speak from the bloodied past, the failured venture;
Speak from the broken vows and the shattered pledges;
Speak from the ruined marriage of flesh
Where joy danced and was denied,

And the harsh croppage of time
Reaped its rue in those dolorous arches.

Dance. Dance.
Dance out the troubled dream.
Dance out the murderous pain,
The mutilated silence.
Dance out the heart in its narrow hole
Caught in the clamp of that brittle hunger.
Dance in the rags of an old remorse,
In the tattered garments of trust,
Ripped from the narrow thighs,
Thrown to the crickets.
Dance and be spent;
Fall in the long gasp,
The heart too hurt, the spirit
Cut too quick—

All gone, all broken,
Smashed and smithereened.
And none to know, ever;
None to heed.

Be through with it then.
Be finished.
Close out and complete.
Look. I am come.
Like a whirlwind
Mounting out of a foaming sea.
I suck all inward.
I shriek.

Dance! Dance!
Dance out the sad bereavement of flesh,
The broken suture.
Dance out the weight of the prone years.
Dance out denial.
Dance it out in the heave of that hope,
Sprung from the proud immortal flesh
That shoots up its flower.
Dance out the sharp damnation of time
That sets the crow's-foot

Crafty under the blear eye
And has its instance.
Dance it out, all,
And be brought low,
And be low broken,
And be brinked.

Now in a black time I come to you
Crouched in your corner of hut by your meager blaze.
Now like a man out of a madded dream
I come from my cleavage.
I come running across the hints and notches of a glacial year.
I bear brash on my back.
I wear an old woe.

Be joined.
Be clipped.
Be crouched and crotched,
Woman, woman!

Bring me that moaning mouth: I stop it.
Bring me the knock of that hurt-impacted heart:
I grind it out.

I level.
I level the last of my life in your life.
I hammer harsher than hooves.
I gnaw like knives.

Give me that past and that pain-proud flesh.
I come with the hurled and howling North:
A mad naked man.

VI

Of such touch given;
Of such sight—
Your eyes, where the warmth lives on from a late loving,
And your palms,

Placed—

Speak you?

That word wears out the woe of the world.

But now as your mouth on it shapes for a sound,
As a sign,
As of some sign given
Long ago, between man, between woman,
So on your lip it loudens,
Through those chambers of the mind
Where all past in its slumber
Lives on, lives on.

You speak.

And the chimes,
The bronze bells of those death-departed years
Are all awakened.

EPILOGUE IN A MILD WINTER, FROM THE COAST
COUNTRY

Woman, I sing to you now from a new season.
I sing from the freshened creeks,
From the autumn's waning.
I sing where the wind runs in from a wide sea,
Wakens these winter-wet fields to new growth,
A new greening.

I sing from a fallow year that has since been broken;
From a drought, a year that has died,
Gone down into deadness.
Known now of your mouth, known of your healing hand,
I sing to you from a richening joy,
A ripening gladness.

I sing to you from the spacious river of love
That flows in me now to its sea

With its mild murmur.
I sing from the little leaf that lurks in the bough;
The winter bud that has its hope
And will find its summer.

I sing from the barley germinal in the rich acre,
That will sprout and break in time
From its winter mantle;
As in me now the quickening self puts forth,
Uncouth, come with my head unkempt,
But my hand gentle.

I sing. I have been fulfilled in a winter season,
Wakened under a rain;
Like the seed of the mustard,
Like the seed of the vetch that is harrowed into the hill,
Rolled in the mulch of the lifeless slope,
In the leafless orchard.

I move to meet you now in a greening time.
I come with wind and with wet
In a soft season.
I bring you my hand.
I bring you the flesh of those fallow, fallen years;
And my manifest reasons.

Sebastopol, California

THE SPRINGING OF THE BLADE

(1947)

THE SPRINGING OF THE BLADE

But when the blade was sprung up,
and brought forth fruit,
then appeared the tares also.
                    MATTHEW XIII, 26

PART ONE: TIME OF YEAR

THE IRON DIMENSION *

It wears.
Even the young perceive it.
Even the infant,
Before he hardly has any perspective,
Moves with a wakeful wide-eyed caution
Into time's change.
That house-law he lives by:
Discovers one day its true substance,
A mere rule.

But will cross in that testing to the inviolate region,
The true absolute of human pain,
Entered with some injurious act
That can't be forgiven and will never be forgot;
The hurt and the hurter
Strung in the iron dimension,
Fixed there forever.

In our town, when I was a boy,
A man ran off with a grass widow,
"A woman of good looks and scant morals,"
Left to his wife
Only the children and a galled pride.
What the father was she blocked from their minds,
An exorcism of silence.
The eldest, grown out of girlhood,
Kept a suitor for eight years before she decided.
They were to marry in June;

---

* At stanza three, line three, "scant" replaces "loose"—a change Everson made during his
editorial work with the projected *The Achievement of William Everson* during the summer of
1993.

In April the woman
Caught them together on the parlor sofa
In the naked act.
She came to my mother;
I heard from the near room;
Her sobs shook through the house:
"Why couldn't they wait!"
Over and over, choked in the wet kerchief,
"Why couldn't they wait!"

It is hard to wait. In the drab parlor,
Under the drapes, under the faded pictures
And the papered walls, the stained and papered years....

But that does not redeem.
In the woman's heart, the old mother,
There that terrible cry burst with its burden,
To see the sin
Substantiate in the reckless act;
And the lip that never trembled in public,
Sustained in pride while the lean years grated,
That lip broke,
And the stringy throat gave its giant grief,
That splits, and like the wolf's howl on the winter crag
Shivers the overhanging snow
To start its crumble, its monstrous slide.

But no. Nor the blind hurt
Ran out no brutal, bloody course.
They made their marriage;
In proper season blessed with a babe.

But that does not redeem.
Not there, in the old woman's heart,
However she came to dandle that child.
For the taint, like a birthmark laid on a baby's face,
The delineament of an ancient lust
Spied out in the dimple—
And what caught in her throat,
Revulsion and shame and the gagging pride
In a raw mingle....

She went under the clay

Her jawbone clenched on the obstinate
Unobliterable, not-to-be-swallowed
Gorge of reproof:
A sharp stone in a chicken's craw,
Stuck there forever.

ODOR OF AUTUMN

And in the cooling weather,
Over the canyons,
Over the sun-invested slopes,
That hold, like tawny wine, all summer's hauteur;
Over the hazy draws and the pine-thicket knolls,
Drifts the unmistakable odor of autumn.

And I am reminded
That once more now it is the season of school;
And on country lanes
Again the school children make their way,
Wearing that openness about the eyes
Where fields have glimmered,
And the ground squirrel pierced his skirling note;
Bearing about them a something restless,
Something unruly,
The charge of freedom,
Nature's benign tolerance,
That will in time be curbed, made docile,
Smoothed as the tousled hair
Before the glass is smoothed and parted;
Sent with them off down the road
To an anxious future that long ago
Lost what they cannot keep.

YELLOW WEATHER

To rankle under restriction,
And seek an out—
As in the municipal environs,
The groomed campus and the kept parks,
One turns at last to the pathside weeds for his assurance,

And sees there, snatched out of confine,
A glimpse of that large pervasive nature,
Thrusting the tasseled head untrammeled,
The spiky thorn shot forth,
A rough challenge
Toward a freer, more ambient order.

So will the guiltful youth,
Too timid to leave his father's house
Yet chafed to remain,
Wander, come autumn, in the rural lanes,
Where the poplar litters its rainy leaf
And the thorned weed prospers;
Where the yellow weather leans over the land,
And summer's harvest, umber, a balm for all burning,
Sleeps on in the smoky fields.

MUSCAT

When the crop is in: fat muscats,
Most nectarous of grapes or sun-shrunken raisins,
The boys will go out in search through the vineyard,
And find the few forgotten bunches
That hang on late near the raggy stumps,
Gain a puckering sweetness,
Till frost drives down the leaves.

All through the empty afternoons will they wander,
Between the picking of the grape
And the pruning of the vine,
And find these better,
The ones not taken,
Rarer to the eye,
Riper to the mouth,
And richer to the mind.

CARROUSEL

For the child,
In love with looking,
The world goes wide to his earthly gaze
And there is no past.
The round eye,
That stares at dusk from the dark sill,
And sees the moon in the tree,
Rough hands on its face,
Fills then to overflowing
With autumn's wonder,
Not knowing what the cold means
But that the moths are gone.

And what lumps in the throat is the music's magic,
Its exquisite trill,
At the October fairs
Where the painted horses,
Bridled in gold,
Leap up, leap up in that lifeless lope,
With the little girls
Who shriek with joy
And shake out their ribboned hair.

It will be years, years!

And the dream will go,
Will keep only the trace,
As of a forgotten fondness,
Wholly lived out in youth's maturation,
But caught now, over the boardwalk,
Just for a moment,
Drifting across the summer music,
Where the carrousel tinkles and whirls.

But out there the sea,
That has been hushed and torpid,
Half asleep under a squat moon,
Scruffs up its strength,
And all the intervening years
Crack in two.

THE AREAS OF CORRUPTION

And the years reveal.
And there comes a time when,
Waking out of a walking dream,
As the child, each day, wakes with a wonder in its eye,
He rouses up the recumbent head
To a knowledge of the past.

And perhaps it is that the splendor of a tree,
Leafing the curb near the suburban mansions,
In the suggestible season,
Will make a meaning of itself;
Will write its own articulation in the cooling of the air;
Will say, with the loosing of its leaf,
All he could say,
Who looks by the marigold, loitering,
His slow shoe scuffing the gravel.

And the pipestem, like the chewn twig of his boyhood,
And the jackknife clasped near his knuckle;
Can these be touched,
Or what lies in them,
That somethingness,
Like a sleep on them,
As if the years had placed them there,
With their special substance,
To be at hand when the leaf fell,
And lead him back?

The sun says, Yes, it is true,
It is the sameness of the light,
It leaned so then.
The bird in the hawthorn,
Near his foot, says it,
Its head cocked in the known way,
The assurance of its eye.
And the lady, so smartly clad,
Whose heel on the flagstone,
In its luxurious clip, confirms it,
And whose glance, behind the flecked veil,
Bestows its fleeting speculation—

Is she not the same, the very same,
Who leaned above the little head,
Touched him, left him laved and swimming
In the lambent smile?

He cannot turn.
The heel-note clips away, smartly;
Out of the clinging clamorous ear
It trips and vanishes, its brief note
Gone like a flashing smile
That left its beckon but would not wait,
Lost beyond the hedges,
Where only an old gardener,
Seamed and serious,
Pokes among the shrubs.

The substance of the years,
Their very texture.
Like the milkweed down,
That drifts with the drifting air,
This time of year,
On the roadsides at home.
Or as the cattail
Lays out its fluff on the placid water
In the dryness of the fall,
Before the rains come in.
The very substance.
Gone with the autumns,
Washed out under a leaching rain;
Gone with the mother's mouldering smile;
With the father's frown
Stained in the earth.
Gone where the schoolmates of the past
Have long since gone,
To their separate lives,
Only the echo of their shouts
Caught in the scrappage of a phrase,
Where that cry persists,
Plaintive and long,

Calling him out to the leaf-frolic game
Before the dark sets in.

And the areas of all corruption
Cockle and fray in the torn heart.
The foxed pages rattle in an unrelenting wind.
And the written word
Blurs, fades as the sight itself,
Worn-out with looking,
Fades in the face,
When the eighty years' infant,
Witless and daft,
Wholly resumes his past.

PART TWO: THERE WILL BE HARVEST

I

Thus in this way, these glimpsings back,
Do I call up the days of my childness.
Thus in these nights I muse at work,
Through corridors and emptied rooms;
A cleaning task the day entails,
A new place, not mine,
The rooms others', their personals;
And I, a stranger of night,
When all are gone, to move in unease,
Fearful somewhat of the unwitting error,
A morrow's rebuke; and made once more
Child in my father's house,
Fearful to offend.

Oh, weakness! weakness! Where now
That strength of self so lately learned?
Come from the camps, measured with men
And known of esteem, found selfliness,
Held up your head, the first time
And at long last sure in your worth!
To be so tottered by a past's hand,
Made child to yourself,
That others' room, others' roof, a foreman's cut

Could so unseat! Where now
That new attempt, that looking toward life,
Learned with hope from one
New found, now wife, of such womanliness
A fallow past sings from its slumber?
So easily lost? So soon obscured?
Routed into that old ruin,
Rushed, thrown back there,
Made boy again, under a father's frown?
And now, the year sloping toward autumn,
To let its old spell
Speak soft in your ear—
That way lies lack, lovelessness,
The self shut off, all regression,
The sweetish smell of disconsolation!
Make a hymn then of other,
Sing of it. Set a hymn
In praise of God's being,
Of man and woman joined in the godly eye,
And made fond there, and fecund, founded in wholeness,
To have a wholeness out of the earth,
In earth's abundance: Sing!

II

Given the rotund and revolving world
Season on season tilting to the sun,
Its orchard-ending hills, its weighted fields,
Its August heat in which the growth is won.

Given the pasture-loving herds upon its plains,
Its hives like humming cities in the sage,
Its vineyards rooted in the level loam
To bring the sunburned vineyardist his wage.

Given all this, all these, these simple proofs,
This common casual promise of the plains,
The very being's recreative yearn,
Only the ultimate gathering-in remains.

There will be harvest, harvest, summer's mastery,

Garnered in fulgence from the fruited trees;
The harvesters come singing from the fields,
And men and women take their mutual ease.

And men and women make their secret tryst
After the blared torrential light is blind,
As all the earth's cohabitants will come,
Creature to creature, kind to pairing kind.

Lord of the vineyard, Lord of the leaning year,
Who burst the vine's forbearance out of the earth,
Tender again the very plenty of your plains
To bring the body its essential birth.

There will be harvest, harvest, autumn's endlessness,
Forever and forever out of the ground.
The strong sons and the seemly daughters rise.
The streams replenish, and the fields abound.

III

And the earth bears. Back of the house
The blackberry riots the fences, swarms the tree,
Hiding the fruited runner under its thorn.
The apple, loosened, launches the long way downward,
Marked in its passage by the leaf's whicker.
All through the hovering deadness of the night
They give, go down. We heard the pears
So fall in the Valley. In the Hood River country
Where the thick Columbia thrusts its flattened weight to the sea,
We heard that sound. And in the orchards of Sonoma,
All night, the round fruit spun out its brief duration,
Limb to loam. And heard now, once more, like a pure pronouncement
Out of the past; in the mind seized, fixed in its fall,
Made absolute in the dark descent; as the round earth itself,
In any instant of its wide reel, may be so caught,
And all its godly creatures struck in their perilous stance—

So the apple, falling. Come morning find them cold, dew-glistened,
Spiked with straw, the mute wind-fallen members.

There will be harvest. For the look of love;
For the hope cried out of the great love held,
Cried out for the child to fill, fulfill, bless the body's being.
For the light that lies on the full of the arm, the roundness,
A slowness gathering under the knee,
The easeful tread of a woman, walking, waiting for bearance.
These make their prophecy. I make my prayer
That the shutback seed may be restored, and the restoration
Blaze with the spring, brood with the summer,
Break forth with the fulgent fall,
Fill the last lack of a life, the hymn be heard.

There will be harvest, harvest. We freighted the handpress
Out of the hills. Mounted at last in the little room
It waits for the black ink of its being;
And the rich paper, drawn out of Europe, it too hand-fashioned;
The work of the hand, all; the love of the hand in its sure sweep
When the bar pulls over; all about it the touch of a hand
Laid on it with care. And borne like fruit, a perfect page,
That testament to the heart's abundance
All work of wholeness executes in the enlivened eye: a godly issue.

There will be harvest. I stand on the verge
Of my manhood's might, I know it.
I cannot read the ripe richness,
Nor estimate in what welcome way
Reward will grow, will gratify.
But how they hail now in the heart!
How the great heart hails to that host,
Shouts its festive charm, rocks in the breast!
I poise for it; I hold out my hands; I hug it in;
As the great heap of the harvest
Is hugged from the fields,
Boxed; the dust of that labor
Drifts over the arms,
Drifts over the deepening fields,
Near twilight, when the dark heels in,
And the crows, high over, a last light on them,
Halloo in from the hills.

IV

And in the mornings
Sun stanches the roof, sinks it,
Floods it in gold effulgence,
Rolls light all-where.
It is an autumn sun, bears autumn's allness,
Makes blest the bough, builds against deadness,
November's sullen norn.

It is a sun of blond propinquity.
I walk to my work in its hallowed light.
We walk together, in the streets of the city,
One man, one woman.
I hold the sun as a sign against deadness,
In autumn's being, when all lies open,
The heart and the hand,
Held open, each, and to each.

Your manhood's might. What had you thought for it,
And what assert? What do you hold in such high assertion,
To speak of it: your manhood, your might?

I hold an earnestness
Under the sky with one I love.
I hold an earnestness edged against death.
I hold it in high assertion.
I come to my own, in living's grandeur.
I speak of what soars in the soul,
As that sun soars, as that sun
Sets its printless course in a clean quarter,
To draw an equinox toward autumn's being,
A demarcative line, a taking course
Cleaved clear between the gray and the gold,
In jovial balance.
I hold all things my own,
Made mine, by what heads in me:
The sun-swaddled earth
Hugged to my heart,
As all harvests, hugged from the fields,
Are held to the heart of the bounteous man,
The human harvester, in God's plenty, toward his highest hymn.
I hold that might in manhood's highest state,
The human family. To speak for now of the man and the woman,
Joined in the godly grace, and the child they hold between,

The union of the highest selves,
Portioned to each its proper sphere,
In the godly dispensation:
The hegemony of selfliness in the selfless trinity.
These things I hold at an equinox,
That pleasant portion, when the lordly sun
Holds temperate sway, and moderates the earth.

V

I spoke of night.
For darkness too holds autumn's imminence,
In autumn's lordly mien.

Twilights come slow, come slipping in.
There is a hush of air that touches wonder.
All waits for it, feels darkness
Draw at the knees. On those boles and trunks
Of archward-towering trees, already in their thicketed branchings,
Gnarled limb and twig, a closeness gathers in, a lack of light.
Then all goes deep. The great dark hangs.
Standing you look on stars.

At Treesbank, turned autumn, came one,
Bird-lover, learned in their ways.
From our low-roofed porch
He hooted the owls up to the house,
In closest dusk, when cypress
Gathered up the gloom the orchard had engendered.
What quavered in the trees
We could not see, but the soft spokenness,
The mutability between those three,
The mated birds, the muted man,
Holding their whispered concourse.

There too at sundown, south,
Saw how the sea-pregnated fog
Crossed on the holding hills.
Eastward it shot its long advancing column,
Always, laying across that portion of the coast

Its deep dimension. Then dark drew down;
We finished chores
Soon under prickling stars, dined fully,
Forgetful of that widened world
That all day long absorbed us.
But later, outside, a trip for stovewood,
Saw how the fog had come, with darkness,
Filling the creekbeds, taking the slope,
Up through the orchard, a soft coming,
A gentle drawing in. There was no noise.
The eye cast up still swept on stars.
Later, the last look, those too were gone.
The trees dripped softly, swaddled in mist,
Raining their lightsome leaves.

Night. All dark. All deepness on the land.
All darkness over the shadow-hovered world.
Darkness on the Pacific, there westward,
Beyond that Gate that goes out to the island-dappled ports,
Where troughs the sea, all darkness.
And plover, upon their inter-polar passage,
Look down on cities, so strewn
In clusters on its edge, faint jewel-like sets
Beneath their own jeweled eyes; their underportions
Gleam back the upcast light as they pass over,
In darkness, toward Yucatan, a southern star,
A haven and a home.

All darkness. Stopping a bit,
A deep-drawn breath, I see how Pollux
Throbs the low east;
I hear a solitary killdeer,
Some local migrant,
And think: long gone it was
I lay upon an open plain
And heard it over, this bird.
It sought some destination, thirsting,
Some waterhole it knew of, off there beyond that edge
Where each star stood upon its certain time
That had not gleamed before.
Or how, beneath a riding full-of-the-moon,
That bird swam through its upper spaces,

And cried its long plaintivity,
The note of sadness, a faint piping,
The lost soul of the wayward world,
Voiced from out of the mystic void,
Reminder to men.

All deepness. But now the city
Sleeps under bird-cry, in dark repose. The last traffic
Sighs through the streets. The late walkers,
Home from over the deep harbor,
Where the greater city
Sleeps on its murmurous hills
Settling toward dawn,
Comes each to his own,
To his roof,
His woman and his world;
Husband and wife to their mutual ease,
A solacing love,
A succumbing sleep;
The replenishing bed where each absolves,
His dream reclaimed,
The separate selves
Resolved again in the soft embrace,
And the older drift toward depth.

VI

And then the rains.
For such is the softness with which all summer is broken.
Low, grayhooded, their undersides darkened to purple,
And running before them the whirlwind couriers of the cirrus,
Wisped and spumed,
As of themselves the sublime benedictions,
Those streaks, those mare's-tails
Far-reaching ahead in a gladsome summons—
In walk the nimbus.
They have been fostered westward in the froth-figured sea.
They have been marshaled together for a great entry,

As autumn's herald, the wide-robed summoners of fall.

They are made of softness and they come with softness.
There is wind but not wild,
Broad-backed, a clean breather.

There is a moistness of it that tells its business,
Warm and wet, and the parched places eastward
Will lift up their dust plumes.
They will twist up those quick cavortings of welcome,
And be glad for the quenching,
For the long condolence of drenchedness,
Those years of renewal, those summers
Gone over at last to the long wetness,
The deep rebirth, a weighted restoration.

There will be sundown with rain in it: the first leasings.
There will be red from up under,
A long hole in the west shot under with amber.
And all cloud-darkened things
Will take of gold on their seaward sides,
And be double; the trees
Flame by halves and dwindle away;
All roofs, each window give back the gold.
Then light bleeds out, west heals over,
All earth lies swaddled.
And then the rain.

And the crop-worn farmer,
Snug under roof,
Will be glad for it,
No longer anxious.
He will call up before him those other autumns
And again be glad:
The harvest hauled,
Dust shin-deep in the drive;
His emptied vineyard,

Its first tracing of color
Clear in the veinéd leaf;
And hear the crisp coming,
That rap on the shingles.

He will walk out in it.
He will hold up the stretched-forth hand,
Feel the cloud-fostered drift of it over his eyes;
Hear, almost, the very root in the earth
Reach up for it, sigh.
He will make his rain-song, a hoarse humming.
He will hum what it is,
What it means to him,
One of the West, of the rainless summer,
What there is in this changing of the year
To make life replenish, a life restore,
Set root down, take stock,
Look to the long winter to come.

All gladness, the good heart's hoard.
All that welcome seated in a self, when the soul
Springs from a deepest source,
Makes of itself that shining in the sheath.
Man on earth, under sky, at edge of sea,
In his own city, set at a hill,
That wears on its summit the black pine crown.
This as a sign. This song, set as a sign:
The singing of the mouth, to make approval;
The final summons when the horns are blown,
And summer sighs out, and mortal autumn, spun amber,
Spangles its latitudes.

And now the city lies wholly quenched under cloud.
A long night of rain,
A winter of wetness,
Walks in on the land.
Far back in the mountains the snow is falling.
The summer-placid lakes

Pucker and seethe where the first flakes enter.
And the black forest
Sinks in the long primordial sleep
That only an age can reckon.

Berkeley, California

THE YEAR'S DECLENSION

(1948)

RAINY EASTER

Rain: and over the thorned, cliff-eaten,
Ridge-broken hem of the east
Dawn slits its murky eye.
Two thousand years. And the Tomb-breaker
Rose from his nightlong ruin,
Up from the raveling darkness,
Rose out of dissolution,
Heaved off that sealing stone, looked out,
Looks out. The faithful follow.
This day the neighboring churches
Clang up the summons. The faithful rise,
Slosh through the drench to the steep ascent.
Eight days back spring foundered,
Shook off the wintry hand, came on,
Comes on, under the downpour,
Splitting its blind-eyed buds.

TWO LIVES

Two lives: a tortuous affinity,
Slowly worked out;
A blind thrusting, without recognition,
Toward a consummate end.

And one looking back will think most of the wind,
Changing south for rain,
Searching across those poppy-freckled fields,
When winter broke open,
And the cold face of earth
Gave grass up, rankly, out of the rank
Dung of cattle.

Two counties between us, the pasture-open land,
And we at that time not known to each other;
But yet your face compels in its past,
And I see it there,
Fixed, your eyes in that sightless interior dream,
As though the tremolo chant of the frogs
Crying and crying out there in the night
Had you wholly in spell;
Not knowing your wish
But the wish required;
Not knowing your own want
But the want decreed.

Look, said the wise, it is only the trouble of youth, that riddle!

But there were two counties between us,
And twenty years.

And you need not walk it ever again,
The winter-runneled road
That yoked those double bitternesses together:
Home, and to school; school, and to home;
Nor scuff at the pebbles,

Your face sullen under its cloud,
To pass on, silent.

Nor need I speak of the maelstrom in which I wandered.

But there was always the wind,
Those turbulent springs,
And one kerosene lamp,
To make you a little center of snugness at night in the room.
And the black wind moved with its mouth on the roof,
Suddenly to lean its weight in a prone shove and be gone—

Who knows where?
—No one knows of it.
How far gone?
—None can tell.

And you spoke the poem that was not yet yours to live.
But what rang in your voice—
(I heard it, have heard; I know it well)
That passion for elseness,
As if the very depth of demand
Could make it be.

No. But there comes a final bringing together,
Almost too late,
As when the exhaustible self is made to learn
More than it ever wanted to know,
And means to give up;
And then a further teaching comes,
And all is reckoned,
Each inveterate ache of the soul
Most wondrously redeemed.

So that one looking back thinks most of the wind,
Restless, ranging the pastures,
Pushing the rank grass here and there,
Thrusting and blind.

**

UNDER A KEEPING SPRING

Under a keeping spring, that country,
Its hills green-headed, its swales water-delled—
A land, you would say, of great softnesses
Any month of the year;
But now, rains into June, drenchers,
The earth steeped in the mortal languor of wetness,
And the swaddling bands of sea-deriving fog
Huddling it in.

It is all out of season, all extra.
In the flush-full gulches the lank weeds flourish,
Quaking grass becks its rustling pod.
Everywhere on the upland meadow
Oat glistens, filaree and jacalac toss to the wind,
While the pale owl's clover thrives in the pasture.
It is all extra. The cows browse on through the hour of milking:
They have to be driven.

And one thinks with a kind of wild exultance:
What a bringing down there is going to be when the sun gets to it!
What a scorching-over July will make!
For as the mind loves luxury,
But drives through its cloy to a strict extreme,
So now, impatient for summer,
It flares with the scything stroke of the sun
Toward a mown finale.

One week of that weather,
Give it ten good days;
And autumn will enter on all as it was:
Chewed over, eaten down, gnawn to a stubble;
And every seed, dry through the germ,
Knuckled up for a rain.

THE FIRST ABSENCE

I

The house is dark;
And nothing within will have suffered change
From as I left it.
I think how a death has drawn you away
In the grim warning of what it can do in its deprivations.
That emptiness behind the door!
That lack in the rooms,
Waiting for one to enter it
And fill up the silence!
Something in there is lost,
A felicity and a pleasance,
As if most of what it was meant to be
Had been withheld.
Roof, walls, beams, floor.
And the unfillable windows,
Letting the vacant night gaze in
On what is gone.

II

This blank unrest,
This hedging dolefulness a minor lack denotes,
When the full loss would send the disjunctured soul
Howling toward heartbreak—in the fond absence
Your meaning richens my loneliness
With its own understanding.

All gathers on your face,
As something behind your smile
Rings like a long halloo
Back down the corridor that leads to childhood.
There everything converges,
Caught forward out of its smoky dissolution—
The child's enchantment, the youth's ambivalence, the grown man's
    fullest need—
A soft incitement half afraid of hurt,

A quelled response, sustained there, dimly inviting;
As what was glimpsed but never seen
Smoulders on in its own dream of fullness.
Back there your meaning moves,
Forming behind the image of your face,
That like a metaphor transforms the past.
Almost in the very room you smile,
And the self smiles back,
Friendly, wondrously fond,
And wholly outside the fear.

THE QUARREL

I cannot squall, though that is what it needs,
And though the rush of rage
Beats you against me like a wearing sea.
There is an oath to use, an edged imprecation
Shot from the lip, to hit and hurt.
If only I could roar,
Render the room a shambles, make you blink!
But all chokes behind the tongue;
And the wide menacing hand, that might have moved,
Checks on the strike.
Even your anger richens and compels.

My love! My love! Leave me a little!
Some necessary certitude to start anew!
Keep me the shreds of selfliness!
For I shall have the need of your regard
To wrap about my bones
When the black storm blows out,
And that wide commonplace of calm
Fairs out the peaceable years
Where we will go together.

COURT OF LAW

The anarchist reflects

Court of the Law.
And over the door,
High out of harm's way,
In the massive masonwork of its wall,
The cleft-winged swift cakes his muddy nest;
From whence, half-social and wholly free,
May launch out into a bright space,
Nimble above the sun-glitter roofs,
Faring briefly back in a lively commerce,
Deft citizenry of the light.

So might, one thinks, convention's own creature,
Society's natural man,
Could one conceive of him,
Here issue forth;
In the bastion's eminence
Protected but free,
Hold an easy intercourse,
Returning for rest from the populous street,
To gaze out over the sun-filled city,
In the wide pulse of noon.

False, fleeting and false!
Swift as the very bird,
Which writes its name,
In its brilliant reversal,
On the breathless mind—
To then be gone,
Lost to the eye and the thought with it,
When the self comes back to the sudden self,

And all unchanged!

O sorrowful breed!
In his little pew the criminal shuffs his feet,
Having nothing to do any more but wait,
Nor cares enough to lift his head
Until the mention of his name.

THE DANCE

The dance. And that whickering of reefs,
Rockheads, the strewn skerries and eaten coves,
Where the sea treads, unendingly champing its graven closures.
There does that serious smiling prevail,
That laughter of light,
A chuck and mumble,
That ambulant pervasion.
What is it of teaching?
Only the indirection,
Charted back toward those sheer revelations
One likes to remember of childhood,
When the self stood free in a naked grace
And was unexcelled.
So the sea exposes,
Over and over and never reckoned,
Done not to remember but just to do.
How the self inhibits!
Lamely preferring the trite little step
They taught you at school.

But that is because of the not trying.
Something of freedom is always retained,
Back there, in the cloudy repositories,
Where all that the child was eager to risk
Has been withheld.
There is a light that lies along a sea, yes,
And that is a teaching.
There is a pucker of water around a rock,
That forthright line in its flex onward;
Or as the guitar, picking and mincing,
Breaks open the heart with its wild sob.
All that is lesson.
Think, in the dance, not of it but of sea
And the dance densens,
Takes that thrust of power out of the surf where the comber hovers,

That multitudinous pounding of watery feet in the dredging quarries.
And oh! Its birds! Its birds!
Their breathless way they take up height in a close spiral!
They have always known.
It was only a matter of prime discovery
And then they had it.
A means of exposure.
The stamp, the step, the sudden twist;
Even the recklessness of a leap will do for a start.
Once back into sources
Skill compels; the earnest compliance
Calls up the sheerest governance of foot
Because that opens out.
The rest is dead.

THE DUSK

The light goes: that once powerful sun,
That held all steeples in its grasp,
Smokes on the western sea.
Under the fruit tree summer's vanishing residuum,
The long accumulation of leaf,
Rots in the odor of orchards.
Suddenly the dark descends,
As on the tule ponds at home the wintering blackbirds,
Flock upon flock, the thousand-membered,
In for the night from the outlying ploughlands,
Sweep over the willows,
Whirled like a net on the shadowy reeds,
All wings open.
It is late. And any boy who lingers on to watch them come in
Will go hungry to bed.
But the leaf-sunken years,
And the casual dusk, over the roofs in a clear October,
Will verify the nameless impulse that kept him out
When the roosting birds and the ringing dark
Dropped down together.

END OF SUMMER

The Berlin Airlift, 1948

Something that woke me out of sleep
Got me up in the pinch of night to haunt the house.
There was a drench of moonlight,
Rare enough on this fog-sealed coast to draw me out.
It was still September,
But looking up I saw fearful Orion,
His dog-star raging at his heel,
The fierce winter hunter
Rough on the innocent edge of summer;
And strangely beside them the great womanly planet,
Sad and maternal,
As if bearing some meaningful reassurance,
Waiting to speak.
It was like coming out of the depth of sleep on some deep divination.
Orion reared with his violent club,
Threatening the east,
And serenely beyond him the matronly planet.
What omen was meant?
What ominous warning and what grave reassurance?
Under the east the dawn lay waiting,
Breathing there on the edge of entry,
This much I knew.
And took the portent back to bed
Where the heavy hours could shape the oath
A million deaths might certify
Or a million lives reject.

IN THE DREAM'S RECESS

Let from no earth-engendered thing your friendship be forsworn.
Not from the Scorpion, that arcs its poison-shafted barb?
Not from the Spider nor the quick claw-handed Crab?
There is a place where all snake-natured things obtain,
Where squats the Toad: see there between his eyes
The carbuncular gleam break forth! The Sow Bug breeds there,
And the Sphinx Moth takes her vague compelling flight.

These are the dangerous kingdom's least inhabitants.

For deep in the groin of darkness, in the dream's recess,
Far back in the self's forbidden apertures,
Where clangs the door, comes forth the One.
Great prince, most baleful lord,
Clad in the adjuncts of his powerful craft;
The brimstone blazes on that unrelenting brow.

How may the soul, in horror hugged, make friends with him?
There lies a world of willfulness beyond one's best intent.
How may one reconcile it? There lies a universe of darkness
Far past the reaches of the wish. How may one
Civilize that obdurate realm? Deep down
The Scorpion lurks. The Salamander
Twists his chilly flesh. Deep down
The Horned Toad and the Crab consort.
All evil copulates. Each loathly thing
Peoples the dark with its sloth-gotten spawn.

Great God! Give me the cleansing power!
Scour me out with brightness! Make me clean!
The sullied presence crouches in my side,
And all is fearful where I dare not wake or dream.

DEAD WINTER

This is the death the wintering year foretold.
And the encroaching cold
Clamps on those hills the light knew;
And the frost-discolored pastures,
So naked and inert that suddenly the rank heart
Throttles on deprivation and goes blind,
Shuts down the long dream,
Caught there, beneath that rib,
Where all that was willing to let it go
Sinks and dispels.

This is the death.

But the human future,
Gathered upon that upsurgent stroke,
Breaks the year's declension,
Refuses to deflect.

Berkeley, California

AFTERWORD, RETROSPECTIVE
Bill Hotchkiss

He was already Brother Antoninus when I first met him that spring
of 1963 at the University of Oregon. He'd been Antoninus for more
than a decade, and he was thought by some of my fellow graduate
students to be half-mad or wholly so—a religious poet, a mystic, a
charismatic, one who had the capacity to cast a spell over his audience,
to hypnotize, to spellbind. His work, I was told, celebrated the external
landscape while at the same time investigating the terrain of the psyche.
Possibly he was a mere *poseur*—or perhaps a contemporary saint. But
prior to his conversion to Catholicism, he had been William Everson, an
agnostic pacifist, a man who had grown up in the small town of Selma
in California's sun-baked San Joaquin Valley, had married his high
school sweetheart, and had declared himself a conscientious objector,
refusing the draft during World War Two. The poet's repudiation of
military conscription and of war in general resulted in his being interned
at a forest camp for conscientious objectors, over on the coast not far
from Eugene, at Waldport, Oregon—a variety of minimum security
incarceration in those days known as "alternative service."

For several days before his arrival at the campus, there had been a
good deal of discussion over coffee concerning this priestly poet. I
listened to the scuttlebutt and then proceeded forthwith to the library,
where I checked out the 1948 New Directions edition of *The Residual
Years,* by William Everson. I opened the volume, and the title "Tor
House" caught my eye—a poem depicting the home of Robinson Jeffers?
In Professor Bill Nolte's course on "major American authors," we were
reading Jeffers, another California poet whom I had known only in
passing until that term but whose narrative "Tamar," among other
works, had left me stunned, shaken, humbled. What was the
connection, between Antoninus and Jeffers? Had the two men actually
known one another? Why would a Catholic demi-prophet-to-be have
written of the house and rough stone tower built by one John Robinson
Jeffers, a poet whose hands had come to know the magic of stone?

> Now that I have seen Tor House,
> And crouched among the sea-gnawed granite under the wind's
> throat,
> Gazing against the roll of the western rim,
> I know that I can turn back to my inland town

273

And find the flame of this blunt headland
Burning beneath the dark beat of my blood.

For I have stood where he has stood,
And seen the same gaunt gulls,
And all the tide come pitching in from Lobos Point
To shatter on this coast....

Everson's poem was one of reverence, of awe, indicating the younger man's need to draw strength from the vision of Jeffers, to avail himself of the power that came "pitching in from Lobos Point." Only later would I hear Everson-Antoninus speak of the Carmel Master as the one who had unlocked the younger writer's poetic gift.

Indeed, Everson's verse at times had a Jeffersian ring to it, was able to rouse itself to what Longinus called "the sublime" when need be. For a poet whose reputation suggested extremity and Dionysian release, the work seemed to me remarkably controlled, the images lucid, the ideas a constant challenge to the reader, with even the most unusual perspective taken in calm observation, at times almost journalistically plain, drawing together "opposite or discordant qualities" with the apparent easy familiarity of a great master.

But where was the linch pin? What sustaining concept held things together, providing cohesion and consistency to the work? In a sprawling poetic sequence entitled "Late October '39" (included in the present edition of *Residual Years,* but heretofore unpublished), the poet asserts, "This poem is the word of a religious man with no god to worship"(Section XIX).

On the other hand, the perceived principle which lay at the center of Everson's thought (prior to his conversion to Catholicism) and which in large measure generated the thought of the self-professed "religious man," was an Entity greatly resembling *Wyrd* or perhaps Thomas Hardy's "Crass Casualty," that somnolent, amoral God Force which informs Hardy's poetry in general and which is depicted specifically in "Hap." In his own poem "Circumstance," Everson tells us the following:

He is a god who smiles blindly,
And hears nothing, and squats faun-mouthed on the
    wheeling world,
Touching right and left with infinite lightning-like gestures.
He is the one to pray to, but he hears not, nor sees.
   ...

He is the god to pray to; he sits with his faun's mouth
and touches the world with hovering hands.
He is the god—but he sees not, nor hears.

Such was the god-concept the poet found compelling, albeit
unattractive, frightening. The god Everson saw, apparently, was not
Jeffers' "Beauty of Things," but rather a force that, oblivious to
Mankind, was presented as being almost demonic, blindly smiling,
creating out of pure whim. In "The Knives," Everson cries out to the
"poor virgin":

...you forge your own knives,
And whet them too keen to be carried.
The lusts that you loathe, as the soul you adore, were made
     by the God;
And nothing [that] exists needs praise nor condemnation,
     but shines its own splendor....

The Jeffers echo and connection were clear enough, but ultimately,
at the poet's own word, the gods conceived by such thinkers as Hardy
and Jeffers would prove insufficient in one crucial way, for they allowed
no interactive communication with mankind. The need for a Personal
God would be the force which was to draw Everson into spontaneous
conversion to the Catholic Church, Christmas Mass, 1948. In
Prodigious Thrust, Everson-Antoninus asserts, "...without love God is
nothing. This, in its essence, is the thing that would make me a
Catholic. Love, the prime existential fact, is sourced in personality, and
the person is analogous to God"(85).

This was a poet of the land, the "autochthon" as Rexroth was later
to call him, a man who had tilled the soil, who had repaired fence along
property lines, who had taken clusters of newly picked grapes in his
hands. He was, so to speak, a commoner. Nor was he a university
person, for twice he had unsuccessfully matriculated at Fresno State. It
was clear to me that Everson had read immensely and that he knew
rural California on the basis of close association. He found verses
amongst the Muscats and in the shine of the plowed earth:

Before my feet the ploughshare rolls the earth,
Up and over,
Splitting the loam with a soft tearing sound.
Between the horses I can see the red blur of a far peach
     orchard,

Half obscured in drifting sheets of morning fog.
A score of blackbirds circles around me on shining wings.
They alight beside me, and scramble almost under my feet
In search of upturned grubs.

Of his native San Joaquin Valley, he wrote the following:

This valley after the storms can be beautiful beyond the telling,
Though our city folk scorn it, cursing heat in the summer
    and drabness in winter,
And flee it: Yosemite and the sea.
They seek splendor; who would touch them must stun them....

Everson cultivates the inward landscape as well, and, as he has said in public on several occasions, he is in general a far more self-analytic poet than Jeffers was. He sees his life as a pilgrimage, and he's engaged in a search for meaning, a discovery of purpose. This impulse would ultimately require him to reach out to the God-Man Jesus, both as Divine Agency and as Inward Principle: for the poet himself was to play the role of self-crucified deity, an Odin enduring immense pain in an attempt to determine the fates of the gods and of humankind, the one who discovers truth through delight as well (a different sort of crucifixion), the one who realizes that meaning comes through endless effort, almost in the sense of Browning's "Apparent Failure." Struggle is vital, and, in Sara Teasdale's phrase, "The heart asks more than life can give. / When that is learned, then all is learned...." Consider these lines from Everson's "Outside This Music":

These verses are lies.
Who bends the hard hand over the lines,
Shaping the words, feeling the gust of an ancient mood
Blow through the room, the weight of the night
    and the broken hills,
Hammers no truth.
    ...
The eyes will be blind, the throat shattered and mute
In the wave of thunder of the fallen sky.
    ...
And the feeling of tough wild weeds straining all outdoors,
And the bruised mouth, forming the shape of a word,
Turning toward night.

In "Trifles," Everson imagines the archetypal poet, as it were, doing battle with the unchanging order of Newton's predictably mechanical cosmos, which is no friend to Mankind. Rather, humanity writhes

> ...under the long dark in the agony of destruction,
> The great sky and the flaming west riding our eyes,
> Gathering in from the heavy hills, and the tides of the sea.
>   ...
> And you and your shouting burst up before us;
> We taste that wry and sterile bitterness,
> And pound with our hands on the dark.

With the horrors of World War Two rising before him, Everson was driven into one of a number of "impossible choices," for he speaks of himself as "the living heir of the bloodiest men of all Europe." He attempts to shoulder the guilt of his Scandinavian forebears—guilt that those Vikings, the *Wichinga* in question, probably never felt at all, and as he tells us in "The Vow," written autumn 1940,

> I flinch in the guilt of what I am,
> Seeing the poised heap of this time
> Break like a wave.
>
> And I vow not to wantonly ever take life;
> Not in pleasure or sport,
> Nor in hate,
> Nor in the careless acts of my strength....

As noted earlier, the consequence of that vow-taking was to be the camp at Waldport. Everson's long poetic sequence "Chronicle of Division" reveals both the schism deep within the national psyche and the separation of man from woman (certainly true for those in the military and also for those who were conscientious objectors), and of the greater division enforced by the weakness of the human spirit, the failure of nerve, the shallowness of commitment suggesting that absence makes the heart grow fonder *for someone else*, and so it was to be with Bill and Edwa Everson. He would become "wifeless at thirty," and for all the spiritual growth and all the artistic accomplishment that were derived from the Waldport experience, ultimately the war would be concluded, and the men in alternative service would be cast back into a society in which everything had been "changed, changed utterly," to use

Yeats' phrase. Whether any "terrible beauty" was to be born, however, remained to be seen:

> He will be given again to the indifferent world,
> Go south to a city,
> Muse over coffee in small cafés,
>
> ...
>
> He will stare up the dark through the tall invisible storeys
>   up above him,
> Where men and women place mouth to mouth
>   in their old exploration,
> And will watch through the roof the small hard
>   and unquenchable stars
> Make their overhead arc....

By mid-summer 1946, with the Great War concluded the previous year, Everson was indeed out of the alternative service camps and had ventured south to the Bay Area, where he'd set up his old handpress in an empty apple dryer at Treesbank, a farm operated by Hamilton and Mary Tyler near Sebastopol. As fate would have it, poetess and artist Mary Fabilli was invited to Treesbank as well, and the two fell fortuitously in love. They danced their dance of courtship, and the old, inveterate force of mating drew them together. Fabilli was also divorced, but as a Catholic she remained married in the eyes of the Church. There was to be trouble ahead. But for the moment, Everson was smitten and could think of no one else, as he tells us in "The Sphinx," even as he sought to solve once again the ancient riddle:

> All day my mind has fixed upon your face
> That drew me in the dance and was alone,
> Saddened with a sorrow of its own;
>
> ...
>
> Our years between us like twin rivers ran.
> The dance you danced was on a nether shore;
> Our bodies gestured but could do no more;
> Like mutes we looked across that double span.
> The years drew out their desultory roar.

In the final stanza of "The Blowing of the Seed," the whole of the poem addressed to Mary Fabilli, the poet presents himself to his new love:

> I move to meet you now in a greening time.
> I come with wind and with wet
> In a soft season.
> I bring you my hand.
> I bring you the flesh of those fallow, fallen years;
> And my manifest reasons.

Bill and Mary would first live together and subsequently marry, June 12, 1948.   Fabilli was drawn back to her faith, and Everson followed her to the Church.   Since, in the eyes of the Catholic hegemony, Mary was still married, and since the Archbishop could not countenance so young a couple attempting to live together even as brother and sister, Bill and Mary parted, June 30, 1949.   Everson was subsequently baptized at St. Augustine's Church, July 23rd.   The final poem in the 1968 edition of *The Residual Years* is a piece called "Dead Winter," which concludes thus:

> But the human future,
> Gathered upon the upsurgent stroke,
> Breaks the year's declension,
> Refuses to deflect.

That was 1948.   But now more than fourteen years had passed, and it was spring of 1963, rain falling softly, and Brother Antoninus (in his Dominican robes) would read poetry to a packed house in the Erb Memorial Union at the University of Oregon.   The more traditional members of the English department sat with arms crossed, resisting the force of the spoken word, while the rest of us leaned forward in our seats, caught up in the torrent of language that poured over us.   The reading began with "A Canticle to the Waterbirds," composed shortly before Everson's acceptance as a lay brother (donatus) into the Dominican Order, a poem that is, even now, perhaps his best known and most loved, and ended with the magnificent ode to the great Carmel poet who had died a year earlier—Jeffers, of whom Everson would proclaim a few years later, "Robinson Jeffers was my father."   At some point about midway through the reading, Everson addressed the concept of freedom through violation—how a rupture or breaking of traditional patterns of expectation and of normative values can produce a great upwelling of spontaneous energy.   At this point Antoninus lifted his water glass, hesitated just long enough for the audience to focus upon the object, and then casually and quite deliberately he poured the contents out upon the floor.   An electric wave of something akin to a sensation of violation passed through the crowded room. A few cried out in surprise, as though lashed with a whip. Somebody groaned, "Son of a bitch!" and the tone was one of pure shock, utter disbelief. Antoninus strode back and forth, returned to the podium, and began to read his dirge-like tribute to Jeffers, "The Poet Is Dead," the strophes set off by pauses that seemed each time to be unbearably long. When the performance was concluded, we all continued to sit there, unnerved, uncertain. No one moved until the poet gestured, in effect granting us permission to rise and to leave.

James B. Hall was the director of Oregon's creative writing program at that time (1963) and Jim had been instrumental in bringing Antoninus back to the Oregon campus to read—even as Hall would later be instrumental, as Provost of College 5 (now Porter-Sesnon) at U.C. Santa Cruz, in hiring Everson to teach the course that would come to be known as "Birth of a Poet" and to function as master printer for the university's revitalized Lime Kiln Press.

Those of us who were Jim Hall's students in novel-writing were to meet that night after the reading—at Jack Taub's rented house down Thirteenth Avenue. Present, to the best of my recollection, were Taub, Sharon Brown, Lucy Paine, Bob LaRue, Dirk Jellema, Bob and Dar Mansergh, Frank Kendig, Bill Borcher, the old salt Charlie Wallace, and myself. Dr. Hall arrived in the company of Antoninus, something none of us had expected. J.B. brought the meeting to order, and Jack Taub read from his book-in-progress. Everson nodded occasionally and in the round-table discussion which followed said little. He seemed as one who felt out of place. I recall that Sharon Brown attempted to engage him in the discussion, and in response Antoninus spoke a few words of general writing theory and encouragement for Jack.

The meeting was at length adjourned. Professor Hall and most of the workshop members excused themselves. A couple of us stayed, and in this smaller group, Antoninus was fully willing to speak his mind. Taub protested that a poet could not be a *religious* and still be a poet—that the church, any church, would not allow sufficient freedom. Antoninus smiled, nodded, and gave us a short discourse on the necessity of religious awareness in poetry. Identification with the church, he contended, provided a great aid to expression rather than any hindrance thereunto.

After Antoninus took his leave, Taub and I continued to talk for a few minutes longer, as though unwilling to admit the amazing night was in fact complete, *perfected*. But soon I too went down the stairs and out the door onto Thirteenth Avenue. The hour was past one in the morning. A soft, warm Oregon rain continued to fall. I wasn't quite certain how, but I knew that the reading at Erb Memorial and the poet's unexpected presence at the fiction workshop had somehow changed my own focus and possibly the onward course of my life.

Eleven years thereafter, in 1974, I would complete a dissertation on Jeffers. I mailed a copy to the poet whose own work on RJ had stood me in good stead. Antoninus was once again William Everson. He'd left behind his persona as a monk, having in December of 1969 at the University of California, Davis, read a sequence of erotic poems inspired by young Susanna Rickson, with whom he had fallen in love. At the conclusion of the Davis reading, Antoninus removed his Dominican robes, hung upon the podium microphone a gold crucifix he'd been wearing, and exited, *solus,* with emphasis.

Everson returned a note of thanks for the copy of my dissertation, and a portion of his letter was devoted to an enthusiastic response to my *opus.* He invited me to visit Kingfisher Flat, north of Santa Cruz, the elder Jeffers scholar thereby extending his hand to a younger. Thus began a personal friendship that would endure to the poet's death twenty years later.

The Residual Years spans the period of 1934 to 1948, comprising the "Pre-Catholic Poetry of Brother Antoninus," as advertised on the title page of the 1968 edition. With painstaking scholarly work, Allan Campo has added a significant body of hitherto uncollected or unpublished poems drawn from the archives at UCLA and Berkeley, beginning with "Gypsy Dance" of 1931 (Everson was eighteen when he wrote this poem) and concluding with an untitled piece [*For there is a place where the water hovers*] dated December 20, 1948, just a few days before Everson's conversion to Catholicism upon the occasion of Christmas Eve Mass, St. Mary's Cathedral, San Francisco—the last poem, so far as we know, written before that intense moment of spiritual turning. He was thirty-six years old. The poem Campo places before this one, also untitled [*As in all that country*], is likewise December 20th and depicts the poet in a halcyon mode of perception:

> As in all that country,
> Will find, unbeknownst,
> That sheen, that glimmer as of God,
> When what was holy
> Hits out to the heart,
> Hits home.

The poet's psyche, as revealed in the verse, is open and perceptive, as though awaiting some great turning point—solstice, perhaps, the year's hinge. Nonetheless, the poet-speaker seems oblivious, unaware of what was about to transpire—would indeed transpire—within just four days. The "glimmer" he speaks of is not God but *as of God*. Yet the spirit searches and, "Filled with all that southward light," the potential of spiritual enlightenment, his protagonist imagines himself going "forth in it...."

> So it is in mid-December,
> Cold, many days fog-bound, rain-holden,
> Many days of inclement weather,
> To have a warm Sunday,
> Filled with all that southward light,
> And go forth in it....

However many echoes of and parallels to the work of Robinson Jeffers one may discover, one can hardly be unaware of the overwhelming difference—that of the impersonal Jeffers and the intensely "autobiographical" Everson, the poet committed to scrutiny of his own actions and his own thought processes as a means of elucidating the human condition, just as Wordsworth did in *The Prelude* and indeed in much of his work. *Ecce homo!* This is what it was like to live within the mind and body of Bill Everson—these are the heartaches, these the joys.

In number XXIII of the "Late October '39" sequence (uncollected / unpublished section of the present edition, noted above), Everson speaks the following words:

> Do you think from this poem I am blind to its danger?
> When you open yourself for the world's eyes you run
>   your own risks,
> You will feel the thin minds prying the pages,
> The frigid and acid tentacles of their lust,
> The mean mouths saying:
>
> "Look. This is the man.
> By his own admission,
> In his poems he tells of it—"

With Eliot and Pound as models, American poetry in this century has at least pretended to avoid the merely personal, the self-analytic, the

self-congratulatory. In criticism a major shift has occurred, away from
the poet *qua* poet, his life and times and psychic landscape, in the
direction of art for its own sake—possibly even to the point where, with
Oscar Wilde, one might suppose nature to be imitating art. One should
approach poems, we were told, as though they'd been written by
anonymous authors. The New Criticism moved wholly in this direction,
was formalist in nature, and was insistent that the poets should avoid
being tendentious. Didacticism was abhorrent, as was celebration of the
self. Whitman and Wordsworth, to invoke the ghost of Yvor Winters,
were two other limbs of the devil. Poe's verse was an art designed "to
please the soul of a serving girl," and Jeffers (for whom didacticism was
the poet's weapon and specific antitoxin) should emulate his own
characters and forthwith commit suicide.

The passage of but a few years, however, can change much in terms
of scholarly opinion and academic *dicta*, so that at present, the neo-
Marxian, deconstructionist, gender feminist, politically correct, cultural
diversity, ecological movement would value poetry and all literature
simply as a means of correcting taste (promoting the kinds of causes that
were embraced by the generation of the sixties). Thus even the haughty
Robinson Jeffers may now be championed by gender feminist critics, for
was RJ not opposed to war and is he not a patron saint (along with Muir
and Ed Abbey) of the environmentalist movement? On the other hand,
while Everson is comparably anti-war and environmentalist in his
overall orientation (as featured speaker at the Earth Day 1970 festivities,
for instance, he presented his "The Poetry of Earth" essay at the
Coliseum at U.C. Berkeley), he's apparently viewed by some as a sexist
and as one devoted to the cult of the self rather than to the presumed
needs of the collective. In the poet's own words, words immediately to
be recognized by all who knew him well, "I'm a patriarchal male."

As individuals, we enact various roles throughout our lives, just as
we are often allowed to speak more than a merely personal witness. The
allegorical element abides and grants much deeper meaning than simple
description of happenstance human events. Even before Everson was
drawn to the study of depth psychology and to the concepts of such as
Pierre Janet, Sigmund Freud, Wilhelm Reich, Victor White, and C.G.
Jung—and to the Catholic mysticism of St. Augustine, Hopkins, and
Merton—his artistic affinity for the realm of the Archetype was certain.

"I'm a much more personal poet than Jeffers was," as Everson-
Antoninus said (not for the first time) during preliminary remarks to his
reading of "The Poetry of Earth," at a subsequent Robinson Jeffers
conference. For Everson, the events of one's life, all the details of one's

existence, are fraught with implicit meaning, and it's the poet's task to unearth these meanings, to perceive and to comprehend and to learn from the drift and flow of his own life. Thus it comes as no surprise to hear Everson addressing Susanna, Rose, Mary, or Edwa:

> Edwa, when we met, that autumn in the hush of darkness
> Under the mulberry close by the corner of the old house
> We made the pledge. We clung together in the pouring dark
> Too young to know, too wild with love and desire and the sweet
>   hunger of adolescence
> To know ourselves, or our inner purposes, or the shape
>   of our lives. (XXIV, "Late October '39")

The penultimate poem included in the 1968 edition is entitled "In the Dream's Recess," an artistically shaped record of the unconscious mind in process, a poem Everson placed immediately after "End of Summer" (perhaps just following his 36th birthday, since he specifies "It was still September"; Campo supplies the information that "...the earliest drafts are Oct. 1, ...and [the folder in which the pages were contained] is titled by E. 'The Omen'").

"End of Summer" is subscripted with the phrase "The Berlin Airlift, 1948," a joint American-British operation begun on June 28th of that serendipitous year, some sixteen days after Everson and Fabilli had been legally married. Significance of the subtitle? Perhaps the sound of an airplane awakened the poet—if I may be permitted a lame guess. This poem is equally one based upon or generated by a dream, for the author tells us, "Something that woke me out of sleep / Got me up in the pinch of night to haunt the house. / There was a drench of moonlight...."

In the next few lines, Orion is described as "fearful," while beside the "fierce winter hunter" is Venus, the "great womanly planet," and she appears to bear "some meaningful reassurance." Orion's "club" threatens the east, and Everson sees both "ominous warning" and "grave reassurance." Under the east, as he tells us, "the dawn lay waiting, / Breathing there on the edge of entry...."

Placed after "In the Dream's Recess" is "Dead Winter," a poem wherein the author says, "This is the death the wintering year foretold." In the present moment, "the rank heart / Throttles on deprivation and goes blind, / Shuts down the long dream...." A spiritual crisis is near. The bride and the groom, so recently in love, are now throttled "on deprivation."

The body of "In The Dream's Recess" depicts scorpion, spider, toad, and sow bug—a physical reality that is at once both offensively intimidating and yet one to which the speaker seems inevitably drawn. The door clangs, and we are shown "Great prince, most baleful lord, / Clad in the adjuncts of his powerful craft; / The brimstone blazes on that unrelenting brow." The image is that of Hades or of Hephaestus, the former having abducted Persephone and the latter having been cuckolded by Aphrodite herself.

Stanza one ends with, "And the Sphinx Moth takes her vague compelling flight." The "Sphinx Moth" is associated with "The Sphinx," and hence with Mary Fabilli, for the fragile and beautiful creature is drawn fatally to the lit candle and yet at the same time poses the riddle of identity. Is that "Moth" also to be possessed by the "most baleful lord"?

The prince of darkness, the Lord of all that is temporal, secular, profane, is the shadow-side of Jesus and perhaps must be accepted (in physical terms) before it (He) can offer spiritual redemption. The poet demands, "How may the soul, in horror hugged, make friends with him?" The poem ends with this stanza:

> Great God! Give me the cleansing power!
> Scour me out with brightness! Make me clean!
> The sullied presence crouches in my side,
> And all is fearful where I dare not wake or dream.

From "End of Summer" to "Dead Winter" encompassed the passing of a season and represented the interval from equinox to solstice. It had been, I think, a season of discontent, even as it was a time of spiritual crisis. The draw of the church, at Mary's lead, was increasingly powerful, and "Under the east the dawn lay waiting." In *Prodigious Thrust*, the poet gives us the following closehand account:

> ...her struggle toward God, deflected by me, was not annulled by me, though I made my attempts. Rather under the anxieties of such an adjustment it intensified. She attacked without mercy the loosely formulated ethic of my own impeachable orientation. A man of deep evasions, I learned to dread her redoubtable certitude, her excoriating facts, as the sickling dreads the potent ministrations of the physician; and when, driven to the wall, I turned in truculence and smashed the closing web of truths that hemmed me round, in those defeats she fled, and found her refuge in one or another of the mystifying practices she had recovered from her Catholic past. (76)

The final poem in the "uncollected / unpublished" appendix, as I said before, is dated December 20, 1948, and concludes with a response to Everson's own question, "Where have the gulls gone?"

> The mystery prevails
> Like a soft enchantment,
> As does the quality of wonder
> When what invokes but never answers
> Lingers its why beyond the eye's retention.
>
> There is a scope of quietude that may be stirred.
> There is a newness waiting in the self
> For the gulls to go again
> Across the smoke dis-[/ ∪] water
> Across the gulls' descant.

With these verses, the era of "the residual years" is concluded. The anarchist poet Bill Everson would disappear for nearly two decades before reemerging in the aftermath of that dramatic U.C. Davis reading of late 1969, and the charismatic Brother Antoninus, the "beat friar" as *Time Magazine* was to dub him, would emerge.

At Treesbank Farm, with the handpress set up in the empty apple dryer, and with his mind's eye set upon the face and form of Mary Fabilli, Everson wrote these words:

> Woman, I sing to you now from a new season.
> I sing from the freshened creeks,
> From the autumn's waning.
> I sing where the wind runs in from a wide sea,
> Wakens these winter-wet fields to new growth,
> A new greening.
>   ...
> I bring you the flesh of those fallow, fallen years....

By late December of 1948, the "residual years" were past, and the "veritable years" were about to begin. It was Christmas Eve Mass at St. Mary's in San Francisco, and in a moment the poet would rise and walk down the aisle toward the altar:

> And gazing now across the multitude between me and the sanctuary
> I saw the tabernacle, set back upon the altar, contained in its own

reservation, as mysterious and impenetrable as some thoughtless stone. "Unknown God," I said to myself, "what can you be that I should come here and wait for your word? If the hills and the sky and the stars have not spoken, what hope from you? O lifeless bread housed in the lifeless bronze! If the vast cosmic god hears not, nor cares, why should any man speak to you?" (*Prodigious Thrust*, 86)

The nuns had placed fir boughs about a miniature stable, as Everson describes the situation in *Prodigious Thrust* (78-79), and "...there came to me the resinous scent of the fir trees. It cut across everything else my senses had to contend with in that place, there in the heart of the great alien city, far from my early home and the reassuring simplicity of my old life.... I could look with my eyes to the place from which I knew the scent was coming, the somnolent odor of forests, and I saw in the miniature stable the several statuettes...."

For a moment all was stasis, all action merely potential. Directly the anarchist poet—farmer-poet turned conscientious objector turned printer—would rise and walk down that aisle and ultimately into the faith and into the identity of Brother Antoninus.

—Bill Hotchkiss
Munger Creek, Oregon
January, 1997

APPENDIX A

A SELECTION OF UNCOLLECTED AND UNPUBLISHED POEMS

INTRODUCTION
Allan Campo

As I indicated in my Foreword, this "Selection of Uncollected and Unpublished Poems" is meant to round out both our presentation and the reader's awareness of the work Everson did during the period which encompasses *The Residual Years*. The "Selection" begins with "Gypsy Dance" from 1931 and concludes with poetry from late December of 1948.

The uncollected poems are those which have been published in periodicals or other venues, but which Everson did not choose to integrate into either *Single Source* or the 1948 and 1968 editions of *The Residual Years*. There are, in fact, only a relatively few such poems, and not all of them are included here. The verse he contributed to the Selma High School yearbook, *The Magnet*, in 1930 and 1931 is omitted, for, aside from showing Everson's youthful knack for doggerel, they would serve no real purpose, as this 1931 example attests:

Future Farmers

From morning until darkness
These tillers of the soil
Sweat and slave and labor,
Work and delve and toil;
And then after their supper,
They gladly hail the night;
And what these farmers do not do
Beneath the pale moonlight!

Also not included is an early version of "Orion," published as "Poem" in *The Phoenix*, I, No. 3 (autumn-winter 1938). Two poems—"Here The Rock Sleeps" and "We Walk The Young Earth"—were, until now, among the uncollected. However, due to Everson's reappraisal of them in the later 1970s and his notations in his personal copy of the 1968 *The Residual Years*, each has been chronologically incorporated into the *canon*. The uncollected poems contained here have been situated chronologically within the "Selection"—the facts of their publication given by way of footnotes.

The great majority of poems presented here are those which have remained unpublished. In my examination of Everson's surviving

291

papers from the *Residual Years* period, I was able to identify more than seventy unpublished poems. Some of these are fragmentary; some, basically complete but obviously unfinished; and some, virtually finished but, in the poet's judgment, apparently unworthy of publication. To the extent possible, each of the poems selected here is given either the date of its draft or the time period during which Everson worked with it.

Various of the unpublished poems were found as individual works among Everson's papers. However, a substantial number of them belong to two groups of verse that Everson had gathered together. The first group is here entitled "Late October '39"—the designation he gave to a holograph manuscript of fifty-four pages, containing thirty-seven poems, of which only twelve have been published. These twelve are "We Walk the Young Earth," "The Sign," "These Have the Future," "The Illusion," and eight of the poems making up "The Sides of a Mind." In preparing his manuscript, Everson left the poems untitled, distinguished as individual works only by spacing obviously meant to separate one from another. The poems as printed here are given Roman numeral designations. Where no objective source of dating a specific poem was found, one can only say that it had been written before the end of October 1939. Speculative dating based on textual considerations or subject matter goes beyond the scope of this volume. Where later drafts of a poem from this group exist, the printed text is derived from the latest version.

The "Late October '39" group of poems has a special significance that should not be overlooked. For his 1966 collection, *Single Source*, Everson pulled together several poems that had been separately printed in *The Masculine Dead* twenty-five years earlier and joined them as a single sequence, "The Sides of a Mind." This sequence was not, as it might have seemed at the time, an arrangement constructed in hindsight, but was, as the 1939 holograph shows, an attempt to return the poetry to something of its original sequential perspective. Indeed, in several manuscript references to the holograph, Everson noted it as the "long poem." In fact, six of those poems had been printed in *The Masculine Dead* as a sequence, "And From Bad Dreams"—an earlier title of which was "Introspections: A Sequence Of Adolescence."

In other words, this early use of the "confessional sequence" not only presaged the prominence this poetic form would attain for Everson throughout his mature work, but it preceded by some twenty years the 1958 publication of Robert Lowell's justly acclaimed *Life Studies*, which generated the important critical attention that the form would thenceforth receive.

The other group of poems is a gathering labeled by Everson as "Waldport Rejects," and is so designated here. Again, Roman numerals are used to head the otherwise untitled poems. These poems were written almost exclusively during the 1943-1945 period he spent as a conscientious objector interned at Camp Angel, located outside Waldport, Oregon, before he was transferred to other camps prior to his release in July of 1946. As might be expected, these poems express the concerns also present in his wartime sequence, "Chronicle of Division"—his pacificist situation and his troubled marriage. Of the twenty poems making up this group, twelve are included in this "Selection."

In preparing these unpublished poems for their appearance here, the only editorial changes made were the correction of misspellings and the occasional insertion of obviously needful punctuation. A blank space corresponds to a blank left by Everson. At times, in such instances, Everson placed metrical markings for the as-yet-unselected word, and these markings have been reproduced here. Although Everson usually allowed his penchant for British spellings to be editorially "normalized" for publication, we have retained them in these poems. Lastly, although Everson seemed to prefer the variant *staunch* for the verb *stanch,* we have used the latter throughout to avoid confusion with his adjectival use of *staunch.*

Specific acknowledgments and thanks are in order here for the poems comprising this "Selection": to Selma High School, Selma, California, for "Future Farmers," reprinted from *The Magnet* of 1931; to the Scarecrow Press, Inc., for "November First Nineteen Forty-Five" and "To My Ancient Enemy," reprinted from *Take Hold Upon The Future*; to Occidental College, Los Angeles, for the 1936 poem beginning "What there is fiercely now in the world," from the William Everson/Lawrence Clark Powell correspondence; to the Bancroft Library of the University of California at Berkeley, for "The Forms," "The Portrait," "You Know the Land," and the three translations; and to the William Andrews Clark Memorial Library, University of California, Los Angeles, for the remaining unpublished poems included here.

GYPSY DANCE *

Flowing, glowing music drifting through the tangled trees,
Ringing through the midnight on the light and dancing breeze;
Flashing figures whirling in the pale light of the moon,
Sweeping, leaping gypsies spinning to a lilting tune!

Down upon the creekside where the tules sway and nod,
Out upon the meadow in the glowing goldenrod,
Deep within the shadows where the moonbeams never pierce,
Everywhere is music ringing fiery and fierce!

It is rising, flinging, falling like the Northwind in a tree,
Or a joy-mad ghoul a-whirling in an ecstasy of glee!
Strangely woven in the music; in the eery wail and sob
Is the age-old thumping rhythm of the tom-tom's savage throb.

Oh, the whirling, swirling figures of the gypsies, everywhere
Are a-spinning, dancing, leaping, in the fire's fitful flare;
Like a merman in a maelstrom swishing through the seething sea,
Is the band of swaying gypsies crazy-mad with melody! [1931]

---

* *The Caravan* (Fresno State College), V, No. 1 (December 1931), 40.

DESERTED GARDEN *

A naked wall to left and right,
    And cold, bare earth, beneath,
The sun choked by a sodden sky,
    A wind with needle teeth.

A twisted tree, a tangled bush
    Forgotten how to bloom,
With green and yellow lichen scales
    That glisten in the gloom.

The roses used to blossom, here,
    And tulips used to grow,
And oh, the sun was mellow, here,
    So many years ago.

COMPENSATION

Starve the flesh, and freeze the bone
    And face the bitter storm,
But never, never cage the soul
    To keep the body warm!

---

* "Deserted Garden," "Compensation," and "Autumn Song" appeared in *The Caravan*, VIII, No. 1 (November 1934), 16, 28, 31.

AUTUMN SONG

Take my hand, dear, let us wander
　　Once again those gusty ways;
Let us roam the long, gray reaches,
　　As we did in other days.

Once again the road is luring,
　　Twisting up the hazy hill!
Once again the tree-tops beckon,
　　Blazing in the Autumn chill!

Ah, the plover, piping, piping,
　　Singing out that gypsy song!
Oh, to feel the cold wind blowing —
　　We have tarried over-long!

Take my hand, then, let us go, dear,
　　On into the glowing day,
Tread again, the misty miles,
　　Out and off, and far away!

[UNTITLED] *

You nations of Europe, dog-snarling dolls in your nook of the world,
Bristle among your pieces of earth and fight again:
Go wolf-mad and savage—
Leap at the throat, sink the white fang, tear and be torn.
When you have spent yourselves, lick the deep wounds and look East.
I think you will see a real menace. [*Summer 1935*]

---

* On the verso of the poem's draft is a holograph note dated "Carmel 1935." Everson had
visited Carmel in July 1935.

[UNTITLED] *

What there is fiercely now in the world:
Tyrants and warring: the continents throb with the beat of the nations;
There is over Europe the cadence of thunder;
The speaking drum.

Old paper reveals no phase of the world's changing
But held terror and anguish, and men now centuries dead
Regarded the next time only with terror.
For thousands of years the future's been ugly,
And the old wheel running; the same sky darkened,
The dream of security troubling the scared mind under the cloud.

What seems true:
The age of the past is the age of the future
And for what there is coming armour the heart or wade the dark river;
But terror's futile: one way or the other gone sanely
And no dread for your goad.

So far: peace, sound health, the love of a woman;
This place for labor where the clean light sky-falling floods on the land,
And night-time the stars that lit Carthage, huge in the sky;
The wind wide; the fields loaded;
This earth and this labor: good.

---

* This poem was included in a typescript of sixteen poems toward the work collected as *San Joaquin*. A mutual friend, Fay Porter, sent the typescript to L.C. Powell in the fall of 1937. The typescript is included in the Everson/Powell correspondence at the Library of Occidental College.

THE FORMS *

Over the land the clouds of the storm
All day blowing up from the sea,
Dark and somber, all day under the February wind,
Driving and blowing.

Growth and your marriage: this one wide country;
To breathe through the very pores of your flesh
Mood of region and mood of woman,
The essential presences, the forms of contact;
They have shaped your growth to the meaning of each.

Out of the west the endless drive of the February storms,
Bringers of beauty; and this woman,
Her grace in the rooms of the quiet house.
You, most fortunate of men,
Who early in life have resolved the great answers,
While better than you in the breeding towns,
Frustrate, are seeking and blind. [*Winter 1939*]

---

* In a letter to Lawrence Clark Powell, dated July 14, 1939, Everson refers to a group of poems, including "The Forms," as "a winter's work." The letter is included in William Everson and Lawrence Clark Powell, *Take Hold Upon the Future: Letters on Writers and Writing, 1938-1946*, ed. William R. Eshelman (Metuchen, NJ, & London: The Scarecrow Press, Inc., 1994) 106-108.

THE PORTRAIT *
For Hubert Buel

Back of his board he reaches and moves,
His hands working to break through the shell of my face;
To get under the bone;
To bring to his brush what is shining out of the shape of all things;
And the oils go on;

Still is the air of the afternoon.

Outside is the earth, shining green, yellow-green,
Sweeping west from these walls,
Enclosing the houses and hidden towns.
At the valley's head the puckering hills tighten and gather,
The rivers score them, branches straggling in from the slopes
Till the one trunk breaks to the sea.

And the walls shut out that beautiful country,
Letting us fashion these forms of our own,
Our eyes unblinded, some pattern out of an inmost need,
Here in the room in the afternoon
While the great earth beats at the walls. [1939]

---

* The poem is dated by its placement in a typed booklet of *The Masculine Dead*, prepared by
Everson in lieu of actual publication. An undetermined number of these booklets were
prepared by Everson in 1941 and distributed to friends. A copy is included in the Everson
collection at the Bancroft Library.

THE SIGN *

Under the docks the dark water slurs, swashes,
The men look down to it, their thin lips straighten:
At the given word they move pier-ward, close-packed,
Their eyes hard with meaning.

The men on the narrow street
Gather together: few words spoken:
Twos and threes out of the gutter-dusk:
The groups form. One man moving among them
Talks quickly, the quick short gestures:
The groups thicken.

And the wind: slow on the Rockies
The wind prickles the eyes of the last hunter, the last fur-taker:
He sees the far plane high on the peak of the Great Divide
Burn west and vanish.

In box-car corners, roaring through Kansas, roaring through Utah,
Two men talking, three men speaking,
One man dreaming alone in the loud darkness,
Not hearing the wheels, not seeing the stark poles
Flick on the moon as the miles break under.

And one man in the thundering dark
Guiding the tractor hour by hour,
The thin light piercing,
The great blades ripping the loam,
Hour by hour, the one man, dreaming his one dream
    through the blind hours,
Guiding and dreaming.

You see them heel-squatting night after night,
Round all the hidden fires of America.

When the freight pulled past he lay in the weeds,

---

* William Herber [pseud.], *Poetry: A Magazine of Verse*, LVI, No. 2 (February 1940), 243-45. Everson dates this poem in his letter of February 19, 1940, to Powell (*Take Hold Upon the Future* 154).

His heart pounding: he heard the long whistle far down the tracks:
The speed gathering: and seeing the bull turn finally back,
Broke for it, plunging out through the first dusk,
And sprang, and catching flung back on the car, and held,
And pulled panting into the suck and safety of the inside cleats.

You see them night after night:
They meet on the corners,
They say few words, quietly, and part quietly,
They go on their way dreaming the one dream,
In a whore's bed, or a ship's berth, or a bum's blanket,
Sad and persistent, running through the lonely rivers of their minds
The one dream: like a bond: the one future.

And he in the field, hoeing,
Heard the near train,
And watching the cars saw who huddled in the cold light,
And their hands lifted, a sign,
A symbol between them,
The one sign caught between earth and sky,
Like the meeting touch of their palms. [*Summer 1939*]

"LATE OCTOBER '39"

I

There are rivers out of the high plateaus that bear no names,
Secretly starting under the stones,
Tiny fingers of water straggling down from the snow-naked peaks
    and roofs of the world.
Under the arches of the highest trees they grow and gather;
Under the edges of the lower hills they gain their bulk.
They break on the plains, and their banks go under.
The marshland lies in the stretch of the sun
Till the sea takes it loud at the land's edge.

There shall be hundreds who squat on the lip of an unknown stream,
Squat on the broken edge of a bank, their hands on the pebbles,
Their palms at the face of the smiling earth, listening to water.
Who pause at the oar in the surge of a channel,
Letting the water sing its own song,
Letting the suck of the hunger of water
Sing at the oar, and the boat's side.

When they have heard
They shall turn their eyes to the murky shore
Where the sun never beats to the boles of the trees,
And watch, thinking.

There shall be water;
There shall be rivers breaking new ways to the granite,
The hunger of streams when the old nights break on the new worlds,
And the mountains go under.

And I, who lie in the dark,
These thousands of years before they have broken,
Hear in the fumble that shakes in my wrist,
The future loud in my blood.

And turning my head, seeing the great shafts and lances
    of the star-thrown light
I think of those rivers. I know the burst

Of streams in the gorges of the world.
I have in me loud the thunder,
The presence,
The dark desire, the knowledge and the purpose
That sucks at the roots of the hills.

II

This country so new from the hands of our elders
All their by-play we hold up for wonder.
We long to feel back of us not merely the tree's past,
Not merely the past of the grass, the game thick in the tules.
We long to feel back of us fullness, firmness,
Generations deep in a valley, the songs built there,
The forms of conduct shaped to a land.

Here were few men, a thin ripple of home-hunters
Laying their streets on the seeds of the grass.
We long for tradition: we hold in our hands a fifty year's axe
And endow it with centuries.
We hunger the feel of our own past, and we starve for tradition.

That is why, when forcing a bend on a mountain road
And a meadow opens, and black in the meadow an old barn,
Ancient with winters, its boards falling,
Something comes up in the throat that you cannot tell, some mood,
The feeling of all the gone past comes new in us.
We pass it in silence,
The hill close behind.

III

Who reads these poems will say to himself
With some suspicion and with some contempt:
This has happened before.

Hundreds there are who gave themselves off,
Who poured themselves out for a page's ruin,
Slobbered it out on a clean page,

Puked up their souls like a dog on the street for the passing eyes.
Flick these leaves to the thumbs of your scorn,
Mark the undiscipline, the vagaries of the Romantic mind,
The tricks and the twists I have used till they reek.

You seeking deep meter,
The level measure and the noble theme,
Hunting-hounds down the track of all verse,
Be warned.
This is the running stuff of a sore
And the words match it.
Who reads this poem knows what I am.
I have no defenses. [*October 1939/February 1940*]

IV

I leaned in a booth of that little town
Set on the Bay and the Santa Clara plains.
I spoke in the box, waited,
Heard presently out of that summer night
Her voice, speaking after the empty weeks.

I stood in panic, trying to frame in articulate speech the want
     and the hunger.
I could not; the time was waning, the time was draining out and away,
And suddenly I saw in my mind the wires set on the slender poles
     binding the towns,
I saw the thin strands climb on the Pass,
And go down, and the haze and the splendor of San Joaquin
Fade out before them. I saw the women bent at their boards,
Placing the sockets. I saw the flow that bore our voices flash
     and go out.

And I stood in the booth,
My tongue breaking over the stumps of words,
Her voice and her longing blind in my ears
And the night alive on my face.

V

The sun climbs,
The blue wind slides on the fields,
Over the trees small birds, westbearing, drive and are gone.

Out through this open door sight of the sun,
The track of the wind on the vineyard top,
And some mood on you, half-shy, half-heavy,
Without compulsion and without an end,
New coming after the sterile days.

No poem: the good gust quiet,
But the mood hangs, and tasting it here in the quiet light,
Knowing the color and weight and meaning it has is surely enough.
Purpose: force all to an end: the mark of the time.
But the mood drains out, untouched and illusive,
And the wind's track fades on the vines.

VI

We lie on our sides under the steep roof
Shedding the light of the northern stars.
Facing, our eyes unseeing into the dark,
Our mouths close, our knees touching.

"Listen, the wind. I have lain with you now—"

"Do not count them, let them go down,
Let them go back of us, building behind us."

"I have lain with you times back beyond—
Strange roofs, the unknown walls,
The unknown noises in the unknown street.
We lay in the rooms of towns where the rats were noisy
in the hollow walls.
We lay in the grass far under strange skies.
We lay in the wind's suck, in the sound of the ants
in the brittle grass."

"Let it go down: let it lie back of us,
Full, the stream of event,
Let it lie."

    "I remember the man westward from the city gate,
    I remember the old woman watching the gulls.
    I remember—it comes to me, in these sleepless nights—
    And this room, how many before us,
    Sucking their bodies together, twining their loins,
    Plunging their mad loins, their knees hugging,
    Their thighs hugging, their tongues sucking,
    Their seed plunging.

    How many before us, caught in this room,
    In this very bed, caught by the pressure of their own need,
    As we, now, my hand on your thigh—
    They were all here before us,
    Whores, lovers, lechers, pimps—!"

"Let it go down,
Let the night take them down with the dead past.
Hush.
Touch. Now. The Present.
Touch."

VII

They watched from the slopes for the evening star,
Listened under the pitch of their roofs for the wind's sound,
Saw sun, followed at dusk the low flight of birds.
They fashioned their temples on the highest hills.

The glass on the mountain stares and annuls,
The double lens on the cluttered bench
Stares, sees, breaks under surfaces, sees, stares.
Back of us ten thousand years,
The growth of beliefs, the shaping desires,
The shaping hopes, the forming hungers.

The glass stares, annuls,

The double lens on the laboratory bench,
Sees, stares.

What is it crowding up in my lungs
When the long light breaks on the crusted earth?
What is it singing under the flickering blood?
What are the forces of affirmation singing into my mind?
The trees flaunt their blossoms on the swirling air,
The birds, their beings breaking with music swing down the sky.
Far on the fields lies the golden light,
The sun falls at evening,
Beautiful, the great waves gather for the shores' assault,
The lightning springs and startles in the heavy cloud,
Beautiful, by every test and pattern of our aching past
The world blows in to us sweet to the eyes.

Glass stares, annuls,
If there be god, show me his face.
Seeing, the glass, staring.

We are caught between epochs,
We have in us straining and tense the hopes of the past,
We see the golden leaves and ache to believe,
We see also the hurt flesh, the skin scalded,
The bone shattered and the blinded eyes.

You hordes of the future,
Inured to the lens' look,
Unhampered by hope, untouched by the fever of a fallen past
You will look in your eyes and out of your own blood,
Without aid, without deity,
Will pattern survival, and live all your days
In the honey of life,
Till death lifts in darkness over your eyes
And you feel our old fury in falling.

VIII

What is it, blowing your throat in the strident light,
Thrusting your hands?

We sat in a room, the sun came through in a yellow glaze,
The shadow of leaves lay on the cloth,
Over that breakfast south of here in a sunny room
Our words fell.

Now, calling it, the odor of coffee hung in the room,
Wakening eight years after
The shape, the color of light,
The transient impalpable color of lost days,
Some illusive and long gone time
Brought over the eyes in a soft ebb of recollection,
And it comes colored with memory,
The shape of her face, the head turning,
The tilt of her head.

We have broken it with time,
We have beaten it under the light of suns,
We have covered it over.

What have we said?
What words have we spoken
To ripple and stir subtly under the levels of thought,
Recur and beat up lonely and gone far down the years,
The sound, the sight,
The odor of coffee hung in the air
And the tilt of a head?

IX

I lie on the roof,
Beneath me the great boards tremble and shake,
The engines below me turn and gather.
The walls tremble, the great plant shakes in the summer night.

Above me the stars,
Jupiter leans in the south, high and clear in the Milky Way.

X

The wagons rolled on the plains, lurched on the passes under the pines.
The oldest men remember.
The ships found the channel at Golden Gate in our grandfather's
    morning.

You think of some young poet in his skiff on the Thames,
Watching the suck of the dark water,
And feeling the force of his past beat on those shores.
The men who saw that channel burn in the light centuries before,
Who gathered it under the points of their pens, broke it to words,
Reduced it down to the syllable's span.
He feels their presence,
He drifts with their presence under the light,
The words shape for him.

Long rolls the sun on the San Joaquin,
Long rolls the wind over California.
This is the end of the western drive,
This is the last pile-up on the shores of the continent.

And the earth:
Broken under the share of a plow but not of a pen,
There have been few before you to gather the gust of this long level
Into their eyes, hammer it down to the lean line and the lift
    of the phrase.
There has been no past.
You feel the long drive of the sun flat on your shoulders,
Unresolved through the words of a thousand men.

There have been none here before you to temper the drive
And let it expand in the chest.
The books that you read talk of another coast and another valley.
You sit in the dark and feel it lonely and huge over all the raw cities,
And the words you will write were not shaped to these plains
Nor the look of these mountains.

XI

Her head turns on the pillow,
Her eyes watch you, through that one wisp of her let-down hair
     her gray eyes.
Under the cover, soft and young the movement of her waist.

Outside, the dusk, the one owl.

Take her, roll into those thighs and loosen within you the wells
     of desire,
Feel it come seeping and yielding,
The impalpable juices oozing themselves
To swell the current,
Pour crashing up to the tumult of completion.

Yes be emptied! be drained!
Pour shining and loud between those good knees the stuff
     of a dozen poems,
Spill it out to the last fertile ounce,
Rise in the morning dry, cold of creation,
Know the frustration of that barren page!

Fool: the nuzzling breasts, roll, take,
And between you build a poem to ring in your blood forever,
Make a music that under its draught blows paper and ink,
Breaks walls, cracks roof, lets night and the Wain and the hidden tern
Rush in the room: these are the times
When the pausing and musing of this careful life
Go down and go under.
Build a past out of your strength to leave at the grave
More than the dry swish of a turning page with a few marks on it.

The eyes are asking,
The restless motion of those ready knees asking, asking.
The owl's in the dark, the tern's in the sky,
And high and thin in the luminous night
The Wain is clearing the roof. [*May/October 1939*]

XII

Under the lean of the low hills
Slow wind running and pushing the leaves of the trees.
The wind turns, the leaves flare sideways,
The wind twists and drags on the edges of leaves.

Turning your head, your eyes take country far to the east,
By the turn of your head shutting out country, taking in country,
The edges of sight excluding, including,
Imposing a margin, the momentary boundary rigidly forced at the edges
    of your eyes.

Your head turns,
And you fill into those wells long vistas of earth,
Miles of it, the waver and fall of ridges,
The slow hills, the deep color of earth.
You have the power.
Turn, turn with the wind,
Impose your eyes, shut out, take in,
Drag inward over the lengths and the slopes
And strike it in on the mind.

XIII

What I want of this poem more than any one thing is youth in its lines.
What I want is the young blood to sing down the sky, or straggle,
    or falter in flatness, or fall, or be broken.
I feel back of me more gust and vitality than now I possess.
Better poets than I have dried at this age.
I have tried all my life to bind in a lyric the weight that it needs.
Before I grow old I want in a poem a youth's strength
    and a youth's daring.
In three years I am thirty.
Perhaps I can write then poems like a rock of the earth in a hand.
But now for a time let it grow like a bramble,
For I will be old in a moment.

XIV

And the yellow of the leaves,
The blue wind of September,
The green and the blue and the yellow of September
Mingles in the wind,
In the desert of the sky, the falling of the sun,
Great south-falling sun in the channels of the wind,
The wide light of the valley,
And the vineyard, and the vineyard,
In the ripple of the wind and the wide light of September.

Go down Sagittarius,
Go down you stallion-bodied runner of the sultry south,
Give over to winter, go south-west down in the gather of September
To the leaning of the light, and the plunder of the year.

XV

What lovers before us in all the broken ages,
Stealing under the river dusk,
Touching, the eyes asking, the lips curved for the answer?
They met in the gloom of innumerable dusks,
All through the forbidden nights of the human past they touched
     in the twilight,
Whispered at midnight.
They came burning through every wave of the world's changing,
And the words there always, the sucking lips, the thighs, madly,
The phallus sunk in the aching flesh,
The eyes, forever the asking eyes.

And we: the low wind coming leans on the wheat,
Curves on the hand.
What words have been spoken?
They ring at our ears like the sound of the ages,
But we do not listen,
Here on the earth, in the leaves, in the grass,
Under the moving night. [*March/May 1937; October 1939*]

XVI

Toilers under the summer sun,
Heat-drinkers, laborers under the California sky,
Here at our hands is the work of the valley.

Young men feeling under the skin the long muscles knot up the flesh,
Old men feeling the tendons wince, the vertebrae grind,
    ruptures give signal.
We work, and the heavy wealth of this yielding earth is heaped
    for the cities.

We work: under our hands the labor and life of the world,
By this sweat and this effort the towns grow, the farms blossom,
The long trains high on the inland grades roar through the mountains,
On the continental slopes the men of our kind are lifting and straining,
They breed their children in the wayside shacks.

Fruitpickers.
Roadmakers.
I have seen you beaten in the Fresno streets,
I have seen you labor all your lives and die poor at the last.

Night wind over the Spanish ridges,
Rain on the hills, refugees under the high whine of the hidden planes,
Stumbling and trudging, the bombs falling, the blast, the mangled flesh.
The broken Jews under the eaves of their city.

Where can we find salvation when our own acts are the acts of treason?
Where can we find what it is we are seeking with the fungus
    of sloth ingrown on our eyes?

O men my brothers, here with you over these Fresno fields
I have seen hate in your eyes, the narrow prejudiced minds.
I have seen you quarreling in the vineyard dust.
When fortune finds you, you pour out your souls in a slut's belly,
Go down to every evil that bled you: false wealth, false pride,
    bigotry, greed.
You who bear yourselves beautifully under disaster

Annul all your good—a lynching, a lie, the rusty knife of a sneer.

Where can we find salvation when our acts, our very acts?

Give us the task,
There is all around us the shadow of doubt.
We believe our own lies.
We blunder and grope and are duped by desire.
Give us earth to be moved,
Give us the job to close our eyes and let the sweet strength of the
    earnest bone pour itself out.
Someone show us what to believe
And we can level mountains.

XVII

Wind for a week; we heard the suck, the surge,
The trees roaring and seething,
All the new leaves hissing and pulling on the strain of their stems.
We had in our mind the image of air
Rushing the hills at the valley's head,
Flooding down to the plain, brunting and nosing over the towns.
We walked in wind till our ears forgot it,
Till our flesh forgot the thrust and nuzzle.
We slept at night soundly, the nerves inured to the heavy sound.

Then suddenly one sundown, a slow draining of light in the lemon sky,
And stillness, the air hushed,
The far sounds floating mile and mile.
We lay in our beds restless, in strange quiet,
And thought we could hear the noise of stars
Had a cricket not drowned them with clangor.

XVIII

What was spoken is nothing.
Say one word and feel the past falling behind you,
The mouthed tonalities spending themselves ripple-wise into the air.
Hunt deeper for what will abide,
As the times McKelvy, here in this room,
For all his words, which are gone, for all the clear edge of his mind

Speaking through stillness—they have passed, they have gone.
But the spirit, the man's quality,
Somewhere now he is moving through mountains.
I know him, the hardness, the honest and earnest eyes
    seeking perfection.
I pour myself out to blacken a page,
Express, shout, give off, exude.
Clear-eyed and quiet, McKelvy watches, perceives,
And, if you ask him, can give an opinion.

XIX

If you see in this poem looseness,
If you see in these units diffusion, slackness of texture,
Know the fury and confusion and uncentered quality of the age.
I feel in me all the power of the human past, and no center to hold it,
I see the beauty of the outer world, and the terror behind it.
I feel the weakness and the frailness of flesh,
The weakness that never can stand to the force that drives it,
The weakness that chokes at the last and sends us staggering
    into the earth.
This poem is the word of a religious man, with no god to worship.

XX

We are those who went out in the Great Depression.
We stood on the streets in the cold afternoons with our hands
    in our pockets.
We remember the banks, their doors locked, and the men
    with long faces.
We remember the Blue Eagle screaming out of the empty stores.

I remember also the camp in the hills where they sent us,
The officers, their proud and vulturine faces,
Swindling us at every turn.
The drunken boys in the valley towns

Rootless, nervous, hungry for home, for a woman, for the work
    they wanted.

We went out to the world in the Great Depression.

This poem is as rootless and lost as the time that bred it.
It is out of the age, it is born of confusion,
And the failures it holds are its mothers'.

XXI

We stood in the evening light of his room
And told him. He, lifting his face: "You have children?"
Behind him the wall, the dark curtain.
"We have no children."
He stared, the last light ebbing from those naked hills.
"You want this? You are *sure*?"

I felt her beside me.
We stood together in that little room
Having come there out of so urgent a need
And our strength blew between us.
At the knee and the arm we touched for a moment
And the touch welded.
"We are sure, doctor."

There gathered across us one of those times
When the future roars from its dimness,
Hangs on your head, immense;
The implications that will alter your life
Hang, and you meet it,
You drink it deep with your eyes wide,
With your nerves straining.

We stood together in the evening light
And gathered our aching past upon us
And spoke, and he saw our eyes, and turned in the room,
And the stroke fell.

And however we change,

However the years will twist our desire
And leave us empty, and the bitterness of an old mistake
    blacken our age
We will have known the strength to act as we saw,
To face our beliefs, and shape our desires,
However it turns and we taste our error
And curse ourselves in our age. [*October 1939/February 1940*]

XXII

I walk through this town
And feel from occasional windows
The curious and indulgent eyes.
I am a poet.
I am of that rare breed
That chants over daisies, soulful,
That clasps its hands to its wish-bone breast
And speaks its rapture.

I feel the eyes of housewives,
I feel the puzzled and suspicious eyes
Of those good men, the merchants.

I am a poet.
I walk through these streets
With the knot in me tight as a fist.
Whatever I think of these people:
Their petty pleasures, their narrow minds,
The ruts of their prejudice guiding their lives,
I should like to live here where my past lies,
Where my boyhood sleeps in the vacant lots
Not marked by their eyes,
Not under the mark of their curious eyes,
Forever avoiding the questions they put,
And the look of their eyes. [*October/November 1939*]

XXIII

Do you think from this poem I am blind to its danger?
When you open yourself for the world's eyes you run your own risks,
You will feel the thin minds prying the pages,
The frigid and acid tentacles of their lust,
The mean mouths saying:

"Look. This is the man.
By his own admission,
In his poems he tells of it—"

If you want peace and contentment be secret, be still,
The inner flame huddled within you,
No glimmer, no spark to shine from the lidded sight.
If you would save yourself wounds and the filth of the street
Guard yourself closely.

World, great crashing plane seeking the level,
Like a rusty nail in the wood you are trueing I heave myself up.
Go under I will, be smashed, be broken,
But all I can hope when that time passes:
A nick in the bright of the blade. [*October 1939/February 1940*]

XXIV

Edwa, when we met, that autumn in the hush of darkness
Under the mulberry close by the corner of the old house
We made the pledge. We clung together in the pouring dark
Too young to know, too wild with love and desire and the sweet
hunger of adolescence
To know ourselves, or our inner purposes, or the shape of our lives.

We stood together and pledged what was not ours to pledge:
What was beyond us: the future.
In the pain and splendor of adolescence we placed it between us,
And bound it under the ache of our meeting mouths.

Edwa, between that time and this I have given you anger
And agony, and staring nights,

And the hopeless gnawing that eats at the heart,
And maybe some pleasure.

We have learned,
We have seen how the low tide of coming events
Can snare the knees,
And drag a runner choking and gasping into the spume.
To be wild with hope and longing and high purpose
In the fine fever of youth is good.   [*October/November 1939*]

XXV

He dragged himself over the edge of rock, bleeding,
By his arms' strength
His maimed legs serpent-wise, raking the leaves.

   She found him there on a little ledge,
In sere grass, under the junipers and the last light.
   His eyes blazed fiercely against her:
"You bitch: let me alone: you southland she-devil.
I heard your legends and I came:
I broke the gates: I swam those rivers as no man before me.
I broke the gates, and dared those dark halls
And now I lie like a ham-strung ox."

She knelt down beside him; and took the great shaggy northland head
   in her arms
Saying: "Hush: you have not long to live,"
And rocked it gently against her breast.
The strength and the hate drained out of his limbs,
And he rested, in deep peace,
"If you had shown me such pity—your gown will be bloodied,
Your people will flog you through the public streets."

She did not answer, and later he died.
The dogs of the watch were maddened by blood,
And sprang upon her, and falling she thought: "I died for love"—
   but that was a lie.
And the guard who leaned above them under the torches,

Said soberly, with compassion:
"They died for love—it was a great and noble death."
But that was a lie,
And the night wind sucking up from the gorges
Touched them,
And blew across them, and flattened in patches the heavy pelts
Of the panting and bloody-mouthed dogs.

[UNTITLED]

November foundered visibly and winter
Like a persistent creditor arrives; we saw it dozing
In grimy crevices; the old black bark of trees,
The north exposure, had its dull tolerant air.
The gradually less effusive sun
Suffered all shadows to increase;
It hardly touched the wet things sleeping there.

The poet lover of the San Joaquin
Nurses and charts the humours of the fog;
He sniffs his orchard avidly and looks
Among the horse dung for the prints of God.

But God has come to live in this old city
And laid his loving blight on once green sod.

YOU KNOW THE LAND

You know the land;
Falling south and west it drains to the river;
There are fences strung by the country lanes,
And those tall strong weeds.
Riding these roads see great barns rotting in the homestead yards.
The track slanting south through the empty pastures
Rusts in the rain.

You know the land.
Year over year and those spinning seasons
Cover the face of it.
Cow-country, grain-country;
Its last weeds strewn on the flank of the roads
Yield the rank smell. [*February 1940*]

SEEKERS

Night on the river, the doors closing inward darken the faces
    and the knees,
The hands fumble in the loose cloth.
Back of the eyes the long line shining in the closed column
Sings in its splendor, and there is no sight:
Only the curve, the round, the buttock jerking in madness,
The mouths meeting and hanging, and the touching tongues.

Women giving themselves in the summer nights to unknown men
Seek only the male presence, the masculine flesh;
Locking their knees round those dark loins
They couple in lust, are left in the weeds depleted and gasping,
Their bellies burdened with strange seed.

The slave girl sold to the far country suffered her master;
The sailor who rose from the loins of the Negress
Knew the African twilight over that land.

And the whores, the priestesses of love,
In the metropolitan alleys
Passionately mixing the bloods of the world,
Consuming power and hope and terror,
Building it into their supple bones,
Bringing it forth in the hidden rooms
To suckle the very breasts it had handled.

O seekers at nightfall, whisperers,
Couplers under the city roofs,
Children leap from your act the living mockery of restraint,
In the lewd beds, in the wayside weeds,
The flame running in the hollow bone breaks surface:
The preacher trembles at the furtive door,
The seed bursts within the roaring womb. *[January/June 1940]*

[UNTITLED] *

Love, who have in new maturity
Turned unto another not your age,
Moved by some long-resisted lack in me
That warped the marriage bed to make a cage.

What he knows not, only the years can teach,
That wifery is knotted deep in need,
And by what slow assimilative modes
The rootings of its old engrossments freed.

This he would learn, enamouréd of one
Younger than he, ignorant in youth,
Holding her body's sweetness as a jewel,
And blinded to its strong, self-hidden truth.

But you, the senior partner of that pact,
Never could stint the knowledge, in your want
Bruising his body with an unstanched need
Importunate beneath that stringent taunt.

For you, moved though you were by tenderness,
Solemn with love, half-hesitant with doubt,
Have too long eaten of such stringent fare
To leave the *entrée* of the banquet out.

You will go forward faster than he follows,
To such advancements of the coarse-grained flesh,
That he, though he has heard them told and tallied,
Is not yet [*incomplete*]

Or, say, you tutor him, and he, all willing,
Retraces unoffended your fast course,
What of the deep divisions he will measure,
Forming between your fury and his force?

What then will mar the doting of his gaze
Marking your body's beauty, its clean grace,

---

* This poem was included in Everson's letter to his wife, dated Nov. 14, 1943, wherein he
states that the poem "shows my misunderstanding of the true situation.... Perhaps it will offend
you. I would never write it now—but as I say, I didn't understand.... I don't expect to work
on it further." Everson's letters to his wife, Edwa, are among his papers at the William
Andrews Clark Memorial Library, UCLA.

And what becloud that innocence of eye
That he brings to you in his trusting face?

When you, carnivorous, feed on each other's flesh,
And through your limbs the beaked sensations fly,
In what compulsion will he ever cover
The uneradicable presence which is I?

Wound in your knees, what visions will he hold
Of me entwined before him, our thick speech,
And fastened by the brute embedded dowel
That pins the sweating torsos each to each?

What time the love-scent reeks within the bed,
The sea-stench increment of your elation,
How can he drive the crowding vision down,
Of our loins laved in that evisceration?

Nor will his hands, regardless how they press,
Ever erase the indentures of strain,
We set there in some late-discovered stance
That whipped the wasted nerve to life again.

All our love-postures, the infinite ancient acts,
He can but duplicate, nor his invention try
Some game we had not frolicked at before
He ranged into your favor-finding eye.

He will, arousing, struggle back to sight,
Behold your visage inches from his own,
And see my features stamped upon the face
That he had thought was yours, and yours alone.

Then every line upon it will denote,
Some incidental aspect of our past,
That beggars him with hopelessness and doubt,
And warns him that its luring will not last.

Then will my years confront him, and my name,
And all our seasons, and our good and bad,
And you will be remote, and he will writhe,
Struggling to win back what he never had. [*August 1943*]

[UNTITLED] *

And do the indulgent lovers
Weave their arms in the April twilights,
Home from the river-runs,
From the straw beds in the hay heaps,
Broken of grass,
And marked maybe with the small sign
A woman leaves when her drouth has been broken?

Ask no man here.
The country girls may laugh in the leaves,
On the straw beds,
In the hay heaps,
But none here know it.

Ask no man here,
For he cannot tell,
But will speak instead of a dream,
Some snatch of his thoughts,
Sharpened to shape in his sleeping sight
And not anything more,
Being beyond that time,
And quite unable to say. [*August 15, 1943*]

---

* This poem is actually the earliest of the "Waldport Rejects," but is placed here for its
chronological appropriateness.

[TRANSLATIONS] *

LE MAL
Arthur Rimbaud

While the red spewings of the shot
Whistle all day through the infinity of the blue sky,
While, scarlet or green, near to the king who rallies them,
Flow the battalions en masse into the fire;

While a terrible madness crushes
And makes of a hundred thousand men a steaming pile;
—Poor dead! in the summer, in the grass, in thy joy,
Nature! O thou who made these men holy!—

There is a God, who laughs at the damask cloths,
At the altars, at the incense, at the great chalices of gold;
Who in the lulling of hosannas falls asleep
And wakes when mothers, crouching
In their agony, and weeping beneath their old black bonnet,
Proffer him a fat penny tied up in their rag!

---

* The following three poems resulted from a joint effort between Everson and Robert Walters, a fellow conscientious objector. Walters supplied interlinear literal translations, and Everson, with the further help of a French dictionary, would render Walters' version into the translated poem. This collaborative effort was principally maintained during the late summer and the fall of 1943. "Le Mal" was printed in Lee Bartlett, *William Everson: The Life of Brother Antoninus* (New York: New Directions, 1988), p. 55—where *Walters* mistakenly appears as *Walker,* due to Everson's misspelling of the name in his letter to Edwa (October 17, 1943). The poem accompanied the letter.

LE VOYAGE
Charles Baudelaire

I

For the child, in love with maps and prints,
The universe is equal his vast appetite.
Ah! How wide the world is in the light of lamps,
Within the eyes of memory, how the world is shrunk!

One morning we depart, brain filled with fire,
Hearts puffed with rancour and with harsh desires,
And we proceed, tracing the rhythm of the wave,
Lulling our infinity upon the finite seas.

Some, joyous to flee an infamous home-land,
Others, their cradle's horror, and some,
Astrologers drowned in the eyes of a woman
Tyrannous Circe, dangerous with perfumes.

To shun the beast's conversion, they get drunk
Of space and light and blazings of the sky.
The ice that gnaws, the copper-colouring sun
Slowly erase the markings of the kiss.

But the true travelers are those who leave
Just to be leaving: hearts buoyant as balloons,
From their fatality they never go astray,
Nor knowing why say always: Let us go!

These are the ones whose cravings are like cloud,
Who dream, as the conscript dreams the cannon,
Of vast sensualities, transitional, obscure,
Of which the human soul has never known the name.

C'EST L'EXTASE LANGOUREUSE
Paul Verlaine

It is the ecstasy of languor,
It is the fatigue of love,
It is all the shivering of the woods
Among the clasping of the winds,
It is, through the gray limbs,
The choir of the little voices.

Oh the weak and cool murmuring!
It is like the soft cry
With which the shaken grass expires...
You could say, under the water which veers,
The deaf rustling of the stones.

This spirit which mourns
In this deep sleeping sigh,
It is ours, is it not?
Mine, say, and thine,
Which the meek anthem breathes
Through this tepid evening, so low?

"WALDPORT REJECTS"

I

But at last we learned,
Who had railed and brooded,
And eaten our hearts in their isolation,
That life in its knowledge
Teaches and /
Nursing the prisoners' sorrow, the prisoners' rage,
Bawling the [*incomplete*]

Outside we were fixed,
Engrossed in our little limitation:
A wife, a job, and a shelf of books
That had its returns,
And we loved it,
As the foetus, shielded and snug,
Loves its little world,
Lags and resists when time thrusts it,
Shaping its mute mouth for the whimper
It yet cannot make.

Are we then to return?
Can we return,
And take up again our thoughtless function,
Living between the clock and the car?
No. Not now. Not again will that suffice:
What was learned at such cost,
Such loss and such anguish,
Is too dear to forsake.
A little glimmer of what can be
Has been revealed.
To deny it now
Denies the mind,
Denies knowledge,
The whole wide teachings of life. [*November 18, 1943*]

II

Is the soldier less brave,
Merely because he has breached Hell for nothing?
His haven lies only in errors.
All he endeavored he did coolly and well:
Mastered the mind,
Subdued the raw ruin of fear,
Imposed the hardness of human will
Upon the brute blood
And bore hell,
And stared down death.
Who paved the highway to Hell's high gate
With his good intentions.

Give the soldier his due.
His virtues are clear.
The evident error of his perception
Will be rendered by time;
As even now it leaches and bares,
Sorting speech from motive,
Motive from need,
To leave only the act,
Simple and terrible,
Revealed in its consequential might.

We are all in error,
Bound in the limits of our perception,
And can only proceed,
Waiting the future unfolding
That approves or rejects.

But after so many thousands of years,
Each one of them marked,
Each one of them bearing its duplicate anguish,
Stanched in pain, and riddled with torture,
Is not the final factor apparent,
Plain in the cluttering wrack of the years,
The clear elucidation of life,
The simple truth, serene and revealed,
For even the blind to behold? [*January/February 1944*]

III

But the healer is time.
The healer is time and the truth-loving mind
That subdues and adjusts.
The days winnowed under
And brought in their span the old associations,
Old habits and forms.
They had spent so many years together,
And their ancient love.

She moved in the room,
The light lay on their flesh,
The days thawed out the ridges that lined her face.
They fell to the lot of their old rhythm
Between bed and board,
And that was all good.
The soreness was healed.
She was honest and good
And life was made sweet.

And clearly he saw how hard was the heart,
That clung and / ∪
Clutching its own,
Hanging on to its old known engrossments
But they had to go.
She was honest and good.
All that she did she had her motives,
And they were enough. [*May 3, 1944*]

IV

He went back to his North when the time came.
And she to the man in the far city
And he held no hurt;
Seeing it clear in his mind's eye,
And a thing to be / .

The sun swung in the south and climbed up again.

They met in the fall,

A week in a house that fronted the sea,
And was filled with its sand.
They were easier then.
And one night over wine,
Without thought or premeditation,
They finally spoke.
And there in that room,
All the old bars that were raised between them
Were then dissolved.
For the first time in their long union
Spoke cleanly together,
Delving up the old secrets,
The little restrictions that none had
And could not have known;
All of it bared,
Dug up,
Pulled out of the cramped and twisted past
And shown, half-shyly, with pain,
But finally shown as one will show some terrible scar he had kept
    close hidden.
She showed him indeed what the other had brought her,
And all his mistakes rose up around him,
That he never knew,
That she herself had hardly known,
Till the other man came
And merely by being
Laid them all bare.

He returned to the North
And she to the man,
But whatever they did,
He locked in his / ∪
And she in the city's rented rooms
And another man's bed,
This was not to divide them,
Who had learned by so / ∪ and hard a way,
That nothing is whole,
That richness is gleaned

Between the great needs
That are not to be filled.

Having seen to that center
What then was time?
A thing to endure,
A thing to endure and
They could come together
Bearing their separate pasts upon them,
To place each at the other's feet. [*May 3, 1944*]

V

What then is God,
That he should ride in the ripple of the long sea,
And not in men's hearts?
That his presence should sleep in the sloping cloud
And not inhabit the mind?
The furred animal crouched in its tensile fear
Embodies his ⏑ / ,
And the loving woman
Arching above her mattress mate
Reflects his vast hand.

Let the criminal kill,
Let the rapist rage in his violent act,
Let blow be brunt,
The tentacles of rapine open and close,
And the sleeping babe,
And the tern in his animal torment go south,
God breeds and burns,
God tingles the pubic hair,
Tempers the virgin's foot in its tread,
And the lyric voice,
Arch in the orgasmic timbrel of want,
Keen his clear name. [*August 31, 1944*]

VI

But all fluxes, flares,
Time twists and turns,
The river deposits its temporal reef
And takes it away,
And the man walks on in his ∪ / trance,
Turning right and left,
His head swinging out to reciprocal twist,
And it breaks about him,
Flows in his room,
Bestows and removes,
And sends him on down its vast current,
Cleansed of his vows,
Reduced of his hopes,
Cut from his little schemes and his foible,
Intact yet in the five senses
That glower and reach,
And refer back to the mind
Their small discoveries
For it to compare.
But where he began and where he will end
Are not to be known.
Let the motion suffice,
In a world of motion
Let motion suffice. [*August 31, 1944*]

VII

Once more in his world,
The little world on the land's lip,
Perched between hills and the huge sea,
And its confinement.
Can he come to terms?
The terms are not his.
Only on her,
Torn like a top between her two men,
Does his time dangle,
And he cannot resolve it.
Only can wait,

And let patience prevail,
Seeing her in her plight,
Flung on her own in her separation,
And no hold on the time.
Of this he is sure:
She holds no deceit,
Or only such as will spare him pain,
Nor for her own ends.
And who is he,
Who had schooled his life on tolerance's teaching,
Knowing the complex needs of the mind,
The heart's hunger,
The violent rages locked in the line?
Who is he to clutch and demand,
Make the bed-oath law,
Enforce the lawyer's line—
Or else sever the limits
And let her out on a [*incomplete*]?

The years between them!
Whose hand but his
Will close her again when she needs such comfort?
Not her lover's palm:
That is for playing between the sheets,
That is for stanching the restless want
When the body,
Too long denied,
Takes its fate in its hands.
But never the heart.

And he?
He too wears his hurt:
When they lip in their spasm,
Do not the years he cannot compass
Lie too in her eyes;
Are they not also his border,
The beam he can't break?
Does he hate the husband?
Does he in his dark
Beat hand on her brow,
Stamp at the vision,
Wear the central hurt,

Seeing always non-wholeness of life,
That lets fulfillment glimmer
And then cuts off,
Half done,
Its little parcel of need
Eked and pinched off?

And she?
What hurts must she harbor,
Wearing the mark of conventional guilt,
But knowing this truth:
The disparate heart,
That never knows what it really wants,
But runs from haven to haven,
And has no hold?

The man cannot rancour,
But seeing all,
Suspicious of woe,
He yet is woeful,
Distrustful of such inured engrossment,
Cannot break its mould.
How, in his moments,
Lift the black pall of mind,
The steamy cloud introversion festers,
Its black ramp,
Its clammy warp,
Its brute judgment,
Its fell laws, its anarchic myth!

Ah bruit and blather,
Cries the hurt horde—
How long can he bear,
What metal is heart
That it must grind,
Like a rock in a piston,
Month after month and no surcease—
Only progression
To accept or reject,
And that is all hers,

And that is not offered!
Howl madness!
Wail your rancours of the hot blood,
Break with your hands,
Stab past and murder.
Slash time.

He cannot do it.

But yet can he know
How thin wears the metal,
How worn is the [incomplete],
How hard blows the weather in the heart's kingdom
And by what flawed and delible props
Does temperance keep peace with its recourse. [October 15, 1944]

VIII

But that too is of this life:—
That hooded hounding.
Sitting each day in the long room,
The male faces bent above food,
The male speech,
The male laughter,
The male [incomplete]
Such hurts are the time's.
And he knows now the soldier,
In a strange land,
A strange region,
Far and away over stranger seas,
And knows his hunger,
When the fond letters lessen,
And the dutiful phrase fills in the scant page
Where [incomplete] once flourished,
And knows the hard hurt that sends him
To town for his torment,
A bottle's boon or a harlot's hug,
And the hate that flares in the frayed nerve,
In at last in war's welter,
He finds before him The Enemy,

Hunched over hulk,
And stabs and slashes,
And all the stored tumult breaks its bonds,
And murder prevails.

For the man, that is closed.
He has schooled too well the hard wants
To know that as succor.
But chancing across the news sheets
And sees in its pages
Their haggard eyes, their haggard hands,
And all their loss,
Their wasted world,
Their speechless hunger,
The baffled hope that heaps at the hurt ego
Hung in its howl,
He looks in his heart,
And sees what hunches there like a toad, puffed with its bile,
And dimly somehow, he understands. [*October 15, 1944*]

IX

But is not this, indeed, the true progression?
In his early hurt,
Engrossed in his loss,
He had thought to proceed,
But such was his hurt,
Could not hold his head its new direction,
But must look to his past,
Keeping it close at hand
For the heart to hutch in its new misery,
And savor its loss.

But now like one who has lived too long
With an old anguish,
Must he throw it off,
Cough up the gall
That lived like a toad in his central region,
And spew it out,
All bile,

A black bruit.

So the world,
Who once went to its war with a high shouting,
And the words of reform,
Has forgotten all but the anguish,
And grinds on,
A great deadly rasping,
Its gaped wounds pussed and infectious,
And loses every ideal,
Wanting only to be done, be done,
And will drop to its knees in utter exhaustion.

The man comes to conclusion with a great breath,
And lifts up his head,
Wants once more to laugh,
And cripples on toward his future
With something near to elation,
And marvels how it can be
That one can be glad
When all he held dear is dead.   [*December 16, 1944*]

X

And may this not, perhaps, be a purer progression?
That the past is all dead,
Cut off in a terrible act of the will,
As a trapped wolf,
Who has trod all night
His bloody dance at the chain's end,
Gnaws at last the caught knuckle,
To cripple off to his haven hill
In the rifting dawn.

Let all that suffice.
The man, guarding his maimed stump,
Faces out toward the future,
And does not count the cost.
For the world is all there,
A vast totality

That exceeds definition,
But must be met.
The multiforms of possibility
Lie there for perusal,
And the explorations of experience
Reverse the accident of birth
To its own betrayal.
So moves the man.
And he will touch with his hand
The preponderance of substance,
The tangible reality forming beyond the intangible dream;
And the weathers will break,
And weave their fluid casuistry
In a hundred subtle ways,
And have no end.

He will go out and behold the murderess
Framed in her rage,
Regard the hacked hands,
The dissevered thighs,
The trunk-murder corpse in its makeshift coffin,
Riding the fast express to a distant port
And the all-receiving sea.
He will touch the thief in his shrewd scheming,
The racketeer, bland in his vantage;
He will watch the rapist,
Discover the nun,
Observe the abortionist
Extract with his / ᴜ
The humeric deposit,
And the sprung foetus
Dive down the drain
To the intestinal tubes
That feed the turds of a city
To the omnivorous sea.

He will look up out of city streets
And see over its top the flat wind,
Prone on its roofs,
Go out and off over huddled forms
To the tall ranges,

The sky-breakers,
Where the naked rock
Towers and piles
Toward an all consuming God.

And bloody Europe stanches her wound and groans,
And the tyrants seethe,
And all about
The anarchic man,
The anarchic woman,
Meet above board,
Seek food, discover pleasure,
Play the couplers' will between two sheets,
Till the next generation
Groans out of their loins
And opens its eyes.

And all consumes,
Withers, fades and goes out,
Totters down to the grave and topples in,
And the future generations
Trample over that place to their own edge,
And go under.

And the man laughs and exults.
What was his past
That all the days of his youth he sought resolution,
Built a solid home,
Bought comforts,
Married a woman,
And poured out his passion,
Poured it word by word,
By sight, by the velvet touch,
Poured it out in semen to the breathing womb
Seeking resolution,
The still center,
The whirlpool's orbit,
The consumed area in the tornado's spout
Where pure stasis exists,
To fix forever at that blank center,

And stare out against time?

The man laughs and exults.
For look, that is dead.
He will run down the long slope of the world
And be glad for motion.
He has now no alliances,
But only the omnivorous self
Bent upon knowledge,
The processes of discovery,
Of revelation,
Some insight at last
To the great goals that the eye leaps for
And always,
The great one,
The god,
There like a wind for the hand to hover,
For the eye to enclose,
For the tongue to touch,
For the foot to fondle,
For the groin to gain,
And the stripped self,
Naked at last like a wand in the wind,
To react and deflect,
And bend its blade on the energizing world
That beats all bright at the eyes. [*January 1945*]

XI

And what is man,
In his move against time,
The lean face thrusted toward achievement
And the bulged brain
But pure volition?
Over his head the gulls hold their transitory passage,
Like a clear articulation,
And the subordinate sunrise,

Frozen and fixed in the channels of his thought,
Forever a flag.

And now
He picks up the great sidereal watch,
Where the seasons are held,
Exact and certain,
And sees Venus move toward Antares,
And the northern wheel
Spin on the pole in its huge revolution;
And must the heart in him burst,
The great lungs so labor,
And all the im / ⌣ chemistry of blood go through its changes.
Rather shall he find resolution,
Faced by so many imponderables,
And know within him the range of possibility,
Where all things may form,
The blunt brain hub of so many transitions,
The unimpeachable hands,
Holding within them the range of creation,
His own Adam,
To stand forth from his chaos
In vast amazement
Stunned by the knowledge of what he has been,
Of what he is,
Of what he might be.

By the little shoals he finds in the hollows
Some scattering of shells,
Where the fish-camp tribes who roamed this coast
Cracked open their clams,
Or stands on the mouth of that
Little creek where the visionary preacher came over the hills
    to found a new world, a new union of love—and bred bastards;
Out of such renewal,
The old sea, old in its purposes,
Old in its use, old in its intention,
Casts up its driftage.
He pokes among leavings,
Finds sticks, blocks,
Old piecings of ships,

Or those mussel coated floats the Japanese fishers
Pump out of the Aleutians,
And find their way down,
To / ∪ our shore when the wind blows east:
The glow in the hand,
A green crackle, the glaze on them of imperfection,
That is the finder's gain,
For they have beauty.
Or take that seaman
Planted there on the / spit
Where the sea-grasses crowd,
And the shore pines edge over the spare grass;
His fellows took teakwood to mark his place,
And cut his name and the date '98
In a country so new, so pastless in all that pertained
    to their fluctuant lives,
They could conceive of no other ninety-eight:
For them there was only one century,
But now the time halfway toward another.

For there is such [*illegible*] on it,
There is such soft alteration;
None may know his own face:
Look in the picture.
See some childhood scene,
And yourself: Who is this?
Half my size, the face chubby,
A mop of [*illegible*], and the baby's face;
Showing only weakness,
Like what you held to be Nero's—
But was this not indeed the continuation of infancy—
The body wound in its senses,
Running from pleasure to pleasure,
No holds, no checks within it, none but the parent's restrictive hand
That breeds bitterness,
And warps all a life with their well-meant restraint?
So that the child weeps,
Wails, wailing deprivation,
Already inured in loss,

Not having, of nothing ∪ /.

In the nights on the beaches the sea rustles and moves,
Gathers its great harvest,
Brings it down. In the spring
You see the sea lions in great herds
Go north, close in, riding within the wave,
Just where the combers break,
So that you see their shadow forms,
Lifted a moment against the light,
And then gone, a thing not seen,
But that fleeting glimmer.
They know their way.
In the caves south of here they mate.
The bulls roar and combat.
This may be seen.

But all this not to speak of the man,
Who, seeing them thus in their remote migrations,
Fixes himself:
How shall it be with himself,
The time come for new changes,
The self emergent,
Crying for some attainment
Looking this way and that,
Seeking alignment?

It is the fate to be human.
But fix on the past the blazing eye,
For it harbors the future.
The stars flux and give over.
In Europe the nations now stanched
In their blood
Emerge, clear out the wreckage
And hunt a home.
There is no loss:
How can there be pure deprivation,
When every new phase is its own
Gain?
Shall he talk of deprivement?
There is not a thing within him

He would revert,
In all its involvement,
Not a thing.
It is gone;
It is behind him:
Shut off, closed.
And the inner intensities
Shaping for some new alignment,
Some new progression,
Like the infinitely fertile sea:
Who can rob it of its possessions?
Forever and ever it forever reverts,
And cannot be canceled. [*July 18, 1945*]

NOVEMBER FIRST
NINETEEN FORTY-FIVE *

All day the wind,
Veering south and west,
The sea's quarter,
Strengthens to storm,
And brings the dropping dusk,
Hard on our houses,
And rain on it.

And I write this poem now to that lost girl my wife,
Whom I blunted in youth with my haste,
And learned too late to recover.
She sleeps in a far country,
She stirs in her own dream,
Moist and warm in her cover.

And I coax the liability of black ink on paper,
That holds no respite,
And con the riddle of error. [*November 1, 1945*]

---

* This poem was included with Everson's letter to L.C. Powell, dated Nov. 3, 1945 (*Take Hold Upon the Future* 495).

TO MY ANCIENT ENEMY *
(doleful stanzas in the Shropshire manner penned after
reading *The Function of the Orgasm* by Wilhelm Reich)

Father, underneath the crust,
You breathe the old ancestral dust;
Accept the tribute and the tears
Of one who fought you thirty years;
Who crawled between you and your wife,
Ate your food and marred your life.
Though I made miserable your past,
Know now you have won out at last.
She for whom we rivals warred
You now can claim beneath the sward,
And may resume the full embrace
Undivided by my face.
When she died I broke the band,
Shunned your face and spurned your hand;
And yet when you encoffined lay
Was drawn eight hundred miles away.
Within your loins exhausted lie
The sons who never will defy.
The one who did must now acclaim
Your heritage, and wear your name.
Though you precede me to the grave
Be sure that I am still your slave
And flinch to hear your strident voice
Decree my portion and my choice.
Grin in the ground. You are not dead.
Your old commandment holds my head.
Only your body empty lies:
Your anger aches behind my eyes. [*May 1946*]

---

*
   This poem accompanied Everson's letter to L.C. Powell, dated May 6, 1946 (*Take Hold
Upon the Future*, pp. 535-36).

From "THE BLOWING OF THE SEED" *

It heaved in its hole.
It opened its eyes.

It looked out.

It shook the ground from its face.
It lidded open its blear eyes
And looked out.

It lifted its head from its hoar hole
And the cracked lips parted.
It looked out.
It was dead,
But it broke a patch in the crusted earth
And put forth its face.

When the wind warmed it
It put forth its face from the raw earth
And looked out.   [*December 18, 1946*]

---

* Written as part of the sequence while Everson was living with friends at Treesbank, Sebastopol, CA, this proposed section was revised in February and June of 1947 in Berkeley before being abandoned on Nov. 23, 1947, according to the poet's manuscript note.

THE WOMAN WITHIN: IV *

But give her good leave,
Who has in her holding
Her plenteous hoard!
Give her good leave,
Her clear generation,
Her exquisite fancy!
Form-fed,
Made most of, of any;
Slow in her surcease,
Young in her yielding.

Does the truth tear?
That the self is whole,
Is undivided?
The man and the woman
Androgynous,
Wound in the haft
Of the body's bond?
Is it hence so hollow,
Now, that the inner is all,
Substantive pattern
By which all judgment
Marks its measure?
Self one with the self,
Woman within
Rich in reward?

For see: she moves,
May be found!
Her eyes in that gloam
And her forming face,
Sweet-kneed and knuckled,
Of the pliant thigh,
There on the shore,
Where the water

---

* Meant to be the final section of "In the Fictive Wish," this version, revised as late as July of 1947, was superceded by the Section IV subsequently included when the sequence was printed.

Soothes and sulks
In the scupped stones,
And the wave withdraws...

Oh have her and hold!

For she breathes,
She bends,
She brims all beauty;
And sworn of the answer in her eyes
Will ever be. [*July 1946*]

[UNTITLED]

Crown Oedipus king,
He rules this world.
Great monarch of the mind,
And the heart's red master,
Regent tyrannous,
Throned in the kingdom of the soul.
On his right hand dries the blood of the fathers.
On his left hand dries the blood of the sons.
Crown Oedipus king.
He rules supreme.

Or nearly so.
For I see now how maybe some few,
Gifted in luck,
Maybe some whom as in earliest age
Fate spared,
Let a true ambiance of being
Dwell from the start,
Some father fond in his role,
Some natural son
Given that innocence of eye
To thaw the rectitude of a father's frost
And in kindness bestowed,
Grow beside him,
With kindness blent,
By kindness blessed—

Father: if I could reach you my hand,
Through the borderlands that lie beyond life,
Press through that painful place to what once was,
Reach to that germ, that natural love—

No. But rather will all my sleep be wronged.
Rather will my life's small triumphs,
Hugged, like those childish toys,

A little fardel of hope to my heart,
Slip from my hands,
When you trouble the edges of a dream
And I waver,
Anxious, uncertain, and all afraid.   *[September 1946; July 1947]*

[UNTITLED]

Old Man, was I your imp? Were we
The weak uncomprehending three:
Sister, son, and little brother—
And tearful, easily-injured mother?

For surely, the love that was there,
Lost in the omnivorous ego,
Starved between debts and dullness—

"Look," you would say,
The heavy hands of Justice shown,
"These hands,
They keep you alive...."

There are many to pity the pain of a child,
Choking before the knuckled threat
And the adult scorn.
But who will pity the grown man,
However trapped by a drab duty?
He made his choices.

Ah, choices, choices!

Turned forty, you passionately wanted a family,
But turned fifty, and the brats not ten?

Dead now. But only with us will you wholly go.
Live on, there in the fearful center,
In the remotest region of childhood's anxious dream,
Ill-tempered, boastful, passionate, abrupt and cruel—
But never mean. There was always about you
The unconscious heroic assertion of self;
We were justly proud.

If I could reach you my hand,

Press through that painful place to what once was,
Touch to that earnest joy,
That natural love—

No. But rather will all my sleep be wronged.
Rather, hugged like those childish toys,
My wholest needs,
A little fardel of hope to my heart,
Will slip from my hands,
When you trouble the edges of a dream,
And I waver,
Anxious, uncertain,
And all afraid. [*August/November 1947; February/March 1948*]

[UNTITLED]

Springtime. All churchbells blessed our native roofs.
Herded too soon to the family car
We squirmed in fidget.
From his starched unease,
When mother tarried,
Father sounded the horn.

A grievous blunder.

Yet that womanly wrath,
We wondered, was it really worth it,
That blaze, as, cheated out of the mirror's blessing,
She gave the final angry yank,
And came through the door,
Blood in her eye?

But now, seeing this waitress,
Her heaped elaborate coif,
Eyebrow peeled, an incredible arch,
Mouth preened at the glass to a purple gout,
I understand.

For the moment at the mirror,
Was it not supreme?
The phantasy stabilized forever in the final prink,
That seeming otherness of soul,
When the vision emerges,
And the self smiles back,
Handsome, dapper, well-disposed—

Oh lost now!
Pulled down with the platter,
The next order
Yelled over the shoulder.
How human and how droll,

A pathos lurking in the smeared mascara,
An innocence, naked and naive,
In the simple oath of the burnt finger.

Let the coin on the counter
Pay tribute to the needful attempt,
The partial success and the perfect failure,
Played out before our fifty faces,
Her hurried curtain-call.

And I see my sister in my mother's hat,
And the thought smiles.   [*August/November 1947; February/March 1948*]

TIDEMARSH

There was a road out of town toward the back-water bay
And I took that first.

For a time, trees, till trees gave out with the weak soil
Into scrubby fields.
I crossed a pasture with a barbed wire fence
And waded out through tough-grained grass
Till field and fence slipped off somewhere behind my sight
And left me alone.
I could smell the stink.
After awhile the grass gave up.
I picked my way from clump to clump
And came out at last on the salt edge of what I sought.

I, the history-hating man
Who spurned the image of the hanged god
Nailed high against heaven:
No hope of mine.

And I saw the pelican
Flap the slack air on its massive wing,
Spiral up out of its vast lineage,
That strung back there almost unchanged
Toward a remoter provenance
Than the demi-ape's prototypal skull
Grubbed from the hill caves.
I saw history as tide flat,
Acrid and alluvial,
Rapidly secreting an eventless present
In bottomless slime.

And when the tide went out,
To leave the bald sun sovereign of that manless waste,
It was like some final exodus,
Some vast withdrawal,
Stanching the very impulse toward being,
Relapsing back to some inert state before cognition.
Even the gulls were gone.
There was left on the mudbar

Only the claw mark
And the faint slur left by some spineless thing
Dragging itself out with the withdrawing wave
To weather out the retreating age
Till history could gather up the will
To try again.

I didn't wait,
But turned on back till I found the field
And the road beyond,
Glad enough when the evening lamps
Led me into town.

But it took me more years than I care to count
To get the point.

Some day I'll go back
And pick my way down to the edge where the grass gives out,
And smell the salt, and try to see
Creation as more like what I am
And less like what I was.   *[September/October 1948]*

[UNTITLED] *

As in all that country,
Will find, unbeknownst,
That sheen, that glimmer as of God,
When what was holy
Hits out to the heart,
Hits home. And the city-pent man,
Hemmed, at last goes forth,
And finds that fragrance of earth
But more: that look, as of merely the thrust of grass
At a fenced line,
And all breaks open and blazes,
Dances there in a wild descant
At the tip of the sight.
And those hills, those hills,
Their long line slopeward,
Or the subtle way they bend a flank
In a smooth flowing.
So it is in mid-December,
Cold, many days fog-bound, rain-holden,
Many days of inclement weather,
To have a warm Sunday,
Filled with all that southward light,
And go forth in it,
And see that earth,
As it has always been,
So virginal and serene,
As what one suddenly remembered
Out of remotest past,
[incomplete] [December 20, 1948]

---

* This and the following poem, both dated the same day, represent the final surviving poetic efforts by Everson before his Christmas Eve occasion of conversion.

[UNTITLED]

For there is a place where the water hovers,
A cove, and on it at dusk looking down from a height
See how those congregational gulls,
That have come together from all the shoreline,
Bred in who knows what isolate rookeries
Seaward in that ribbon of coast and in those rock-bound skerries,
Those gulls, now come together,
Search out over the placid water
A hovering line, straggling,
What do they do?
What is it they are seeking,
Down there, so wavering, dipping,
Dipping and wafting?
Feeding, most likely. But that smoke-like line,
That / ∪ [*incomplete*]

Gone. The dark takes it.
And that private beholdance,
Gone with it. Something mystic and untoward
There in the gull-line
Over the green-dark water,
Over the slow passing of the swell
That plashes gently,
Far down there,
On the pebble freckled shore.
Something was completed.
Something revealed, and a resolution.
Something is made at rest in the self
To have looked in on it.
Where have the gulls gone?
Unseen. The dark over them.
That coarse persistent repetitious cry
Comes up from below.
All quit. The stars have it.

But the mystery prevails
Like a soft enchantment,

As does the quality of wonder
When what invokes but never answers
Lingers its why beyond the eye's retention.
There is a scope of quietude that may be stirred.
There is a newness waiting in the self
For the gulls to go again
Across the smoke-dis / ∪ water,
Across the gulls' descant. [*December 20, 1948*]

APPENDIX B

WILLIAM EVERSON

September 10, 1912-June 2, 1994

In the course of his long life, William Everson passed through three distinct phases as a poet. Growing up in the heart of California's San Joaquin Valley (in the town of Selma, not far from Fresno), Everson discovered his true poetic vocation in his 1934 encounter with the poetry of Robinson Jeffers—an encounter that led Everson to aspire toward the creation of a body of poetry drawn from the material of his valley, as well as from his own personal experiences. His initial use of the confessional sequence was twenty years in advance of the mode that ultimately gained currency from the late '50s onward. There in the Valley of the San Joaquin, the poet and his high school sweetheart, Edwa Poulson, were married following Edwa's graduation from Fresno State, and the young couple leased the old Wenty Ranch, where the poet tended grapevines and wrote. The Second World War interrupted this San Joaquin isolation when Everson was conscripted as a conscientious objector and spent over three years interned in federal work camps. At Waldport, Oregon (his primary place of internment), he was instrumental in the founding of the Untide Press and in the establishment of the Waldport Fine Arts Program—projects which were to contribute to the development of the San Francisco Renaissance of the 1950s. The War years saw the breakup of Everson's marriage to Edwa, and, after his release from "alternative service," the poet eventually settled in Berkeley with his second wife, poet and artist Mary Fabilli.

On Christmas Eve of 1948, Everson underwent a conversion from his proclaimed agnosticism to Catholicism; and, because the Church could not recognize their marriage, Bill and Mary were obliged to separate. In 1951, Everson became Brother Antoninus of the Dominican Order, at St. Albert's Priory, in Oakland, California, where he wrote *Prodigious Thrust,* a book destined to remain unpublished for forty years—until it was issued by Black Sparrow in 1996. Indeed, the post-conversion years gave birth to the second major division of his career. Through the publication of his three major collections of

365

religious poetry and his readings throughout the country from 1958 on through the 1960s, Antoninus became known as "the Beat Friar" and achieved a measure of fame quite beyond that of the earlier period.

After eighteen and a half years, Antoninus' situation was, again, abruptly changed—this time by virtue of his leaving the Dominican Order in December, 1969 (a year short of his final vows), to marry Susanna Rickson.

Resuming his secular identity, William Everson, his new wife, and his adopted son, Jude, moved in 1971 to Kingfisher Flat, in Big Creek Canyon, some fourteen miles north of Santa Cruz. As poet-in-residence at Kresge College of the University of California at Santa Cruz, he spent ten years giving a series of meditative lectures and resurrecting the Lime Kiln Press. This latter project not only brought Everson new fame as a master printer but enabled him to nurture an entire generation of creative printers and artists. To match his earlier handpress printing of the *Psalter*, executed during his first years as a Dominican, Everson and his students at the Lime Kiln Press produced a series of acclaimed editions, including *Granite and Cypress*, a collection of Robinson Jeffers' poems in a volume that has been hailed as one of the masterworks of American fine-press printing—as, indeed, the *Psalter* had been twenty years earlier.

During these Santa Cruz years, Everson created more poetry, brought forth several handpress volumes, became a recognized first-rank critic and scholar of Jeffers' poetry, continued his public readings, and added further essays and interviews to his growing body of work—even as Parkinson's disease took its increasing toll on his physical capacity.

On the occasion of his eightieth birthday, Everson and his wife Susanna separated and were subsequently divorced. Struck down by pneumonia in the fall of 1993, the poet survived the nearly fatal attack and returned to his beloved Kingfisher Flat home where, a few months later, after an interval during which he was visited by a constant stream of friends, scholars, former students, and fellow poets, William Everson died in his own bed on June 2, 1994. Following a memorial mass and funeral services at St. Albert's Priory, he was buried in the Dominican Cemetery in Benicia, California.

Hailed by Albert Gelpi as "the most important religious poet of the second half of the twentieth century" and by Diane Wakoski as "one of the most essential and dynamic American poets of the mid-twentieth century," Everson received various honors and awards, from a Guggenheim Fellowship in 1949 to the silver medal of the Commonwealth Club of California, the Shelley Award from the Poetry Society of America, and the PEN Center West Body of Work Award.

Finally, and perhaps most heartwarming of all, Everson received the Santa Cruz County 1991 Artist of the Year Award.

William Everson has left us about fifty published volumes, including some thirty-five of his poetry, several books of Jeffers scholarship and criticism, and various volumes of superb handpress work. At the time of his death, he had completed half of his projected autobiographical poetic epic, *Dust Shall Be the Serpent's Food.*

❧❧ ⚏ ❧❧

CHRONOLOGY:
WILLIAM EVERSON

*For purposes of reference, the editors have compiled this sketch of the
poet's life, set against a scattering of events of general historical
significance.*

1912:   The sinking of the Titanic. William Oliver Everson is born in Sacramento, California, September 10, 1912—at home, 2120 H Street—the second of three children, older sister (Vera), younger brother (Lloyd). He is the son of Louis Waldemar Everson and Francelia Maria Herber. The father is a self-educated Norwegian immigrant and a successful commercial printer (The Everson Printery), a local bandmaster in Selma, California, and a district Justice of the Peace. The poet's mother is of German-Irish farm background. Raised Catholic, she is fifteen years her husband's junior. She converts to Christian Science after the marriage.

1913:   President Woodrow Wilson is inaugurated.

1914:   World War I begins; President Wilson issues a proclamation of neutrality; Panama Canal informally opens to commerce, August 15; in California, Mt. Lassen erupts; John Muir, spiritual father of the environmental movement, dies.

1916:   The death of Ishi, the last "wild Indian" in America.

1917:   U.S. Declaration of war against Germany, April 6; Russian Revolution, November.

1918:   World War I ends, November 11; in California, Mt. Lassen ceases its eruptions.

1919:   Versailles Peace Conference; treaty is signed; the Eighteenth Amendment to the Constitution (national prohibition) is ratified.

1920:   The Nineteenth Amendment to the Constitution (women's right to vote) is ratified; President Wilson receives the Nobel Peace Prize.

1922:   A treaty of union, adopted on December 30, founds the Union of Soviet Socialist Republics.

1926:   Sinclair Lewis refuses to accept the Pulitzer; Byrd and Bennett reach the North Pole.

1929:   Great stock market crash, October 24.

1931:   The Depression worsens; nine million are unemployed, and 1,294 banks fail. William Everson graduates from Selma High School, Selma, California.

1931-2: F.D.R. is elected president of the United States. Everson attends Fresno State College for fall semester, 1931. The Fresno State *Caravan* publishes Everson's "Gypsy Dance," December, 1931. Everson drops out of college and thereafter works in local canneries.

1933:   The Twenty-first Amendment to the Constitution (end of national prohibition) is ratified by vote of ratifying conventions in each of the states.

1933-4: Everson works for the CCC (trail crew) at Cain Flat, on the road to Mineral King in the California Sierra Nevada, in Sequoia National Park.

1934:   Everson returns to Fresno State College and renews his relationship with Edwa Poulson, his high school sweetheart. He discovers the work of Robinson Jeffers: "It was an intellectual awakening and a religious conversion in one.... Jeffers showed me God. In Jeffers I found my voice." Everson begins to write *These Are the Ravens*.

1935:   Everson drops out of college "to go back to the land and become a poet in my own right, to plant a vineyard...." He publishes (through Greater West Publishing in San Leandro as well as through The Everson Printery in Selma) his first book, *These Are the Ravens*.

1937:   *Poetry* magazine publishes "We in the Fields" and "Dust and the Glory" (subsequently retitled "Attila") under the combined title of "The Watchers"; *Saturday Review* publishes "Sleep."

1938:   William Everson and Edwa Poulson are married. Shortly
         thereafter they move to the Wenty Ranch, where, after
         completing *San Joaquin*, he writes *The Masculine Dead*, *War
         Elegies*, the first *The Residual Years*, and *Poems MCMXLII*.
1939:   Publication of *San Joaquin*, introduction by Lawrence Clark
         Powell (Los Angeles: Ward Ritchie).
1941:   Japan bombs Pearl Harbor, December 7, and the United States
         enters World War II.
1942:   The Japanese take Manila; United States forces are driven from
         Bataan; Doolittle bombs Tokyo; the Japanese are defeated at the
         Battle of Midway Island and at Guadalcanal; U.S. bombers
         make their first raid on Europe; British and American forces
         land in French North Africa. Everson publishes *The Masculine
         Dead: Poems 1938-1940* (Prairie City, Illinois: James A.
         Decker).
1943:   Roosevelt enunciates the Allied intention to seek unconditional
         surrender of the Axis forces; saturation bombing of Germany
         continues; America defeats the Japanese at the Battle of
         Bismarck Bay; Allies invade Sicily and the Italian mainland.
         As a conscientious objector, William Everson reports for
         alternative service at Waldport, Oregon, January 21; six weeks
         later, Edwa turns to mutual friend Kenneth Carothers for
         companionship. Everson becomes director of the Fine Arts
         Project at Waldport and works with William Eshelman,
         Kemper Nomland, Adrian Wilson, and Vladimir Dupré,
         establishing the Untide Press. Everson publishes *X War
         Elegies* (Waldport, Oregon: Untide Press); the marriage of
         Everson and Edwa progressively deteriorates.
1944:   America defeats the Japanese in the Battle of the Marshall
         Islands; Battle of the Anzio Beachhead; Rome falls to the Fifth
         Army; D-Day, Normandy Invasion; Allied troops enter Paris;
         Roosevelt re-elected; Battle of the Bulge. Everson publishes
         The Waldport Poems; *War Elegies*, ; and the first *The Residual
         Years* [actually issued 1945] (Waldport, Oregon: Untide Press).
1945:   Roosevelt, Churchill, and Stalin meet at Yalta; Iwo Jima falls;
         U.S. troops cross the Rhine; President Roosevelt dies, and
         Harry S Truman becomes president; Germany surrenders, May
         7; atomic bombs are dropped on Hiroshima and Nagasaki;
         Japan surrenders, ending World War II, August 14; Everson
         publishes *Poems MCMXLII* (Waldport, Oregon). Waldport
         closes, December, 1945; on December 26th, Everson reports to
         Cascade Locks to await demobilization.

1946:   While in San Francisco on furlough, in February, Everson purchases a Washington hand press; the poet reads Wilhelm Reich (first sustained exposure to depth psychology); at the beginning of July, Cascade Locks camp is closed, and Everson is sent to Minersville, in Northern California; the poet is discharged from alternative service at the CO camp in Minersville, July 23; he sets up his Washington in the apple dryer at Ham and Mary Tyler's Treesbank Farm, near Sebastopol; here he meets poet and artist Mary Fabilli; he associates with authors Rexroth, Duncan, Parkinson, Whalen, Lamantia, Broughton.

1947:   Everson lives in Berkeley and is granted divorce from Edwa; he works (for the next two years) as a custodian for the University of California Press.

1948:   Everson publishes *The Residual Years* (New York: New Directions); William Everson and Mary Fabilli are married, in Reno, Nevada, on June 12; Everson converts to Catholicism, Christmas mass, St. Mary's Cathedral, San Francisco.

1949:   Everson publishes *A Privacy of Speech* (Berkeley: Equinox Press) and is awarded a Guggenheim Fellowship; the poet and Mary Fabilli separate, June 30, when the Church rules against recognition of their marriage; Everson is baptized at St. Augustine's Church, July 23.

1950:   On June 25, North Korean forces cross the thirty-eighth parallel, initiating the Korean War. Everson moves to Maurin House, the Catholic Worker house of hospitality, in Oakland, where he associates with Carroll McCool, an ex-Trappist monk.

1951:   Publication of *Triptych for the Living* (Berkeley: Seraphim Press). Everson is accepted as a lay brother (donatus) in the Dominican Order at St. Albert's in Oakland and receives the name Brother Antoninus.

1952:   Dwight David Eisenhower is elected to the presidency. Antoninus begins the writing of his spiritual autobiography, *Prodigious Thrust*; he works at printing the *Psalter*.

1953:   An armistice is signed, ending the Korean War, July 27. Everson continues work on the *Psalter*.

1954:   McCarthy hearings in U.S. Senate; the Senate censures McCarthy. Antoninus experiences a period of crisis of faith— a "dark night of the soul"; he abandons work on the *Psalter* and begins to study for the priesthood.

1955   Antoninus cuts short his attempt at the priesthood and returns
        to St. Albert's. He issues his hand-printed edition of *Novum
        Psalterium PII XII* (Los Angeles: Countess Estelle Doheney).

1956:   Eisenhower wins re-election by landslide. Antoninus
        experiences an interior break-through; he re-discovers depth
        psychology, and, after a brief Freudian influence, through
        Victor White (*God and the Unconscious*) he begins reading the
        work of Carl Jung; he completes the writing of *Prodigious
        Thrust*; he gives his first public reading under the persona of
        Brother Antoninus, at San Francisco State College.

1957:   The second issue of *Evergreen Review* announces the Beat
        Generation. Antoninus writes *River-Root*, not to be published
        until 1976 (Oyez) but subsequently included in *The Veritable
        Years* (poems 1949-1966).

1958:   The poet gives his first public reading outside the Bay Area—in
        Los Angeles, at the Aquinus Institute.

1959:   Antoninus publishes *An Age Insurgent* (San Francisco:
        Blackfriars) and *The Crooked Lines of God* (Detroit: Univ.
        Detroit Press); the latter volume is nominated for a Pulitzer
        Prize. The poet gives readings in Detroit and in Chicago; he
        appears on Irvin Kupcenet's television show, is featured in
        Time magazine and is dubbed "the Beat Friar"; Archbishop
        John Mitty of San Francisco attempts to "silence" Antoninus
        because of the poet's contacts within the Beat Generation;
        Antoninus is banned from further readings; the poet meets Rose
        Moreno Tannlund, beginning an "intense relationship."

1960:   John F. Kennedy is elected president. Archbishop Mitty dies,
        and the "silencing" of Brother Antoninus is lifted.

1961:   The ill-fated Bay of Pigs invasion takes place; President
        Kennedy then orders the first American combat troops to Viet
        Nam.

1962:   America teeters on the edge of war as a result of the Cuban
        Missile Crisis; first gathering of the Second Vatican Council.
        Robinson Jeffers dies. Antoninus publishes *The Hazards of
        Holiness* (Garden City: Doubleday).

1963:   President Kennedy is assassinated, November 22; Lyndon
        Johnson becomes president. Legal divorce ends the marriage of
        William Everson and Mary Fabilli, May 13; Rose Tannlund
        urges Antoninus to enter the Novitiate, and he does so—
        Kentfield Priory, Marin County.

1965:   This year marks the final gathering of Vatican Council II.
        Antoninus meets Susanna Rickson.

1966:   Antoninus publishes *Single Source*, foreword by Robert Duncan
         (Berkeley: Oyez).

1967:   Publication of *The Rose of Solitude* (Garden City: Doubleday);
         Scott, Foresman issues *The Achievement of Brother Antoninus*,
         introduction by William Stafford.

1968:   Richard Nixon narrowly defeats Hubert Humphrey and is
         elected to the presidency. New Directions issues an expanded
         edition of *The Residual Years*, foreword by Kenneth Rexroth;
         Antoninus publishes *Robinson Jeffers: Fragments of an Older
         Fury* (Berkeley: Oyez); Antoninus receives the Commonwealth
         Club of California silver medal for *The Rose of Solitude*; he
         leaves Kentfield and continues his Novitiate regimen at St.
         Albert's.

1969:   On December 7, at a poetry reading given at the University of
         California, Davis, Brother Antoninus presents the love poem
         "Tendril in the Mesh" and announces his intent to resign from
         the Dominican Order and to marry Susanna Rickson. At the
         conclusion of the performance, he removes his Dominican
         robes and exits. Everson and Susanna marry in Mendocino the
         following Saturday, December 13, with Robert and Dorothy
         Hawley and photographer Allen Say present.

1970:   California displaces New York as the nation's most populous
         state. At Stinson Beach, Everson begins life with Susanna and
         son Jude; he writes "Black Hills" and other poems for *Man-
         Fate*, which he completes the following year.

1971:   Everson is hired by the University of California, Santa Cruz,
         Kresge College, as master printer and lecturer. He becomes
         Poet in Residence and begins teaching that fall. He and
         Susanna and son Jude move to Kingfisher Flat on Big Creek,
         north of Davenport. Everson begins teaching his "Birth of a
         Poet" course (which will run 1971-1981)—meditations on the
         poetic vocation.

1972:   Nixon wins re-election by landslide; the famous Watergate
         break-in occurs. Everson resurrects The Lime Kiln Press at the
         University of California, Santa Cruz; under this imprint the
         poet and his students issue *Gale at Dawn* (poems by Everson,
         Hitchcock, Korte, Veblen, Clark, and Skinner).

1973:   The Viet Nam War is concluded, January 23. Through the
         Lime Kiln Press, Everson issues *Tragedy Has Obligations*, by
         Robinson Jeffers.

1974:   Richard Nixon resigns, and Gerald Ford assumes the Presidency of the United States. Everson publishes *Man-Fate* (New York: New Directions).

1975:   Everson issues *Granite & Cypress*, by Robinson Jeffers (Santa Cruz: Lime Kiln Press).

1976:   Jimmy Carter wins the presidency. Everson publishes *River-Root* and *Archetype West: The Pacific Coast as a Literary Region* (both from Berkeley: Oyez).

1977:   Publication of *William Everson: A Descriptive Bibliography, 1934-1976*, compiled by Lee Bartlett and Allan Campo (Metuchen, NJ: Scarecrow Press); Everson is given Poetry Society of America's Shelley Award.

1978:   Everson publishes *The Veritable Years, 1949-1966*, afterword by Albert Gelpi (Santa Barbara: Black Sparrow), and the collection is awarded "Book of the Year" by the MLA Conference on Christianity and Literature; *Blame it On the Jet Stream!* (Santa Cruz: Lime Kiln Press); the first book of criticism devoted solely to Everson's work appears, *William Everson: Poet from the San Joaquin*, by Allan Campo, D.A. Carpenter, and Bill Hotchkiss (Newcastle, CA: Blue Oak Press).

1979:   Publication of *Benchmark & Blaze: The Emergence of William Everson*, (an anthology of critical essays about Everson's work), ed. Lee Bartlett (Metuchen, NJ: Scarecrow Press); the poet is honored as a Tor House Fellow (Tor House Foundation).

1980:   Ronald Reagan wins the presidency by landslide. Everson publishes *The Masks of Drought* (Santa Barbara: Black Sparrow); *Earth Poetry: Selected Essays and Interviews*, ed. Bartlett (Berkeley: Oyez).

1981:   Everson issues *American Bard*, a structural re-arrangement of Walt Whitman's prose introduction to the first edition of *Leaves of Grass*, rendered into verse following the characteristic Whitman rhythms—and thus presenting the work as a poem in its own right, with its presumed original form made evident (Santa Cruz: Lime Kiln Press); suffering from Parkinson's Disease, Everson retires from his position at U.C. Santa Cruz.

1982:   Viking issues a trade edition of *American Bard*, foreword by James D. Hart (New York); Everson is awarded a National Endowment for the Arts Fellowship.

1984:   Ronald Reagan is re-elected to the presidency.   Everson
         publishes *In Medias Res* (San Francisco: Adrian Wilson Press);
         Renegade Christmas (Northridge: Lord John Press).

1987:   Publication of first full-length critical study of Everson's work,
         The Rages of Excess: The Life and Poetry of William Everson,
         by David A. Carpenter (Bristol, Indiana: Wyndham Hall).

1988:   George Bush is elected president.   Everson publishes *The
         Excesses of God: Robinson Jeffers as a Religious Figure*
         (Stanford: Stanford University Press); Lee Bartlett publishes
         William Everson: The Life of Brother Antoninus (New York:
         New Directions); Oregon Institute of Literary Arts award;
         National Poetry Association Award for Lifetime Achievement.

1989:   The "Evil Empire" begins to crumble, with the satellite nations
         moving toward full independence; Everson receives the PEN
         Center West Body of Work Award, May, 1989.

1990:   Everson publishes *The Engendering Flood* (Santa Rosa, CA:
         Black Sparrow); *Mexican Standoff* (Emeryville, CA: Lapis
         Press).

1991:   The United States is involved in the Persian Gulf War against
         Iraq, with decisive victory to the American-led forces under
         General Schwarzkopf; the Soviet Union is dissolved; on
         Christmas Day, the hammer and sickle flag is taken down in
         Moscow and is replaced with the tricolor of the Russian
         Republic; the Cold War, presumably, is over.   Everson receives
         Santa Cruz County Artist of the Year Award and the BABRA
         Fred Cody Body of Work Award; he is a featured reader at the
         International Festival of Authors, Harbourfront Readings,
         Toronto, Canada.

1992:   On September 10, William Everson is eighty years old.   The
         poet and his wife Susanna separate, with Everson filing for
         divorce.   Everson publishes *Naked Heart: Talking on Poetry,
         Mysticism, & the Erotic* (Albuquerque: U. New Mexico);
         publication of *Perspectives on William Everson* (Eugene:
         Castle Peak).   Bill Clinton is elected President.

1993:   Everson continues to live at Kingfisher Flat—editing
         manuscript and working on *Dust Shall Be the Serpent's Food*.
         The poet, a virtual invalid, is attended by Steve Sibley.   The
         divorce from Susanna is now final.   Late in the year Everson is
         stricken with pneumonia—during a two-month hospitalization,
         the poet is several times near death.

1994:   Everson is released from Dominican Hospital in Santa Cruz
        and is able to return to Kingfisher Flat. Publication of *The
        Blood of the Poet: Selected Poems,* ed. Albert Gelpi (Seattle:
        Broken Moon Press). After a long springtime during which
        Everson is once again able to receive visitors—and there are
        many, many of them—the poet finally succumbs to the
        debilitations of Parkinson's disease, pneumonia, and old age.
        He dies at home, Kingfisher Flat, June 2, 1994, and is buried at
        the Dominican cemetery in Benicia, California, with final
        interment occurring on his birthday, September 10, 1994.
        Publication of *Take Hold Upon the Future,* the correspondence
        of Everson and L.C. Powell, ed. William Eshelman (Metuchen,
        N.J.: Scarecrow).

1995:   Publication of *William Everson: Remembrances and Tributes,*
        ed. R.J. Brophy, combined winter and spring issues of
        Robinson Jeffers Newsletter. (Long Beach: California State
        University Long Beach UP); publication of *Quarry West 32,
        The Poet as Printer: William Everson,* ed. Rice, Weisner,
        Young, Vogler (Santa Cruz, CA: U.C. Santa Cruz Printing
        Services).

1996:   Publication of *Prodigious Thrust,* the poet's long-delayed
        spiritual autobiography, the account of his conversion to
        Catholicism, written in the early fifties, ed. Allan Campo
        (Black Sparrow Press); in addition, Black Sparrow schedules
        publication of a *Collected Poems* of William Everson in three
        consecutive volumes titled, in accord with Everson's expressed
        wishes, *The Residual Years, The Veritable Years,* and *The
        Integral Years,* with hitherto uncollected and unpublished
        poems to be included in the new editions. Bill Clinton is re-
        elected president.

1997   Black Sparrow publishes this present expanded edition of *The
        Residual Years.*

INDEX OF TITLES

INDEX OF FIRST LINES

(Parts of sequences within the main text are indicated by asterisks.)

THE PRINCIPAL PUBLICATIONS
OF WILLIAM EVERSON

Verse

These Are the Ravens (1935)
San Joaquin (1939)
The Masculine Dead (1942)
The Waldport Poems (1944)
War Elegies (1944)
The Residual Years (1945)
Poems MCMXLII (1945)
The Residual Years (1948)
A Privacy of Speech (1949)
Triptych for the Living (1951)
An Age Insurgent (1959)
The Crooked Lines of God
    (1959)
The Year's Declension (1961)
The Hazards of Holiness
    (1962)
The Poet Is Dead (1964)
The Blowing of the Seed (1966)
Single Source (1966)
In the Fictive Wish (1967)
The Rose of Solitude (1967)
The Achievement of Brother
    Antoninus (1967)
A Canticle to the Waterbirds
    (1968)
The Springing of the Blade
    (1968)
The Residual Years (1968)

The City Does Not Die
    (1969)
The Last Crusade (1969)
Who Is She That Looketh Forth
    as the Morning (1972)
Tendril in the Mesh (1973)
Black Hills (1973)
Man-Fate (1974)
River-Root / A Syzygy (1976)
The Mate-Flight of Eagles
    (1977)
Blame It on the Jetstream!
    (1978)
Rattlesnake August (1978)
The Veritable Years (1978)
A Man Who Writes (1980)
The Masks of Drought (1980)
Eastward the Armies (1980)
Renegade Christmas (1984)
In Medias Res (1984)
The High Embrace (1985)
The Poet Is Dead (1987)
Mexican Standoff (1989)
The Engendering Flood (1990)
River-Root: A Syzygy (1990)
A Canticle to the Waterbirds
    (1992)
The Blood of the Poet (1994)
The Tarantella Rose (1995)

Prose

Robinson Jeffers: Fragments
    of an Older Fury (1968)
Archetype West: The Pacific
    Coast as a Literary Region
    (1976)
Earth Poetry (1980)
Birth of a Poet (1982)

Writing the Waterbirds (1983)
The Excesses of God (1988)
Naked Heart (1992)
The Light the Shadow Casts
    (1996)
Prodigious Thrust (1996)

383

Printed November 1997 in Santa Barbara
& Ann Arbor for the Black Sparrow Press
by Mackintosh Typography & Edwards Brothers Inc.
Design by Barbara Martin.
This first edition is published in paper wrappers;
there are 300 hardcover trade copies;
100 numbered deluxe copies;
& 20 copies lettered A–T have been
handbound in boards by Earle Gray.

ABOUT THE EDITORS

❧❧ ⸻ ❧❧

ALLAN CAMPO

Allan Campo's friendship with William Everson began in 1958—as a result of the poet's initial reading appearances in Los Angeles, his first readings outside the San Francisco Bay Area—and was sustained by numerous letters, phone conversations, and visits—including many to the poet's Kingfisher Flat home during the last twenty years of Everson's life. Campo was the editor of Everson's recently published "spiritual autobiography," *Prodigious Thrust.* He co-edited, with Lee Bartlett, *William Everson: A Descriptive Bibliography* and wrote an "Afterword" for Everson's *The Mate-Flight of Eagles.* He has also contributed several substantial essays to the study of Everson's poetry, including "The Sensuous Awakening" (in *Poet from the San Joaquin*), "The Woman of Prey" (in *Benchmark and Blaze*), and "The 'Agents of Perfection'" (in *Perspectives on William Everson*). Campo was born in Los Angeles in 1934 and remained a resident there until he moved to Toledo, Ohio, at the end of 1993. He holds both a Bachelor's and a Master's degree from Loyola University (now Loyola-Marymount).

❧❧ ⸻ ❧❧

BILL HOTCHKISS

Bill Hotchkiss first met William Everson in 1963. Eleven years later the two men became friends by way of their mutual interest in the work of the poet Robinson Jeffers. Together, they edited the Liveright (Norton) re-issue of Jeffers' *The Double Axe* (1977). Hotchkiss was co-author, with Allan Campo and David Carpenter, of *William Everson: Poet from the San Joaquin.* With James B. Hall and Judith Shears, he was co-editor for *Perspectives on William Everson* (1992). Born in Connecticut in 1936, Hotchkiss has spent most of his life in California and Oregon. He is the author of numerous novels, including *The Medicine Calf* and *Ammahabas*, and several volumes of poetry, including *Climb to the High Country.* Hotchkiss holds a B.A. from The University of California, Berkeley, an M.A. from San Francisco State, and the M.F.A. and Ph.D. from the University of Oregon. For the greater portion of his teaching career, he has been a member of the English department at Sierra College, in Rocklin, California—and is presently with Sierra College, Nevada County Campus, in his home town of Grass Valley.

❦❦ ⅢⅢⅢ ❦❦

KENNETH REXROTH

Kenneth Rexroth, who died in 1982 at the age of 77, became Everson's close friend, mentor, and even champion during the period immediately following World War II. It was because of Rexroth's connections with James Laughlin of New Directions that the publication of the 1948 edition of *The Residual Years* came about. To cite *Benét's Reader's Encyclopedia of American Literature*, Rexroth was "poet, translator, critic...a largely self-educated man who absorbed and consolidated the ideas of others." For many years Rexroth was a strong, positive voice in behalf of Western American poetry, of the Beat Generation, of the San Francisco Renaissance. His numerous volumes of verse include *The Phoenix and the Tortoise, The Heart's Garden*, and *New Poems*. His translations of Oriental poetry continue to be widely adopted in college and university courses. As a critic, he was the author of *American Poetry in the Twentieth Century* (1975) and others. Like Everson, Rexroth was without a formal college degree; nevertheless, as a highly regarded author and critic, he taught at The University of California at Santa Barbara during the final years of his life.

❦❦ ⅢⅢⅢ ❦❦